T0380263

THE FIGHT OF THE GOSPELS:
GOD'S AND MAN'S

A COLLECTION OF BOOKS

JOSE N. JIJIN

WESTBOW
PRESS®
A DIVISION OF THOMAS NELSON
& ZONDERVAN

WestBow Press books may be ordered through booksellers or by contacting:

WestBow Press
A Division of Thomas Nelson & Zondervan
1663 Liberty Drive
Bloomington, IN 47403
www.westbowpress.com
844-714-3454

ISBN: 978-1-9736-9988-0 (sc)
ISBN: 978-1-9736-9989-7 (hc)
ISBN: 978-1-9736-9990-3 (e)

Library of Congress Control Number: 2023910486

Print information available on the last page.

WestBow Press rev. date: 06/13/2023

TABLE OF CONTENTS

Section III: Was Jesus Afraid to Die?
Fear. Doubt. Insecurity. Commitment. Faith. Sacrifice. Victory.

Section IV: What Is Wrong with Christianity?
Faith. Gospel. Religion. Politics. Law.

INTRODUCTION

The intention of this writing is to somehow bring an understanding in a world of different opinions, where faith and beliefs are so lightly taken by man in his self-sufficiency that it seems as if God is the one who needs our help to fix what man has ruined in his own life. While man is not only using religion and politics to excuse his own actions, which is a natural reaction in man's life, he also easily gets offended when in his rights he is told that he is wrong. The decision of thinking or believing in one's own rights only lasts while the person is breathing, which in every generation may continue, cease, or start all over, creating with the passing of time, something that when we look back, we call that past, history.

Men create a life story that, according to their own convenience or genuine belief, almost never unites them but somehow keeps them together, believing that is unity. And if there is any agreement, it is superficial, because deep down it separates men in their doctrinal denominations and is prevented, then, from becoming one solid unified belief and faith aligned with the wish and the will of God.

This so-called religious faith in man's knowledge and belief appropriates the right to understand God's will as its own—an understanding that for others may appear as a contradiction. It is a controversial approach ignored by the majority of the people that divides their believing faith in the same God, which makes God appear as if He is contradicting Himself and changing His mind in terms of what race of people or what particular person has to believe in Him.

It is in the creation of denominations and religion that the gospel has been divided by man's interpretation and beliefs in a world of spirits, a confusing world where the one who believes may believe that he has the right spirit. Man creates his own rights in a wrong understanding of what God is telling him to do or not to do, making a conclusion based not on the revelation of the Spirit but on his own deduction—and he is under a spirit of confusion. This is a deduction that goes against the wishes of the Almighty. The apostle Paul, through the Spirit, reveals God's will when he writes, "There is one body and one Spirit, even as ye are called in one hope of your calling." The scripture continues, saying, "One Lord, one faith, one baptism. One God and Father of all who is above all, and through all, and in you all" (Ephesians 4:4–6).

In short, Paul is saying to be of one mind, that is, to have the same comprehension of God in the same spirit. Put another way, it is to have one understanding of the only existing God, whose will and joy is to have us in Him as one in Christ.

God's goal is for all believers to be as one, according to His will, and not according to man's understanding of Him in the creation of all the existing denominations. But some of those denominationally profound religious leaders are saying, "But God is God and He can change His mind through the lives of different people who can become His prophets." And that is true. He can change His mind to offer His love, to have mercy on the ones toward whom He wants to be merciful, and forgive anyone who comes to salvation through His love and mercy. But He cannot break His own Word about the only way to come to Him, through repentance of a life of sin, recognizing the Son of God in the flesh, and accepting salvation through the sacrifice on the cross of God's only begotten Son, Jesus Christ.

God, the almighty Father, never said that He will send someone else to bring another gospel of salvation under any other name or denomination to divide His own will. He never said you'll be a Presbyterian, or a Pentecostal, or a Baptist, or a Catholic, or Greek Orthodox—or that you'll be a Muslim or a practitioner of any other religion. On the contrary, the gospel warns us of the ones who will come in His name to preach another gospel of salvation, even when that someone is one of the so-called "New Illuminati" or is any other servant calling himself an apostle or a prophet.

Many people are not paying attention to the warnings and signs spoken of in the Word of God. There is one thing in people's lives that they don't even realize exists when religion is mentioned: Satan's involvement in the creation of a spiritual mirror that shows not a clear picture, but a fuzzy copy of the original that is accepted as original. Not everything that comes from above is from God, just as not everything that shines like gold is gold.

Along with what happened in the Garden of Eden when man died spiritually, that same evil in man's new secular life brought confusion, a confusion in terms of understanding the Word and the will of God. A man who has an inspiring level of intellectual confidence but who is without God's spiritual guidance and is under a wrong spirit of sin, a wrong vision, and wrong interpretations of the supernatural events in his life is what allows false religion to develop. A different way to believe in God results in all the different human-created denominations being deemed right among men, but they are wrong according to the only gospel of Christ.

The only way for a religious person of any denomination to be accepted by God, is if the condition of the person's heart before the Almighty is acceptable, even though they practice what other people may consider to be a wrong belief and have no right to judge. God will look and determine if the person believes according to His will in the gospel or is just an honest, sincere believer of any religious denomination who keeps their heart pure before the Lord. Or that person is a believer who does not want to challenge the spiritual truth of the gospel in their life, living a life of self-confidence based in theological knowledge and not in the world of God's spiritual revelations.

The intentions of a man's heart before the Almighty will save or condemn the said man's soul on the Day of Judgment, whether that person is judged by others to be right or wrong in his faith and belief in God. The Almighty is the only One with the last word about man's heart and faith, the only One to decide his eternal resting place.

Since we have fallen from God's grace, we have undergone a change of ownership in terms of our destiny. The new lord, Satan, is the one whose evil spirits in all their manifestations make men in this secular life do evil things, not only to others but also to themselves. They attack both mind and body, making their lives to be an always open wound that never seems to heal. We haven't gotten far away fast enough from evil, not even with the invention of the wheel, and then the plane, or the space rocket, all instruments that are maybe taking us closer to evil rather than farther away. That same evil throughout all generations has had only one thing in mind, and that is the annihilation of mankind.

Satan got into the lives of people to such an extent that God had to cleanse us, the dirty people, from the face of the earth, with the exception of a few. But even after the Flood, people did not stay faithful to God, so for the second time, He wiped from the face of the earth the degenerate, immoral people of Sodom and Gomorrah by fire, again with the exception of a few who were faithful.

People's understanding about life, regardless of which generation they live in, is always guided by their own self-made laws of conscience or by their unconsciousness. Sometimes an ignorant person who is full of pride and lacks common sense will disregard God's love and mercy, living confused and in despair, desperation, and need. In the end, such a person will be an empty soul with a hurting heart, trying to understand and accept life the way it is, maybe not even worrying about his or her own end. Or maybe they may think about how it might be possible to turn the adverse circumstances around, changing something in his or her secular life, all the while forgetting or not knowing that there is a spiritual life that needs to be found first if the secular is to change too.

The change did not come in us, so God gave us another chance. This time, He became one of us. Now the news of Him is all around the world. Now there is no excuse for people to say, "I didn't know." The rules are established, the lesson is for free, the reminders of the rules and warnings are constant, and the chance for a change is here. Whoever will take that chance will receive a golden eternal reward.

Let's provoke ourselves not only to change our inner beings but also to change the adverse circumstances and take away the lordship of evil in this world, learning what the Almighty has for us. Enough of being indecisive, enough of the excuses, enough of the self-sufficiency, enough of too much intellectuality, enough of religiousness. Don't be a loser; be yourself—and let God be God in your life while you still have a chance to see the light of day. Know in your life the real power of the Creator. Wish for His wisdom; be an adventurer in God's world; try to find His will and knowledge; refuse to be intimidated by the unknown; and be bold. Stop complaining and blaming people for your bad luck, while at the same time trying to trust someone you may think will do a better job for you and your future. Give yourself a chance in Christ and in all the promises He has left for us.

Know the power of the One who has your back covered. Don't doubt in your victory. Let's really be in Him as He is in His Father. Let's look around and feel confident, confessing to the world: "If God Almighty is with me, who can be against me?" Don't look for the Almighty in any man-created denomination. Look for Him in your heart, and He will reward your faith. Let's conquer the armies of Satan, taking from him his rule, all his authority, and all his power, and put them at the feet of our Savior and Lord, Son of the living God, our Father in heaven, as a present for the eternal life given to us by His love and sacrifice, as a present of eternal gratitude for the salvation of our souls. We must not be cowards in this army of God; we will not be crowned if we are not victorious.

It has been said, "Heaven belongs to the ones who conquer it, to the valiant; who am I?" Only you can answer that question because only you know where you stand in your faith, how close you are to Him, and whether or not you are in Him. Give yourself a chance in Christ. If you are not convinced, you may keep believing He does not exist. Or keep believing that you came from a monkey. Or that nature of nothing and from nothing has created you. But don't cheat yourself by thinking that you know better. Now that you have a chance, find out, because after you stop seeing the light of day, it will be too late for anything, even to be sorry. Know how everything started, how slowly man in this sinful world has fallen into corruption in every possible way, and how because of the evil planning in his life, man will create a system that will go against everything that is from God to destroy the souls of mankind in this world through the system of the Antichrist—a system created by the chosen ones, the ones who have been in rebellion since before the time they ended up in Egypt, together with their Gentile followers.

PART I

UP IN THE HEAVENS, A LONG TIME AGO

The Fall. The new life. The fight. New hope. Consequences.

CHAPTER 1

M an has many questions in and about this life, and it is
known that not all those questions have answers. Because
we live in a world of many suggestions and intrigues, hope is one of
the pillars in human life, and we do the best we can to understand
all the whys and becauses.

Learning to get rid of our ignorance takes us to the world of
knowledge, many times a mysterious world of incredible results,
where our imaginations are open fields for the most outrageous
encounters—a world of spiritual and scientific outcomes filled
with wonders and enigmas, where the result of the finding amazes
the mind and soul. Then comes the challenge of finding out the
truth and separating reality from fiction in our own imaginations.
Only we know what we will accept as reality in our intellectual or
spiritual lives, which will last within us to the end of our existence
unless we have a change of mind during the process of getting old,
which is possible, because for us there is no end to learning.

Unless we want to, we won't be able to ignore our own
encounters with the reality of our human spiritual nature when
unpleasant things happen in our lives and corner us in the boxing
ring, hitting our lives hard. Sooner or later, for those who are
interested, the time will come to find out who we are in this world,
what our purpose is here, and where we came from, but what

is more important is where we'll end up, either heaven or hell, whether we believe in "those things" or not. There are lives that we may envy, and other people whom we don't want anything to do with, yet we may get caught right in the middle, looking for a way out.

What can we use to change the adverse circumstances in our lives and not be sorry about the consequences that we'll have to face at the end of this secular, materialistic life—consequences that may touch us in an unexpectedly unpleasant way?

We *must* become interested in finding out more of what we always thought or never knew about our own selves in this secular life. We *must* choose correctly, as we see what is happening not only in our personal lives but also in all the things that seem to be more difficult to reach in this world. That is, we must see the existing and growing dangerous instability in this world created by those who promise us a better future.

Will that moment be the time for the ones who never knew, never cared, or never heard about God to really be surprised? Whether we believe in a Supreme Being or not, we'll definitely try to find out what we know about our own existence. That discovery will be the time to deny God's existence or to accept His life through His Son for a better future.

If you don't believe in God's existence, challenge yourself to consider the spiritual life that you think you have or don't have. You may discover that you really have a spiritual life if only you'll allow yourself to believe and put your imagination toward that denied, ignored, or maybe even unnoticeable mustard-seed spirit of faith you have. If you try to grow your spiritual life without any intellectual deducing, you may find that faith can be a live reality in your heart, not in your mind. The Word of God is something that you have to read to know without any prejudice, because His Word is a spiritual knife, a knife that will cut out any wrong that you proudly carry in your heart. And if your pride feels the pain of the truth and makes you feel uncomfortable, that is God giving you a chance to be with Him in His heavenly kingdom. Don't disregard it.

Hearsay without proof and knowledge is nothing, but knowledge and proof overpower hearsay. When you stop blaming Him for everything bad that is going on in this sinful world and realize both your purpose in this world and what God has done for us to have better lives, your mind will be blown by the acknowledged reality of Him. Victory will be possible in whatever you may want to pursue in your faithful heart in Christ.

You will find out why there are so many things that you don't like or understand, and suddenly in Him you will have the possibility to get rid of those things. You will have the chance to know why life is the way it is and what you can do for yourself and for the ones you love to make a difference—not only in your life but also in this world.

No hero of any science fiction story has the power that our God, King, and Lord has to lead us. We know that He will reward us according to our faith in Him.

Do not believe in your doubts. Do not question God's existence or blame Him or someone else for the mess we are in when you look around and don't see a way out in this world full of problems and evil. Believe in the power of your faith. It doesn't matter how small your faith is; believe in God Almighty. Fight against every negative human feeling or intellectual reason that makes you think fixing a problem is not possible. Believe that everything is possible for God and in Jesus's name. The only thing you need to be directed to the heavens, where the throne of the almighty Judge will acquit you, is your own faith.

The challenge of our lives is to reach His will, understanding that we need to be in Him to be guided by His Spirit and have the revelation of His Word and His will to be victorious. Jesus is saying, "But seek ye first the Kingdom of God, and His righteousness; and all these things shall be added unto you" (Matthew 6:33).

Maybe there is more that God wants from us than just what we know. We must give ourselves a chance to find out more. Let's not guess according to our own intellectual understanding of an inspirational man's idealistic doctrine; let's clothe ourselves without any preconditions in the desire to know the real Truth from the Word of God. Let's put behind us our intellect, give our faith a chance to be in front of us, and try to find out if what we are giving God today is all we have. Let's find out how much we have changed as humans throughout history from the people who left their legacy to us, their descendants.

The understanding of humanity is that we are divided between good and evil: the good, which we are trying to keep, and the evil which is trying to take the good away from us. Whether or not we have noticed, people throughout the generations have not changed much. What has changed is the growing evil in the circumstances surrounding people's lives.

People have changed in their intellectual knowledge and in their material way of living, but they haven't changed much in their own inner persons—in their thoughts, their wishes, their actions, and the intentions of their own hearts. They just accept the good or bad circumstances in their lives. They get used to it, not knowing that a higher power has promised them a way through the things in their lives, things they can accept and change for their own futures and for the secular world. Again, Christ is saying, "But seek ye first the Kingdom of God and His righteousness, and all the rest shall be added unto you" (Matthew 6:33).

But throughout the centuries, the change has been in terms of intellectual and material progress. We have gone from living under a tree to living in a cave, then from a shack to a house, and at the end from a castle to a palace. First we walk, then we ride, then we navigate, and finally we fly. At the beginning we slept under a tree and had no problems. Even when we were naked, we managed to ruin a perfect life. Then, after we got in trouble, we went to a cave. And we carried all the problems and inconveniences of life up to this day, even if we live in a mansion or castle. If we keep living this way, we'll end up going back to the cave with a big hole in it because we do not know our limits.

The spiritual decadence of any man, people, or nation doesn't make anyone better even if they are healthy and wealthy. The lack of spiritual understanding is a problem that causes people to have all kinds of undesirable situations and unpleasant secular adversities in their lives.

First and foremost, when we do not have Christ's life and Spirit in our hearts, we do not hear or understand the convincing voice of our conscience in our own spirits. Our souls end up in a state of moral degradation and then die because they do not understand right from wrong. Respect for any kind of decent human principles doesn't exist because we do not know God or fear future consequences.

CHAPTER 2

U p in the heavens, behind the stars, where man's eyes can't see through the infinity and where the blue sky is clear in its eternity, the last glimpse of an immense peace that man sees with his human eye, is a place in which man cannot participate from his natural world. Where man imagines a million things that could exist in the perpetual beauty of the Divine Creation, he does not have the knowledge to understand what has been created in its configuration to make good scientific guesses about galactic space.

In sidereal space, in which every star is a world in its Creation, man doesn't know the limits of the high frontier, having only heard of the three heavens. Where they begin or end, he also doesn't know. Our world where man lives is a microscopic dot in the middle of what seems to be an empty universe. Maybe for other worlds, we are just another shining star in the infinite darkness of the open sky. The perfect universe, a creation in the will of its Creator, is something that no human knew because it didn't exist at that time—a celestial place in the heavens of such beauty that no human eye has ever seen, the greatest majestic excellence created by the One who is God, Lord, and King of His infinite and eternal kingdom.

A planet called Earth in its plenitude of beauty was and is a place in the heavens, desired by the will of its Creator to be the place where the Lord is the King of His privileged domain. It is a world of spiritual beings who, in the liberty that was given to them in heaven, serve in their freedom the Lord of their Creation, a life that no other has or will have.

The spiritual beings were a divine creation in eternity, where no one knew darkness because the light of the Supreme Holiness was shining upon the infinite kingdom of peace and joy, where misery and sadness did not exist, only the sonorous sound of a celestial praise-filled song to the One who has created everything for Him and by Him. The excellency of His kingdom and the majesty of His throne, where the greatness of His being, with the never-ending power and sweetness of His love, in the purity of His holiness and the tenderness of His grace, with the extension of His mercy and the lateness of His anger, within the greatness of His glory, receives the praise and adoration of His own creation, namely, spiritual beings whose only task is to serve in adoration of their Creator.

The heavens in their extension had no boundary in man's imagination of the reality of life for him in eternity. But something was about to happen, something that would become part of the human race. The planet Earth, which was to become man's home in the future, would be changed by the events. High in the heavens in the majestic open place where the Almighty has His kingdom, His first creation was about to do something that was never supposed to happen.

That first beautiful angel, which God had created for Himself in His eternity, was creating music in his movements and was admired by the rest of the angels for being the one preferred by the King of kings. The respect, reverence, and admiration given to him by his fellow angels made him develop selfishness, arrogance, and prideful thoughts, something he did not know at that moment. That thought was to be the beginning of the end for the one who was called Lucifer. And the end came.

For the first time in eternity, the heavens felt a tremor. God the King, the Almighty standing by His throne, looked at how legions upon legions of angels attacked the rebellious, now evil, spirits. The battle was fierce, and the rebels were cast out of heaven forever. Falling from the highest place, they came down, destroying everything in their path. Overpowered and defeated with shame and hate, the evil, demonic spirits destroyed the stars in the universe, making a big black empty hole on their way down to darkness. Even the universe, in a way, wouldn't be the same again.

This was a long fall from the privileged celestial world to the unknown, followed by countless voices of furious madness in desperation through the galaxies, leaving the perfection of their existence on their way down to their new home, hell. Sin was born, and all the ramifications of that birth came with those rebels. Men didn't know yet, but a big unpleasant surprise was waiting for them. At the end of their fall, all evil spirits and their master ended up in the place that man someday would come to call Mother Earth.

Earth was completely destroyed. The once wholesome mass of land separated into what is known today because of the tremendous impact of the fallen. Everything died; neither the sun nor the moon was shining over the earth's annihilated surface. Darkness now ruled above in what once was the garden of the Almighty King. The living world of beauty, full of amazing nature and creatures of all kinds, big and small, one day became extinct. No more sun; no more moon, stars, or clouds; no more creeks, rivers, lakes, or oceans; and no more of the green that made the life of the world incredibly beautiful. All ceased to exist as such in the middle of the unending universe.

A world covered by darkness and dust, an earth without life, became the kingdom of the new ruler to reign over a principality full of savage demons and evil spirits. Their madness and out-of-control behavior filled them with emptiness as they yelled and howled in their desperate hatred and pain. Hard and hot was the destroyed land; it was not the way of life they had before. Now miseries, pain, hate, vengeance, and destruction was the new life. "And the earth was without form, and void; and darkness was over the face of the deep. And the Spirit of God moved upon the face of the waters" (Genesis 1:2).

Time and more time went by, until the King remembered and looked down, remembering the land of His garden. That beautiful garden was completely destroyed, so He decided to create a new earth. And God created what was a long time ago a new Eden world, with new heavens and a new earth, with the waters from the heavens back to the new oceans, rivers, creeks, and lakes, covering with their given life the beautiful face of the new world. Every living creature that walked, flew, swam, ran, crowed, or jumped in its beauty made a joyful vision and sound of nature. Everything was perfectly done, and He liked it. He was pleased.

But the King of the universe did not forget Lucifer, His first creation, the one who was expelled from heaven for his insolence. Lucifer, now called Satan, and his followers were trembling in fear, afraid that the Almighty would punish them to extinction when they saw Him surrounded by legions of impressive angels.

And the time came when the King saw that the new world that He had created in its beauty was in need of something else. It came to Him that it would be good to have someone to reign over and enjoy His creation, so He said, "Let us make man in our image, after our likeness and let them have dominion over the fish of the sea, and over the fowl of the air, and over the cattle, and over all the earth, and over every creeping thing that creepeth upon the earth" (Genesis 1:26).

Time went by and the Almighty enjoyed the company of man, but He saw how lonely and tired the man was from all his work, so

He said, "It's no good that the man should be alone. I will make an help meet for him" (Genesis 2:18). "And the Lord God caused a deep sleep to fall upon Adam; and he slept: and he took one of his ribs, and closed up the flesh instead thereof; and the rib, which the Lord God had taken from man, made he a woman, and brought her unto the man" (Genesis 2:21–22). And God liked everything that He had created, having this world as a heavenly garden.

But the Almighty posted in man's life a warning: "And the Lord God commanded the man, saying, Of every tree of the garden thou mayest freely eat: But from the tree of knowledge of good and evil; thou shalt not eat of it: for in the day that thou eatest, thereof thou shalt surely die" (Genesis 2:16–17).

When the Almighty had finished His perfect creation and gave the humans the world of this earth, He, with that warning, also gave them freedom, free will. Even when humans are warned about certain things, it is according to their will whether they will obey or not, whether they will follow the rules or break them. It is the freedom of self-determination. The devil knew all of what God was doing, and he was furious. Under his own nose, God was creating the most beautiful place—and he was not able to do anything about it.

Eden was a holy place on earth where no sin existed; its own Creator was visiting the new world with its new inhabitants. But something was about to happen. Satan was on the lookout. He was trying to see how he could do something without compromising himself. With time, observing God's creation, he saw that one of the living creatures was in an attitude different from the rest. A way of communication existed among creatures, men, and spirits, so he perceived that he could approach the serpent. At the same time, he knew that he wouldn't be breaking any rules, so he saw the chance to do his evil deed without putting himself in harm's way.

In his cunning way, and knowing the serpent's attitude, he approached it. The serpent, even though it was more astute than the rest of the living creatures, did not have in it the instinct of malice. Perhaps Lucifer saw it as the one that would do things no other creature would take the chance to do. It was like the "wise guy" of the bunch, the perfect accomplice for the perfect crime for which Satan wouldn't be blamed. He could not force himself on someone, or in anything, and in the end, he found the solution for his plan.

With what looked like a casual encounter with the serpent, Satan in his slyness put his plan into action. The serpent, without knowing the consequences of its action, intuitively accepted in its mind the encounter with the woman, during which conversation Eve's curiosity overpowered her obedience to God in the understanding of right and wrong and of her own self-determination.

Without breaking even one of God's commandments, Satan was in the clear. Finally he had the expected chance to get his way. He found out that the weakness he had could be developed in living beings.

A casual suggestion to a weak will is like an unlocked door for strangers, called a vulnerability, where force is not necessary when the way to enter is easy and leaves no visible evidence. When there is no understanding of wrong or fear, the moment of a pleasantly sweet impulse could lead to an unknown bitter taste in the end.

Why hasn't God called Satan? Because He knew that something like this would happen. He knew who Satan was and what he was capable of. Even when he was outside the picture of what the Lord God was about to do in and for the new creation, the Almighty knew that Satan would be around. That is why in the Bible nothing is said about Satan at the moment when God was finishing His perfect creation in the person of the new man in His image.

God gave to His new creation the gift of self-determination. That same gift is what today humanity still has to save itself. Only man's self-determination will take him back to his beginnings, according to his own decisions and understanding about life and death.

The devil will never use his strength to push anyone to do wrong. What he will do is suggest to your heart, through a very soft impulse by way of your thoughts, feelings, emotions, and desires as brain waves, or whatever they may be, a proposition of a need, in order for you to do wrong on your own, insisting on following your instincts. He will approach you very diplomatically, tempting you, giving you the chance to see or try something different that appeals to your mind as a desire at that moment.

That was the premeditated intention behind the casual encounter with the serpent, an innocent conversation with the suggestion to approach the woman in the Garden of Eden. That is a tactic Satan has always used. The ones who give in, he will own them, having the right to intensify his evil power over their weakness in order for them to do what he knows they are capable of doing.

If you are strong in your will, you will understand that your discernment of right and wrong is still within your control. That understanding leads you to take action against what is in your thoughts, feelings, or desires, giving you the ability to reject what is categorically wrong in that moment. If you should fail, which is Satan's goal, then you become his puppet. From that moment on, the fight according to your understanding of right and wrong becomes a battlefield in your own spiritual life between God's will and the will of the devil. Toward which side you will lean depends on you.

CHAPTER 3

M an didn't know right from wrong; he was living in a perfect world up to the moment of his disobedient decision. The moment he broke his obedience to God, ignoring God's warning, was the moment everything that God had given to him in that perfection was lost. Man once lived on the right side of life, now he is living on the wrong side. He only knew good, but now he knows evil. He was blind to evil, but now he can see it. He didn't know worry, but now he lives in it. Man died spiritually in his holiness; the holiness that he had from having been made in the image of God departed from him. Now he is walking dead in a world of sin. Today we know that if a certain enticement looks, sounds, or feels innocently good, we have to be very careful.

It's kind of late for Adam, the first man, but such is not the case for the second man, that is, us after Christ and in Christ, if we remember, and pay attention, and fight to be first again with God. The first living spiritual man in us does not exist anymore, but we still have the power of free will within us to again become the first man by the love and mercy of God through His Son's sacrifice. Since falling from God's grace, man stopped living in a perfect world. From that moment on, life could go one of two ways. Everything became fifty-fifty. What God has given to man,

man has given to the devil; now the devil not only owns the world, but also has man under his power.

Now came the moment for man to learn who he is. From God, he is far; to the devil, he is too close. Man knows what is good, but his weakness overpowers him and leads him to choose evil. Now he is at war. The only thing that he has in his favor is God's gift of self-determination. How he will use that power of self-determination is up to him alone. The chance he will give himself will determine which way he will go, whether up or down, left or right, crooked or straight.

The painful way of learning has begun. A life without God is no life. A life of no worries becomes a life of stress and headaches. There will be hardship and affliction at every level in a man's life, which will become future companions of the human race. Every evil demon will provide humans misery to make them suffer: physically, mentally, morally, intellectually, psychologically, and spiritually. All the ramifications of sin will be part of man's disobedient life, from killing to lying. It will make no difference in a tragedy of this magnitude.

Disobedience had to be punished, so the Almighty called Adam, who made an excuse, thereby birthing man's lack of accountability in the Garden of Eden. "The woman whom thou gavest to be with me she gave me of the tree, and I did eat" (Genesis 3:12). The woman replied, "The serpent beguiled me and I did eat. And the Lord God said unto the serpent, Because thou hast done this, thou art cursed above all cattle, and above every beast of the field; upon thy belly shalt thou go, and dust shalt thou eat all the days of thy life" (Genesis 3:13–14).

Satan came out clean, and the serpent paid the price. If they were blaming, accusing, or excusing each other, then why didn't the serpent use the same excuse about Satan?

A suggestion is not a forceful idea obligated upon anybody,

but a freely spoken word before a mind that indirectly, or without plain expression or explanation, begins the process of inducing a prospective thought and/or action without being persuaded, that is, without causing the recipient to reflect or analyze whatever action is about to be taken. That action will become the sole responsibility of the actor, with the possibility of blaming no one but himself.

God, being God, knew that Satan would do something, even when He told him not to touch or destroy anything. Just as the Lord also knew that the perfect creation of man, in time, would be tested for his obedience. That is why God has given to His creation the most precious gift ever given to man, besides the life in Him, namely, the freedom and liberty of his own self-determination—a self-determination wrongly used before and now needed if he is to choose his own path amid the understanding of right and wrong for the future existence of his soul.

It was a perfect crime committed by Satan, even against nature. Satan knew at that moment that he had become the new unblemished landlord of this world. He had acted in obedience to God exactly as he had been told. He just used freedom of suggestion to attract and charm a curious will, a suggestion that in the future world would be called freedom of expression, whether man lies or tells the truth.

No excuse for the serpent, but man, after so many generations, still falls for the same trick. The suggested thoughts to a weak heart with a neutralized human spirit still presents a field of opportunities for the evil spirit, with man not yet having learned to defend himself against his emotions, feelings, desires, and wishes.

The good nature of human beings cannot conquer the bad side of evil in them. Knowledge is not enough; understanding of that knowledge is the key. The moment God sent Adam and Eve out of the Garden of Eden, telling them the consequences of their disobedience and the hardness of their future life, was the moment they understood what a terrible mistake they had committed, with nobody to blame but themselves. The hope and guessing had begun in their lives, and with that understanding, they lived all their lives trying to follow what they thought was the right way to live and to do things.

Even when they were out of Eden, God was not far from them, but for them the distance was as long as eternity. The barometer in people's lives is the spirit, but Adam and Eve felt empty because that spirit was neutralized. In their new life, they didn't know what to expect. And if they wanted to be close to God, they had to learn how to do so. Life began to be a very slippery and divided road to reach the school of knowledge—a road where a choice needed to be made, whether to know their new secular world, the spiritual, or both.

Now, it was unlike before when God was coming to them. Now they would have to find a way to get closer to Him, even when He was with them, but in a different way. Man's spirit given by God to humans was a direct way of contact. It was the part of the Almighty's holiness that enabled Him to be connected to man. But that connection had been cut off, interrupted. Now it was up to the soul's heart of man to fight for his survival, a fight for knowledge that would last until the time he stopped breathing.

For man's soul, it was a new world, a new beginning of self-learning, understanding, having goals, and making decisions. The time came when man's soul had no one to intervene on its behalf. Its disobedience pushed the human spirit aside, ignoring the voice of caution, and ceased communicating with its Creator, namely, God's Spirit.

The decision of the soul's heart to try the fruit neutralized the human spirit, which was ignored in its intervention to alert and stop the wrongdoing. Now it is up to the soul's heart to find a way to be reconnected to the pushed away spirit, having its own intellectual will in its decisions.

It won't have the strength it had before, and that will be a challenge—a challenge for both right and wrong decisions, according to the soul's heart's own understood intuition or limited intellectual knowledge. This is a weakness that will exist up to the time when man realizes that to see God again, he will have to recognize his wrongdoing and repent, and allow his human spirit, that is, his conscience and common sense, to guide him for the encounter with the Spirit of God and on to God Himself.

The most difficult challenge man's heart will have is to conquer its weakness, because since man has fallen from grace, something inside him has taken the place of the human spirit, inducing him to deviate from his own understanding of doing good and bad, and of knowing right from wrong. That is a spirit of weakness and confusion and does not come from God.

To God, man's soul is existing as dead because it doesn't have God's life, that is, His Spirit. Man's "life" is a living death, unseen to God's eyes until man's heart repents. And when man repents, accepting Christ as his Savior, God sees and accepts man through His Son's sacrifice.

There are questions such as, what would happen if a man dies without the knowledge of salvation? What will happen to the souls in hell, or Hades, that are condemned to eternity? What is eternity in God's world?

The Bible says, "For who hath known the mind of the Lord [God], that he may instruct him? But we have the mind of Christ" (1 Corinthians 2:16). And in that mind is where love, grace, and mercy should exist in us in the flexibility of our understanding of God's heart. If the Bible says that for God a thousand years is like a day and that a day is like a thousand years (2 Peter 3:8), then it is obviously difficult for us to understand eternity in God's world.

Do the punished lost souls in hell, or the lake of fire, have a chance of redemption? We understand what has been said, that the gospel of salvation will be preached to the last "corner" of this world so everybody can be saved. The answer to the question about the redemption of lost souls is according to the Word of God. Because we have the mind of Christ, we are supposed to know the answer. But there is more to the question.

Even when Christ is in the heavens and He is the only existing God in His Trinity, He is God Almighty. But also He is the Son of man. Even in heaven being God Almighty, He is still being the Son of man in the holy person that He was here on earth. If we have His mind, then we know what He said about there being things the Son of man doesn't know. He admitted this when He was asked by the disciples about when He would be coming back to the earth at the end of times. He replied, "But of that day and hour no one knoweth no man, no, not even the angels in heaven, but My Father only" (Mark 13:32).

There may be a possibility that even when we have His mind, we don't need to know certain things concerning what God the Father may do according to His will and in His kingdom.

For the sake of guessing about, respecting, and accepting what the Word of God says, not denying, contradicting, changing, or adding anything, but analyzing what God may do with the condemned souls, we'll walk through the imagination of what may be impossible and unknown to us, but what is possible and known to God. Knowing who God Almighty is in His love, compassion, mercy, goodness, and holiness, let's imagine in our little brains what God could do with the condemned souls in Hades, or the lake of fire.

In this secular guessing exercise, the main foundation is the holiness of God. It is believed that in this life when someone needs to purify something, he or she must submit to the process of purification, which has different steps. Those steps are taken, we may say, to an extreme if need be. All materials, due to being purified, need to go through a process of testing for quality either during the beginning of their creation or at the end.

The harder the material, the more extreme is the process because of the need to make the material perfect. Some materials are good, but to make them better, perfect, requires different tests and procedures. To test the endurance of those materials, they are put to an extreme test to determine their stability, quality, and perfection. That is akin to the life of a Christian, to go through different fiery trials.

The hard material is the soul's heart in hell. And the good material is those in heaven who will go through a test of resistance after a thousand years, when God Almighty will release Satan from hell.

God the Father, in His almighty knowledge, severely punishing those souls in hell, is giving them a test of His wrath in retribution for ignoring Him. He keeps them punished as an earthly father would do with very strong discipline for his rebellious child, then later giving him another chance. We can assume that the fire of hell, or Hades, is an unbearable punishment, but what will make it worse is the remembering of the rejected Word of redemption, love, and mercy of God through His Son's sacrifice.

Those thoughts will be the ones that will inflame the fire of hell to make it more unbearable for the soul's suffering and torture. It is just for the imagination to think of the reaction of the condemned souls in hell when they are given, perhaps, a chance of redemption by the Almighty, and when Satan comes again to tempt them.

What will the Almighty do with His children after the thousand years of Satan's imprisonment? At that time, when Satan is let free, God will allow him not only to taste the faithfulness of His children who have lived in peace in the world and in the life of the Almighty for a thousand years, a very different life from that of the condemned ones, but also to screen them out in their faithfulness until they come to be purified in their hearts to the point of reaching the degree of holiness that the Almighty desires. Even at that time they will have their self-determination to accept or reject Satan's new temptations.

The process of purifying one's heart to reach a state of holiness, the type that God wants from His children, is done by coming to an understanding of an eternal life with God in the heavens through the rejection of evil temptation and not taking a chance in the fires of hell in the afterlife.

All that has been said is not based on concrete solid knowledge, but is something from a free imagination, whether I am right or wrong in my guess.

Obviously in terms of this matter, people's opinions are quite different according to their understanding of what the Bible says. But no one must think that if in the afterlife souls are given another chance, this is an excuse to keep living in sin.

The real truth might be crueler than that which we have conceived in light of our imagination, even if you are convinced that there is no heaven or hell, especially hell. And this is something that should not be taken lightly. As stated before, it's just a guess.

The evil of weakness in man's heart is what causes emptiness and confusion due to the lack of knowledge of how the enemy works in a man's life. Man needs to know in his inner self if he is capable in his instincts to rebel for his own good amid a foggy misunderstanding of his rights. Man has the intellect to decide for himself according to his heart's intuitive feelings.

The new soul's companion, the ungodly spirit, took the position of ruler of the human spirit, not allowing the man to think straight with a clear mind. The power of this companion seduces the soul's heart to depend on itself, almost like an uneducated person who feels and thinks that in his wild freedom and lack of respectful manners, he has the right to do anything he wants.

Man will not know how it feels to be "domesticated" or "civilized," or to have all the benefits he will need to be accepted in a civil society, if he doesn't give himself a chance. He might not realize that nobody can help him if something happens to him in the "wild".

Man has gotten to the point of no return, unless he decides to go the right way while standing at the crossroads of life—and the correct way is to choose what is right and reject what is wrong. He will do this if he cares, really cares, for his future. With this decision made, he may have the understanding and possibility of coming closer to God. He may be able to turn his future around, but the decision for a better future will not be an easy one to make if he does not put up a good fight.

Whatever good intuitive intentions and feelings are still in man's heart, his heart will encounter resistance from very different evil spirits in his weakness. The greatest task for man's heart to accomplish in order to conquer weakness in himself and save his soul is the recognition of the wrongs he has committed. That recognition and his subsequent repentance will allow him to be accepted by his Creator.

For many centuries, man had to fight for his survival, and when he got to the point where he thought he was doing fine in the liberty of his actions, he did not understand how deep he was under evil's will. He didn't even notice or admit his wrongdoing, and completely forgot about God, destroying himself to such a point that God Himself decided to intervene.

God, seeing people destroying themselves in their wicked ways, felt pain and sorrow. Sorry that He had made man, He said, "I will destroy man whom I have created from the face of the earth, both man and beast, and the creeping thing and flows of the air, for it repenteth me that I have made them" (Genesis 6:7). And God grieved in His heart for man's future, but He did see one man whose heart was right before Him, and He was pleased. God saved Noah and his family, but the rest of the world was flooded and every person and living creature died, apart from the ones Noah took with him in his ark. That was the way God washed people's weaknesses from the face of this earth.

CHAPTER 4

Man under evil control was destroyed, and along with him went everything else that was contaminated. But for the saved ones, a new life was about to begin, and it would be a great mystery to discover. Would that handful of people be different in a supposedly new world? Noah in his generation walked with God in perfect humbleness, humility, obedience, memory, reverence, and gratitude.

Many generations later, man felt confident and secure, and in that security and self-confidence, he began forgetting the teachings of his ancestors: how God had saved them from destruction. Man's humbleness, obedience, reverence, and memory was fading away. Man did not keep his heart strong in the memories of God or in his gratefulness for God. Again he was getting weak and leaving a part of himself open for evil to get in. He decided to raise his head higher than he himself was. Once more in his wicked heart, he felt he had to reach the unreachable by way of his pride. Evil again was at work.

Once more Satan was giving man the thought that it would be easy to reach what he wished for, and man's wrong instincts were challenged by the goodwill of a pushed-aside conscience, the conscience that the voice of the human spirit is always trying to get in touch with the soul's heart. Slowly but surely, the evil spirit was making its way into people's lives, little by little, step by step, in an innocently deceiving way, with unnoticeable corruption to the human heart and mind.

A soul with a heart, a mind, and thoughts controlled by the ego or arrogance in the life of an unbeliever or a so-called believer is always set against the individual. That is when a person defines God's existence as a faraway unattainable dream, a dream of an invisible Being who can never be seen or reached, according to the person's distorted mind and proud, self-sufficient egotism—or ignorance. Or a person might recognize His existence, but under a rebellious spirit, is ignoring or taking lightly the things of God in his life and allowing that evil to grow in his weaknesses.

There are times when the soul, heart, and mind feel empty, without strength, alone, and confused. Such individuals feel lost and abandoned without any real friends or help, and are incapable of finding a way out to make a difference when they are at a crossroads in their lives. That is when they remember in a foggy memory that same denied or ignored God whom they never cared for but now are trying to reach for their salvation.

How important is it for the person to know himself inside his heart, in his feelings, emotions, and thoughts? Maybe he trusts his intellect, knowledge, and instincts instead of that deep inner voice of the conscience that in a soft whisper calls for attention to follow the right direction and do the right thing.

How hard is it for humans to see what is from God and what isn't? Why is it so difficult to have a fighting spirit in us, against everything that we may think, believe, or know is wrong?

Many times, unknowingly, we accept unscrutinized situations or circumstances as if they are something unimportant because they look innocent enough, things that maybe could affect our lives in the future. When people let their imaginations provide them with unrealistic mirages, the devil gets inside them, controlling not only their feelings but also their reasoning, to the point that they have no control over their actions and fail to make the right decisions.

When you are away from your conscience, which is what provides the right reasoning, you have thoughts that diminish the reality of your physical, intellectual, moral, and spiritual state of mind. Your adverse situation is the result of you being confused in your "right" mind, because someone else is controlling it—and that "someone else" for sure is not the Spirit of God acting through your human spirit.

On the other hand, you believe you are in your right mind because you think you know what you're doing, while trying to bring harm upon yourself or someone else, thinking you have a reason in your confusion. The final result is that you are not in control of yourself, nor do you have the right action, the right reason, or an understanding of the reality of the state of your mind or that of your spirit. Desperate times are made up of extremes existing amid circumstances where your lack of reason or rationalization ends in tragedy most of the time.

Your inner being has been overpowered with thoughts and feelings from a spirit that is not from God, but from Satan himself. Your human spirit is completely out of action, unable to intercede for you in any possible way—that is, if you don't allow yourself, even in that moment of desperation, a few seconds of peace in your roiling inner being to hear the soft echo of the voice of reason. That is the understanding that common sense is giving you, along with the chance to see right and wrong. The human spirit is equipped to help you discern between what is evil and what is good in your common sense and conscience when the Spirit of God is communicating with your pushed-away spirit to help your confused heart and mind.

Always remember this: if a person, a feeling, a thought, a spirit, an angel from heaven, a voice in your head, a dream, or anything else is telling or commanding you to bring harm upon yourself or others, it is not, under *any* circumstances, an order or wish from God, because He is not a God of destruction or death. Satan is the one who is of destruction and death, and that is the whole difference between the two.

The purpose of the voice of reason that you may hear is to put an end to the intention of doing wrong to yourself or others. And it will come not from your head, but from deep inside you, because in your head at that moment is a noisy, confusing, desperate turmoil of thoughts, not a good environment for making choices or reasoning. You have to fight that moment of desperate confusion within yourself. Try to calm your roiling feelings and emotions. You may have God's help, but remember that the decision to fight for a better future is the first fight you must do on your own, against your own recognized oppressing weaknesses, in order to allow Him to intervene on your behalf. Listen in your inner being for that completely different voice of peace. It doesn't matter how close to or far away from God you may be, He is always close to help you; He wants your life to be saved, not destroyed. That is why any time that you are directed to take a life, *any life*, you must STOP in the name of Jesus.

Fight that instinct and call for God. Yell from the bottom of your soul, "Jesus, Jesus, Jesus, help me please!" with all your believing strength, no matter who is around you. Fight it and fight it hard because that fight won't be easy. Persist and persevere in your calling to God for help in the name of Jesus until you feel the freedom from that inexplicable oppressive inner force. Fight for yourself, and never give up to any evil temptation or oppression. Do this until the heaviness of your heart is lifted, your mind is clear, and the feeling of oppression is gone from your heart.

After that first spiritual fight, keep on praying or just talking to God as you talk to your best friend, until you fall asleep. And if that happens, don't worry about it; the fight that you will go through will make you very tired, even when it is not a physical fight but a spiritual one. And when you wake up, you'll be a different person. God is not going to let you down because you fell asleep, but you have to finish your own fight first. God is not a pusher; He is a giver. Satan is a pusher and a taker. If you push for your own victory in Jesus's name, then He will give you the crown of victory.

Later on, find a house of God so that you may be helped in the understanding of the gospel and the salvation of your soul. Remember always one thing: man can only help you by directing you to get help, whereas God is the only One who will free you and reward you for your belief and faith in Him. Because there are things in man's life that only man himself can resolve, your fight is yours alone; nobody can do it for you. The more you understand what you are as a human being and what your weaknesses are, the better spiritually prepared you will be to fight. If you understand what is right and wrong in your life, then you have a better chance to win with your human spirit interceding before God on your behalf in Jesus's name. Nothing that is pure, decent, sane, and honest will be a cause for problems in a man's life. But if there is a problem that touches the inner sensibility of a person, any problem making that person feel insecure, the person has to know God is warning them that it is a wrong spirit trying to create a problem. You have to learn to know the difference.

Educated people with great knowledge specializing in different fields of human behavior call the spiritual unbalance in man a state of psychological derangement, for a variety of reasons, such as schizophrenia, bipolar disorder, dementia, hallucinations, autism, epilepsy, neurological disorders, and paralysis, among many more conditions that in the spiritual realm are evil spirits at work in the body and life of a person. These are wrong spirits that have altered the human body and mind, destroying the spiritual connection in its perfect creation.

When man failed to obey God in the Garden of Eden, man gave the devil the right to tamper. Dying spiritually, he gave up his holiness and health; he gave up his perfect existence for an imperfect one, where everything is altered.

God has given us the science of medicine for our lack of faith in many cases, but a working faith and belief overpowers the science of medicine. Which one will we pick? Common sense is a useful tool as well, one that can be put into practice without any religious extremes. Remember, God can perform a miracle by intervening directly, or He might use another person to help you. Your job is just to believe and trust Him, working in faith with your common sense.

The work of evil spirits in man's heart and body is a direct consequence of a spiritual disconnection from the Spirit of God, for which the body is rough terrain. Rocks and sand make the soil incapable of being a productive place to plant, as whatever grows there is good for nothing, unless you replace those rocks and sand with good soil, that is, not only medicine that can be used for a time, but also the miracle of faith and belief, which is the real medicine that cures spiritual and physical imbalances.

God has given the knowledge to man to create medicine. There are things that medicine can't help but faith can, as implied in Luke 9:39–43; Matthew 8:2–3, 9:2–8, 9:29–30, 17:15–18, 20:30–34; and Mark 7:32–35, 10:51–52. Only your faith, not your doubts, deductions, interpretations, or feelings, will move God's hand in your favor. And according to His will, He will heal you in that same moment or over time, through your believing perseverance and a steady or growing faith in your needy heart.

A soul's heart under an evil spell has almost no self-will unless it understands that the possibility of reacting always exists when the heart is given the chance to hear the voice of conscience, that is, its own pushed-away spirit fighting to the last to help it. To have that possibility, we need to understand that it exists when we decide to help ourselves, noticing the right and wrong of the moment.

A soul whose heart has no understanding of its own condition is a soul completely controlled by an evil force from a different dimension where a person is taken by a wrong spirit through mental illness, that is, unpredicted psychopathic or sociopathic reactions; where acts of violence may occur; and where maybe a sometimes unnoticeable physical illnesses, with all its ramifications on the human body, could be present. Such a spiritual condition not only alters but also deforms the thinking of the heart, further weakening the person's already ignored human spirit, to the point of completely neutralizing its ability to warn and to protect the human body from head to toe. Whereas the first victim is the heart, the second is the soul, which may pay the future consequences.

A holy spiritual heart and soul has a transformed body. A healthy soul has no sick body. A knowledgeable heart in the Spirit is a strong, untouchable creation. This is to be in Jesus as He is in His Father. Man has to be very careful with his own feelings, desires, thoughts, emotions, decisions, and actions. If these do not comply with the voice of understanding within his conscience, conquering his own wild side in the will of God, then he won't conquer heaven according to the promise of the Almighty. The strong and valiant, not the weak and confused, will inherit the heavens.

Perseverance will have its day in glory. Good and evil is like day and night, black and white, the two being very distinct from each other; if it looks gray or kind of good, be alert, as something may not be right. Remember, in some things evil can imitate God, and if you don't have the necessary spiritual knowledge of the Word of God or revelation, you may be deceived into believing a lie.

Jesus said that evil will try to deceive even the chosen ones: "Take heed that no man deceives you. For many will come in My name, saying, I Am the Christ, and shall deceive many" (Matthew 24:4–5). A message such as that comes from an evil spirit in a person who is trying to be a good messenger. People who have the Spirit of God in their lives have to constantly be alert. Satan will approach especially the believers, to knock them off the right path, to confuse them in a very subtle way and with such finesse, that if God's Spirit doesn't alert such people through their spirits, they'll be falling for his tricks. And that falling will be because the spiritual believers trust more in their emotions than in the voice of their spirits in the knowledge of His Word.

A normal person who understands what is good and evil can see the difference between something that is right and something that is wrong, while having the understanding to make the right decision. Also, a person can knowingly make a wrong decision for the wrong reasons. Another case is when a person innocently makes the wrong decision, not giving himself the time to see if what he is about to do is the correct step to take. Evil will always put wrong choices in your path, such as opportunities, feelings, choices, interests, and things that you may think are normal and innocent.

If you don't investigate, giving yourself a chance to find out if what is proposed is right, you'll be sorry later. Whatever happens in any way in your life may affect you spiritually, physically, emotionally, or morally—even financially. God wants us to be spiritually alert because in God's spirituality, he declares within us via revelation a higher knowledge of the unknown, the unknown being that sometimes in our own impatience, we accept what we shouldn't. A man's intellectual IQ is only good for the superficiality of this secular world, but God's higher spiritual wisdom given to man will prevail over all worldly things and situations or circumstances in a man's life, including his intellectual wisdom.

CHAPTER 5

W ithout God's Spirit in our lives, we are always in a spiritual limbo, which has an aura of spiritual death, where our soul's life exists in an unknown future of our own determination, whether informed by instinct or by knowledge. This is because our human spirit was neutralized by our heart's decision to ignore God's warning in the Garden of Eden.

When a person knows himself in every possible way, including both his strong and weak sides; understands what is good and bad; and can distinguish between good and evil, then the person pursues the knowledge of God's wisdom in his heart. After that, God will reward that wish for wisdom with spiritual knowledge and understanding of His Word, and with revelations of His will with a working spiritual power.

You always have to remember that just knowing is not enough. You also have to ensure that whatever it is that you know, you also understand, at least putting the effort in. For example, one day, for no reason, you feel as if your insides are empty, as if there is no life, no feelings, no emotions—just complete emptiness. You don't feel your own heart, and you don't understand the why for the feelings you're having, such as sadness, confusion, physical weakness, desperation, unexplained nonphysical pain, and an absence of thoughts and/or strength. That is what you know at that moment. But how can you explain all that? Going to a shrink is not the answer. Taking desperate steps or letting yourself fall into depression isn't either.

The answer is to take the time and learn about yourself and the things surrounding your life. Because that emptiness is the Spirit's wake-up call to your inner life, even when you think that everything in your life is okay. In reality it is not. And the best shrink that you can find for free to help you is yourself.

Believe in God. Or if in that moment you don't believe that He exists or there is something that He can't do to help you, just give yourself a chance. Look up into the heavens with the same sincerity that you would express to a psychologist whom you're paying, and from the bottom of your heart confess your needs, your thoughts, your wishes, and anything that you may think you have to do. Take yourself out of yourself, empty your heart of that incomprehensible internal emptiness, and make your heart confess through your own words.

Look for help with the same honest and sincere intensity in your soul you would have upon wishing in desperation to be saved from the great pain of uncertainty and confusion. It is in those small areas, such as desperation, need, intensity, pain, sincerity, and confession, where God will intervene in your life to help you be honest with Him and with yourself.

Take a chance on God whether you believe in Him or not. Always remember, evil spirits never take a break to stop from making your life miserable. Whatever sweetness you may have for a moment, at the end of the day you will have a bitter and sour taste in your soul. Open your heart to Jesus in your private times. Talk to Him as if you are talking to another person or best friend face-to-face. Be sincere and honest; empty yourself of that inexplicable feeling, and believe, and you'll see the difference. Just talk freely, having Jesus, God, or the heavens in your thoughts, for it is the honest humbleness and sincerity of your heart, in your need to believe, that causes your faith to build a spiritual foundation before the Almighty.

Insist, and God will reward you. Do not listen to that voice in your head that is telling you that whatever you are going to be doing is not going to work. Fight and fight hard, and remember, this fight is not a fight with another human; it's a fight with a spiritual entity. In this battle you don't use your pride, your fists, your body, or your strength; you'll have to use your faith, your belief, and the trust that you may think you don't have or that you may think will not work. It will work if you first show humbleness, sincerity, and honesty about your need.

Get off of your high horse, eschewing your arrogance, self-righteousness, and selfishness, because this fight is quite different. The punches that you feel inside your heart are spiritual, and they hit very hard. You need to learn in the name of Jesus how to fight to defend yourself by believing and having faith in Him, that is, trusting Him. You need to learn how to fight spiritually with faith, and to be a good fighter you'll have to practice, like any fighter in this secular world. The difference is that the fighter trusts himself in his strength, but when you trust the Almighty in your believing faith, He will intercede on your behalf to fight and win against any evil that goes against you. Take the simple secular example of a father and his child when the child is trying to pick up something that is impossible for him to do and his father is helping, encouraging him, telling him, "Come on, Son, you can do it," while the father is lifting most of the weight. Do your part in your faith and belief. When you have that commitment, He is with you, helping you.

This world is a coliseum full of evil people and spirits who enjoy seeing you suffer. You are in the middle of the arena. The adverse circumstances of any stripe that you have to fight are your enemy. The odds against you, with you being all by yourself, are not indicative of a winning proposition. You are smart enough to see that there is no way to win, but if you pick up your faith and belief as your spade and your shield, trust God, and get into the fight in Jesus's name, you will be a winner. After the sweating, having donned your belief, faith, and trust as your spiritual armor and your weapons to winning your fight without a doubt, you'll become one of those people who understand what it means when His Word says, "What shall we say to those things? If God be for us, who can be against us?" (Romans 8:3).

Only then, when you really try, will God fill your empty soul, giving your heart the feeling of full peace and happiness. Sure, you may hear about God, but when you connect with Him, you will *know Him* personally. Then you will really know and understand the big picture.

God and the devil, heaven and hell, holiness and sin, are not only words. These are spiritual realities in a spiritual world, where the intellect is incapable of any understanding. You know what you know now, and it may be a lot or may be a little. Maybe it's right, or maybe it's wrong, but there is always more to learn if you only believe. It's all up to you. Whatever you know, and however much you know, give yourself a chance to look farther for the wisdom of God in your life. How can you change the circumstances of your life and turn the tables? The choice is ultimately yours.

The idea of what it means for a believer to be humble is wrongly understood by many. Jesus said in Luke 6:29, "And unto him that smiteth thee on the one cheek offer also the other; and him that taketh away thy cloak forbid not to take thy coat also." This giving-in action does not apply to our fight with the devil. To win against the devil, we must have faith and humility before God, understanding that without Him and His blessing in our lives, there is nothing we can do against evil, not even for our own selves.

The Lord is teaching us to be passive in our reactions to man, whether the individual we're facing is a good person or a bad person. In Matthew 10:16, Jesus said, "Behold, I'm sending you forth as sheep in the midst of wolves. Be ye therefore wise as serpents and harmless as doves," referring to any person who deals with us unjustly, teaching us how to avoid any confrontation. In this passiveness, we prevent our pride from reacting and getting us into trouble. By reacting wisely, we'll perhaps have a chance to avoid the problem, whether we like it or not. But at the same time, we have the right to defend ourselves, seeing through our common sense and with God's help, the danger in front of us. Trusting God always for our defense and trusting God's wisdom in our lives will help us take the right steps in an act of peaceful resistance.

As for any business against the devil, the Bible says to resist him and make him run. That's a whole different story, a whole different way of reaction where not pride, but knowledge in the Word of God and faith in Him, gives us the right to react accordingly, which is not to pick a fight but to have the necessary spiritual weapons for our defense and victory. This also pertains to when a man with a wrong spirit is trying to fight us or create any adverse circumstances in our lives.

To avoid the miseries of life, we need to know and understand who our enemy is and how we can beat him. Ignorance is not a weapon; knowledge in God's wisdom is. We must trust not in ourselves but believe in the One who stands to the side of our faith, according to the gift given by Him in our lives or the wishes of our hearts. Remember, Satan, out of the blue, will create real problems in your inner being, such as emptiness and confusion, but also through some people in your secular life, whether you know them or not.

CHAPTER 6

A long time ago, a man said, "The only thing necessary for the triumph of evil is for good men to do nothing." His name was Edward Burke. But well before that, apostle Paul said, "For we do not wrestle against flesh and blood, but against principalities, against powers, against the rulers of darkness of this world, against spiritual wickedness in high places" (Ephesians 6:12). What apostle Paul is saying here is that we have a fight against Satan and all his evil demon spirits, who attack us either directly in the spiritual sense or through another person. Satan is controlling and governing this world of spirits, making humankind suffer physically, psychologically, and spiritually.

Paul, apostle to the Gentiles, was the last man to be handpicked by Jesus. Paul was a man who was given spiritual wisdom by God to spread the message of the gospel to the world. God gave him the knowledge and understanding to see the difference in his life after he committed himself to Christ. This knowledge was given for our sake, so Paul could elucidate the condition of a man's life without God and the possibility of redemption for the salvation of man's soul through the sacrifice and acceptance of our Lord Jesus Christ.

We do have a fight not against flesh and blood, but against principalities governing this world. There is nothing better on this earth that describes the division between the two worlds that man lives in than Ephesians 6:12.

One world is from the spiritual beginning of its origin which became distorted in its failure. And because of that same distorted failure, the second one came to be known as secular humanism, a self-sufficient intellectual approach to understanding life that lives well below the original spiritual approach.

Two worlds in one, together but not united, both with spiritual consequences at the end; one to be rewarded upon a person's recognition of wrong, following repentance, the other to be condemned for a person's failure to repent and recognize or admit wrong. From here, the "good evil," or the "evil of good," in man's secular ideals engendered a fight between different beliefs about the gospel and religion, creating the denominations, which instead of uniting people, separate them in their own understandings of faith and belief in the only existing God.

This difference of opinion and difference in understanding did not exist before man fell to the devil's claw. Everything that was pure and clean is now confused, contradicted, and contaminated. Even when the natural fog of nature is kind of white, it is deceiving in its intensity, just like the spiritual fog of evil.

A light is needed for man to see through or doubt that fog of spiritual ignorance, but sometimes that light, in man's deduction, according to his understanding, is not nearly bright enough. This is because the heavy fog prevents the light of man's own intelligence and wisdom from getting through. There is no other light in this world than the light of wisdom and revelation given to man by God's Spirit, which can get through anything that evil in people might create, or anything that makes those people believe that they are correct in their behavior.

A few thousand years back, King David wrote, "Thy word is a lamp unto my feet, and a light unto my path" (Psalms 119:105).

The greatest misunderstanding, as a gift given by the devil to people, is people's belief that they are right in their own minds and in their feelings, deductions, ideas, thoughts, and instincts—without knowing the real truth of God. This is a sort of gift of "goodness" from Satan to confuse people in a very sophisticated, religious, and philosophical way, approaching any area of a person's secular life by way of his or her feelings and emotions. The Spirit of the Almighty is the presence of God in the life of a spiritual Christian who has spiritual knowledge of His Word. The Spirit is the One who gives to the soul's heart not only the real spiritual knowledge of the Word, but also all the words to praise God and to be grateful for the knowledge that is revealed through human words or in the secret heavenly language that the Spirit uses to intercede for us before the throne of God.

Throughout the centuries, people using their good-intentioned wills for their own good never got to the point of achieving any kind of inner peace, either mental, emotional, psychological, or spiritual, by following their own religious beliefs. Everybody is either right or wrong according to their own opinion. And when speaking of certain subjects, the gap of comprehension is as wide as the gap between North America and the European continent, based on each person's experience, knowledge, and beliefs.

In this world, there are two kinds of ideals. One is spiritual and the other is secular. One is from the heavens; the other is from this world. Even though both have spiritual consequences, one is right and the other is wrong. But who decides who is right and who is wrong when each person thinks he or she is right and the other is wrong, even among believers?

Man has determined the truth for himself in politics, religion, science, and every other area of life. The idea of politics for a better future always leads to disagreements even among members of the same party, never mind between members of the other political parties. Christians of the same beliefs also have their disagreements, not to mention the difference of belief among the many denominations. Scientists happen to have their own belief systems too. A different interpretation of any subject in the intellectual, spiritual, or religious arena, in many cases, if not all the time, causes division.

For human beings, division is a normal outcome because man is himself divided between good and evil. But in God's spiritual world, it must not be that way, because God's Word and will is one, and it doesn't change for any reason because it is perfect. And if we are to be in that perfect spiritual world, He wants us to have one mind and one spirit, something that the majority of those who believe in Christ do not have.

Any of man's ideologies, beliefs, or interpretations are, in and of themselves, imperfect because man himself is imperfect; no matter how well-intentioned he may think he is, he is not dependable, simply because of the hidden misconceptions within his heart. For an intelligent man in the secular world, everything has to be tested and proven, and if something should fail, there is always someone or something else to blame. In the spiritual world, on the other hand, things are quite different. God doesn't make mistakes. His Word has no mistakes, and all that He has created is perfect. Everything is clear and absolute. The will and wishes of God for man are crystal clear and are all on the table to be seen.

The lack of understanding in man disables him from seeing clearly what God has given him to set himself free from the devil and his hidden tricks, because he does not have God's Spirit within him, revealing things and guiding him. Even when he first becomes a Christian believer without the understanding of what it means to be guided by the Spirit, his unwillingness to pursue a higher form of knowledge keeps him stuck in a steady, conservative faith, instead of sending him on a faith of investigation. An inquisitive mind is rewarded with knowledge and power for seeking the kingdom of God and His justice. In God's kingdom, the payback for faith and inquisitiveness is wisdom, revelation, and God's power in a person's life, which is never a losing investment.

In this world, nobody can be blamed but man himself for man's lack of faith, interest in, or dedication to the secrets of the will of the Almighty. To achieve victory, one must "conquer" the will of God by submitting to Him in the knowledge and understanding of His Word and by believing in faith. That will be the key to revealing our victory for His glory through His Spirit, according to the wishes of our hearts. He will guide us not only to conquer the many things He promises we will overcome, such as the soul of man within us, but also to cast off and disempower the evil creatures that create misery in mankind through sin.

How can we completely rid our lives of the devil and his evil spirits? Is it possible to eradicate them? Can we try to do that? The answer is either no, yes, or maybe. It all depends on our knowledge and understanding of the Word of God and how close we are to God in our spiritual lives, believing and having a mustard seed of faith.

The Bible says, "Submit yourself therefore to God. Resist the devil and he will flee from you" (James 4:7). But the fact that the devil will run from us doesn't mean he won't come back another time, because he is always hunting us. How do we put a permanent stop to his attacks on us? Can it be done or not? The Word of God is extreme—all or nothing. God is God and there are no maybes, such as the ones in our own minds. The Bible says that God has given the same amount of faith to each one of us. That faith in us is like yeast to the dough when we are going through trials in our lives. It is the quality of the yeast, that is, our belief and faith, that determines whether the dough will rise. If the yeast is of poor quality, that is, if our faith is not firm and solid, then our spiritual growth will never be sufficient to make us into what God wants us to be, namely, efficient and productive, even when He has left us so many promises.

The same Word tells the story of the master who is going away and is calling his three servants to say farewell. He gives to one five coins; to the other, three coins; and to the third one, only one. Each one of them had money, which represents faith. It was not the amount, but the value of what they had, with the addition of their knowledge, understanding, and wishes, that determined how they acted. This is reflective of the way God has given us spiritual gifts. The apostle Paul said, "For to one is given by the Spirit the word of wisdom; to another word of knowledge by the same Spirit; to another faith by the same Spirit; to another the gift of healing by the same Spirit; to another the working of miracles; to another prophecy, to others discerning of spirits; to another diverse kinds of tongues; to another the interpretation of tongues" (1 Corinthians 12:7–10). He continues, saying, "But all those worketh that one and the selfsame Spirit, dividing to every man severally as he will" (1 Corinthians 12:11).

It is not through intellectual knowledge that a person acquires the type of faith that every person must have, but through belief, and belief comes from the heart as expressed in the Word of God. That Word is real in spirit, in our secular and spiritual world.

The reality of the first spiritual life is stronger than the reality of our secular natural existence. So if there is any fighting to be done, it has to be done spiritually. A spiritual person needs to know where he stands as a member of the body of Christ with God's gifts in his life or wishes in his heart. Jesus said in Luke 11:21, "When a strong man armed keepeth his palace, his goods are in peace." To conquer the enemy is not only to make him run away, but also to neutralize him. And neutralizing him doesn't mean to kill him, but to immobilize him, for example, by placing him in jail or prison, where he is under control. The armament of the strong man is his solid faith, which is what makes him confident that he can protect his own surroundings and himself. If the strong man's faith is not solid, and if he has doubts, then another strong man will come and take everything that belongs to the first, who, because of his lack of confidence, will fail to be vigilant and protect even himself.

When Jesus spoke about resisting the devil and making him run from us, He left for us the possibility to understand more by being inquisitive. The example He left for us is the story of the fig tree and the mountain, as follows:

> Now in the morning, as he returned into the city, he hungered. And when he saw a fig tree in the way, he came to it and found nothing thereon, but leaves only, and he said unto it, Let no fruit grow on thee hencefoward forever. And presently the fig tree withered away.
>
> And when the disciples saw it, they marveled, saying, How soon is the fig tree withered away! Jesus answered and said unto them, Verily I say unto you, If ye have faith, and doubt not, ye shall not only do this which is done to the fig tree, but also if ye shall say unto this mountain, be thou removed, and be thou cast into the sea; it shall be done. And all things, whatsoever ye shall ask in prayer, believing ye shall receive. (Matthew 21:18–22)

We must challenge ourselves to seek other possibilities that may exist in the will of God or the wishes of our hearts during the process of becoming more knowledgeable in our understanding of the Word, which will increase our spiritual strength, our belief, and our faith.

The Bible says, "For with the heart man believes unto righteousness; and with the mouth confession" (Romans 10:10). It can be said that man's faith is the "voice" of his soul in his heart, which is the tongue that confesses his faith through man's mouth.

An immobilized enemy or an adverse circumstance is not a threat. Having control over our enemy or an adverse circumstance is much different from allowing our enemy or an adverse circumstance to have control over us. In our case, as Christians believing in the power of God, we need to have control, as Jesus did when He was in this world. But for that we need to stand on a strong foundation called "believing faith."

The devil is not worried about us jumping on him the way he does on us. He knows it takes faith and determination to actively resist him, and he can see that we are having a problem in that area, not knowing how to use our faith directly and effectively against him. If only we had a mustard seed's worth of faith in our believing hearts, then we would allow that faith to take root in our souls. If we doubt in our hearts, then we have no belief, and if we have no belief, then we have no working faith. The soul is the receiver, and the heart is the one that decides to give, take, accept, and reject for the well-being of the soul.

Somehow we are putting up a fight against evil, but not as effectively as we should. It is true that we are able to stop some evil things, but we have a difficult time stopping an evildoer before he does something that causes widespread misery in people's lives across the world. Maybe it's a matter of misunderstanding and lack of interest from our part. Satan is happy to see us in the mess we are in, always in a defensive position instead of an empowered one.

Satan knows we are religious, but he also knows we are cautious, and may be afraid, ignorant, or lazy, about the possibilities evident in the promises the Lord has left for us. Satan and his followers are not afraid of us, even when they know we believe in Jesus. They're just provocatively arrogant. Satan knows that many believers are quite far from being like Jesus.

Jesus said to His disciples, "Oh faithless generation, how long I shall be with you? How long I shall suffer you?" (Mark 9:19). That was His reply when His disciples told Him that they had failed to rebuke an evil spirit. A person who reaches this point is a believer who is short of a believing faith and an understanding of the power given by God to His people to move the hand of God in respect to all His promises, and to suppress Satan and his evil demoniacal followers. What such a person is exhibiting is called doubt or plain lack of faith. He may have a faith that exists only in his thoughts or is expressed from his mouth, but is not at work in his heart.

No matter how many years we have been part of a church, and no matter our level of spirituality, most of us are still children. Faith, knowledge, belief, courage, boldness, and trust are what we need to develop as true believers. We also must admit that we rarely pray or fast, or that we pray and fast without a real, deep knowledge of God's power. If we are so confident that we know the Word of God and understand all His promises, then why is it that we have so many inconvenient things, if not outright problems, in our lives?

It seems to be a contradiction of our faith when we say that we believe in all the promises He left for us while simultaneously refusing to do what He asks of us. Maybe our interpretation and understanding of the Word needs to be reviewed. Or maybe like always, we'll just say that whatever we think or whatever we do is God's will.

The apostles were having all kinds of problems; that is the truth. But you are forgetting something: they were the pioneers, the first Christians. They were the ones who began building on the foundation that Christ left for us, to have and to stand on today, based in the Lord's teaching. Unfortunately, more than two thousand years later, we haven't advanced much in the building of knowledge of how to fight in the spiritual world to defend and protect ourselves.

As a secular example, at that time when Jesus walked the earth, the buildings were made of stone, mud, and wood, whereas today they are made of concrete, steel, and glass. In our spiritual lives, we still build our faith but believe in keeping the old materials (that is, we are passive), not caring much about using materials that are new and more advanced (the promises of the Lord), not even being willing to try them. Many people are even failing to care for the old materials, lacking in the interest to do so because of their own laziness, their hope in man, or their false belief in self-sufficiency.

As written in the story of the virgins waiting for the coming of the Lord:

> Then shall the kingdom of heaven be likened unto ten virgins, which took their lamps, and went forth to meet the bridegroom. And five of them were wise, and five were foolish. They that were foolish took their lamps, and took no oil with them: But the wise took oil in their vessels with their lamps. While the bridegroom tarried, they all slumbered and slept. And at midnight there was a cry made, Behold, the bridegroom cometh; go ye out to meet him. Then all those virgins arose, and trimmed their lamps. And the foolish said unto the wise, Give us of your oil; for our lamps are gone out. But the wise answered, saying, Not so; lest there be not enough for us and you: but go ye rather to

them that sell, and buy for yourselves. And while they went to buy, the bridegroom came; and they that were ready went in with him to the marriage: and the door was shut. Afterward came also the other virgins, saying, Lord, Lord, open to us. But he answered and said, Verily I say unto you, I know you not. Watch therefore, for ye know neither the day nor the hour wherein the Son of man cometh. (Matthew 25:1–13)

Today, we have the Word of God, which is the whole Bible and not the earlier scriptures the apostles had. The first car or airplane ever manufactured today may look like antique, but modern-day cars and airplanes perform the same job, but they go farther, faster, and are much more technologically advanced. This has happened in the secular world where everything is limited, but even so, there is the saying "The sky is the limit." Imagine the possibilities in God's spiritual promises.

It is in our best interests to have knowledge in "advanced spiritual technology"—or a sufficient amount of "oil"—along with the faith and belief to be taken farther in God's will. We must understand that it is in our best interests for God's glory to go the extra mile. When we begin to do so, the Lord will supply the necessary spiritual tools and materials to accomplish His will and fulfill the wishes of our hearts.

God's Word says that in His world nothing is impossible for anyone who has faith and believes in Him. So then we have to ask ourselves, whose fault is it that evil has gone from bad to worse as a result of people's lack of interest in their own supply of spiritual oil? When will we understand that if God is for us, no one can be against us?

CHAPTER 7

We know the devil is smarter than people. Our level of spirituality will determine whether or not we are sure within ourselves that there is no other spirit than God's in our spiritual life that is trying to make us believe that whatever we know at the current time is correct and that we shouldn't look or investigate further. That same spirit causes us to think that what we already know or have is sufficient, so we shouldn't be worried about finding more. To settle this way is to be content in a false sense of confidence in the knowledge that we currently have.

Satan won't push or force us out of the way of God's truth; instead, he will imitate truth to make us believe in our own self-confident spirit that everything is fine. Unbeknownst to believers, he will make them go off the right path or cease from moving ahead, sometimes by using a person who preaches the gospel according to his own ideas of what is right—and those who do this sort of thing today are many—and sometimes by performing "miracles." People fall for this because they approach their faith in the wrong spirit, and this happens because they are not quite knowledgeable in the spirit of the Word.

Spiritual alertness in the real knowledge of the Word will allow the faithful person to remain aware when hearing the Word spoken by anyone who may be doing the will of God. The believer will have in his heart the warnings of his spirit, from God's Spirit, when something is not from God. Such spiritual confidence comes from having a knowledge of the Word through God's Spirit, which is delivered by revelation. Self-confidence and spiritual confidence rooted in the Word are two very different types of confidence.

The Bible says that a person who wishes not to be cheated out of his salvation should test spirits, be alert in his knowledge of the Word, and remain in the Spirit of God. That is why we need revelations, not human deductions or interpretations, or our own understanding, when we read or listen to the Word. It is not in God's will that we should be miserable, when He has repeated His promises so many times. He has told us everything we need to know and has given us everything we need to have in order to get out of this life of misery under the devil's oppression. Being alert and watchful for any otherwise unnoticeable spirits that are trying to deceive us is our main spiritual responsibility. What is our excuse for not being alert this way?

Jesus had to live with only one inconvenience in His life, and it wasn't His problem, but ours: our lack of faith and understanding. People had little faith and understanding two thousand years ago, and the same is true today. Why? If our faith is only coming out of our mouths, that's not enough. It's nothing. It has to come from the bottom of our souls and hearts to really be effective from our mouths.

We have to be interested in the spiritual world of God. We have to be knowledgeable in our spiritual hearts. We have to be sensible to the Holy Ghost, dedicated and persistent, not being conformist and lazy. We have to grab everything that is from God, like a mother who is trying to rescue her child from a deadly situation, convinced to the end that we can do it with God's promises and God's help. If God is with us and for us, who is or can be against us?

The teachers of the gospel and the leaders of the church have to wake up and see that we are here not only to win souls, as many of them believe, but also to fight the evils of the air, as the apostle Paul said, or if it is in the will of God, to conquer them. Like the soldiers we are supposed to be, we must lay them at our Lord's feet, a conquered enemy in front of our general commander. Not just scaring them again and again, but scaring them and defeating them.

Getting defensive and upset over something that we are not used to hearing, something that makes us uncomfortable because our knowledge is short and our faith is mixed with pride, won't be much of a help to anyone if we don't stop and think that maybe, just maybe, the Lord wants to do something greater through us, that is, through our faith and according to the wishes of our hearts.

How do we know that whatever we are doing today for Him is all He wants us to do? We are so sure of ourselves, but maybe we are forgetting or ignoring that we are His servants, His clay. Philippians 2:13 reads, "For it is God which worketh in you both to will and to do for His good pleasure." If we would only open to the possibility of not being so proud, being such "hardened clay", or being so "knowledgeable", then maybe our hearts would be more sensible and would soften up to help us understand the will of God.

Let's not make the mistake of thinking that being spiritually sharp will make us intellectually dull. In Ephesians 3:20 we read, "Now unto Him that is able to do exceeding abundantly above all that we ask or think, according to the power that worketh in us." We have to look for the lessons of His teaching so we can do His will and He can be pleased with us. But that is something determined by the will of each person, whether or not they have the interest, wish, and/or desire to have the real life and the power of God, living in the Spirit of victory.

Somehow the devil has infiltrated people's minds in such a sophisticated way that we are still having problems with becoming one in mind and spirit. Even when we are supposed to have one mind and one spirit, we need to have our hearts ready and our spirits free in God's Spirit if we wish for positive results. When "something like that" is impossible to believe, it becomes a challenge, and we get stuck in the understanding of our own interpretations, knowledge, and faith, and that is all because of the doctrinal differences in our Christian denominations. We are afraid of what we are unsure of, and that is called insecurity.

We are not "spiritual" enough with faith, knowledge, and belief for God to use us in His will. Doubt, religiousness, misunderstandings, misinterpretation, denominations, and pride or arrogance kill the real unity of trust and belief among Christians, preventing them from having true working unity of one mind and one spirit. Where there is no understanding, there is no unity. The day when all denominations, their teachings, and their differences in doctrine are all put aside will be the day when all interpretations become revelations in one mind because of one spirit. When each of us is in our respective places in God's will, that will be the day of victory.

Today the members of the body of Christ are together but not united. Those of man's denominations and doctrines given by Satan are not revelations of God, but interpretations, a self-induced understanding of man, of the Word, and of what is believed to be the will of God. It is the other spirit, the evil spirit, that in a very soft way introduces deceptive knowledge to a person who is blind to his or her own pride, to be accepted as a spiritual revelation in the person's good-intentioned heart, a revelation that many believe is from God.

This has nothing to do with the real spiritual revelation of God's truth. God never separates, but unites. The misunderstanding of the Word of God is a fine intellectual introduction of misinterpretation, where many good-hearted Christian leaders think they are walking the correct spiritual path to a real knowledge of the Word, not knowing that they are following a wrong spirit.

A very fine, almost invisible, line exists in the spiritual world, which can be noticed—but cannot be in the intellectual world, unless it is revealed by the Spirit. The suggested thought given by Satan through the serpent to Eve was: "Ye shall not surely die: For God doth know that in the day that ye eat thereof, then your eye shall be open, and ye shall be as gods, knowing good and evil" (Genesis 3:4–5).

It was purity that was lost in the highest and holiest spiritual world of God, together with man's life—a loss that happened because a liable heart believed in a softly spoken white lie proclaiming "knowledge", a loss that has transformed man's life from the highest to the lowest at its worst, in a world where man still insists on trying to reach the heights according to his own deductions. Deductions, interpretations, and understandings are what is keeping us apart as members in the body of our Lord, and this is the work of the unnoticeable spirit of deceit spreading its own truth.

Together we have the idea that we are united in our religion before the world, but in reality, we stick to our different doctrinal interpretations according to our respective denomination. We have cut ourselves off from the spiritual goal of achieving unity in understanding and working together in the Spirit, which the Almighty requires of us. That is because something is telling us that we are on the right path in our spiritual lives, and we are susceptible to believing it because we don't care to find out why we do not believe in God with one understanding under the same spirit. We also don't question why there are many different doctrines and denominations when there is only one gospel of Christ. Maybe our unrecognized pride with its arrogant attitude doesn't want our egos to let go of "I'm right."

Where does it say in the Bible that God wants us to be of different beliefs, when we have been given the same faith, the same gospel, and the same Word? Who gave us all the denominations and doctrines? For sure it wasn't God. Living according to our own understanding of His Word and Will does not make us okay. Someone will have to answer for the twisting of His Word and the resulting spiritual mess we are in.

The day when we have the wisdom of His Spirit in our spirits, working, warning, declaring, revealing, reminding, guiding, and teaching our hearts of His will, is when as one we'll all have the same knowledge, the same understanding, and the same mind for Him to do His will in our lives. But for that we need to be humble and repent of our own spiritual pride, admitting that we are wrong. Otherwise we'll never be able to reach real spiritual unity, not until we understand the meaning of the will and power of the Almighty through His revelation to us. At the end of the day, excusing ourselves or accusing someone else won't make us right or victorious. God cannot force us to learn how to eat solid food if we don't want to or care to. We need to realize that we must learn how to chew solid food. Christians need to stop being spiritual children all their lives.

Maybe we'll never be able to make the devil run, or get nabbed and placed into custody, even when he sees in us the anointing of the Spirit of God, and the authority and power in the name of Jesus. Why? The reason is that we have not completely grown up in spiritual knowledge, understanding, belief, and trust, and have not experienced the spiritual buildup of our faith in its working power to make us as one in Him. That is our main and only spiritual weapon, a weapon that we haven't learned how to use. Jesus said in Mark 11:24, "Therefore I say unto you, What things soever ye desire, when ye pray, believe that ye receive them, and ye shall have them." As for our asking, He never said, "I'll think about it."

Our doubts, wrong knowledge, and very weak understanding prevents our faith from having the necessary torque to ignite on its own power. If we believe in our faith, we can do what is called the impossible. We may think we have what is necessary, but the powerful weapon of faith that we have in our hands won't work if we don't learn how to use it, believing, trusting, and being confident in the One who has given us that power through our faith. And if that power doesn't work, that means our faith is very rusty, "invisible," or wrongly directed.

We need to know how to use that weapon called faith. We have such ups and downs and doubt because of our weak spiritual condition that the results of our faith are keeping us in a corral. Your working conviction in your faith, in the understanding of His promises, is the only way to be victorious, because it is absolutely impossible for God not to act when He sees no doubt in your faithful heart.

The discrepancies in our understanding of the will of God, such as personal doubts or inaccurate doctrine among the body of Christ, will keep us separated in deeds, beliefs, mind, and spirit, making the conquest of evil impossible. That is not the way to become unified in any way. To open the eyes of the believer is to help him find out to what part of Christ's body he belongs to as a member in his God-given gifts, for in time these will be used in the Lord's will.

According to His Word and promise, we are not the ones who will bring about the destruction of evil or the judgment of evildoers. As believers who are faithful to the Word of God, we leave the judgment and the consequences of any evildoer to God

Almighty. Meanwhile, our failure is that we are not making an effort to gain the ability to neutralize or immobilize evil spirits.

The question is, how does one do that? First, learn the Word of God. Learn the promises of our Lord Jesus. Ask God in prayer to give you what the apostle Paul spoke of in Ephesians 1:17–22:

> That the God of our Lord Jesus Christ, the Father of glory, may give unto you the spirit of wisdom and revelation in the knowledge of him: The eyes of your understanding being enlightened; that ye may know what is the hope of his calling, and what the riches of the glory of his inheritance in the saints, and what is the exceeding greatness of his power to us-ward who believe, according to the working of his mighty power, which he wrought in Christ, when he raised him from the dead, and set him at his own right hand in the heavenly places, far above all principality, and power, and might, and dominion, and every name that is named, not only in this world, but also in that which is to come: And hath put all things under his feet, and gave him to be the head over all things to the church.

Also in 1 Corinthians 15:24–26, it says, "Then cometh the end, when He shall have delivered up the kingdom to God, even the Father; when He puts an end to all rule and all authority and power. For He must reign till he shall put down all rule and all authority and power. For he must reign, till he hath put all enemies under His feet. The last enemy that shall be destroyed is death." And about the last enemy, his destruction will not be our job; it will occur in a face-to-face encounter between God the Almighty and Satan.

Jesus said, "If ye abide in Me, and My words abide in you, ye shall ask what ye will, and it shall be done unto you" (John 15:7). In 1 John 5:14–15, the apostle John said, "And this is the confidence that we have in Him, that if we ask anything according to His will, He heareth us: And if we know that He hear us, whatsoever we ask, we know that we have the petitions that we desire of Him!" All this requires faith and only faith. But if there is no faith, there is no confidence. And the absence of faith and confidence is the product of a heart that is not strong in its beliefs.

Our challenge is to ask. If God says no, we lose nothing, nor bear responsibility for not going the extra mile, but if He says yes, oh boy! Get ready for the fight, because surely you'll be a winner. God the Father through Jesus Christ gave us in His Son's name the most powerful weapon ever given to man.

To what extent do Christians fail to understand the power of this promise? Jesus is telling us about all His promises: "If you have faith …"; "If only you believed …"; "If you don't doubt …"; "If you have a wish in your heart …"; "If two or more people gather together in My name …"; "Whatever you may ask of the Father in My name, it will be given to you." He gives the assurance that whatever we may want, according to the intentions of our hearts, it will be granted. We have to understand that the Word of God is a challenge for Christians. Our belief is a challenge to us. His promises are a challenge. Faith itself is a challenge.

The Bible reads, "But without faith it is impossible to please him" (Hebrews 11:6). The Bible is reminding us that we must have faith and believe all the time. If a person's heart is weak in its beliefs, then his or her soul is faithless. Why faithless? Because it is through the will of the heart in its decisions that the soul receives. So, faith in the Spirit is the life of the soul with a believing heart.

When the Word says all things are possible for those who believe and nothing is impossible for God, but then for some reason we think that something cannot be done, that is called doubt or just plain lack of faith. When using our intellect without spiritual revelation, our deductions won't hold value when we try to understand a spiritual promise or mandate. That is our challenge when it comes to our faith. Faith doesn't work according to our imaginings or deductions. Faith works only in a believing heart.

The only way to understand the Word and the will of God is to be guided by the Spirit in His revelations and to have the courage to really reach the heavens the way God wants us to, the way Jesus did when He was on this earth, through fasting and constant prayer. But it seems to be that we are a little short on faith and are defiant about getting to the deepest part of the spiritual world without any doubts. Christians who do not have the right spirit working in their lives, or who prevent the Spirit from working in their lives because of their own weakened hearts, have been slapped and slapped again by the devil for their lack of proper spiritual knowledge of the Word and will of God as it is revealed.

Who among Christians can challenge himself to know more about God than what is known up to this moment? Why does the Bible say that we will face all kinds of unpleasant situations in life when we have so many promises of help from God? Is it just because God says so, or because He knows we aren't capable of reaching heaven with our lukewarm faith in His Word? And not only that, but we also do not practice our spirituality in our daily lives, preventing us from having a close relationship with Him.

Why are we unable to see farther than our own noses when it comes to what the Word of God is telling us and teaching us? Is it because of the shallow traditional teachings of the gospel in an attempt to reach the ultimate spiritual knowledge, or are we afraid of finding out that we are weak in our faith and therefore incapable of fulfilling His will? Maybe we are just afraid to be spiritual, knowledgeable, and holy.

God said, "My people are destroyed for lack of knowledge." Obviously, God is telling this to someone standing before Him with responsibility as a shepherd, "Because you have rejected knowledge, My people are destroyed for lack of knowledge" (Hosea 4:6). This pertains not only to the Israelites, but also to us Gentiles. Can these words be applied to the leaders of the church today? Or have we become like the Pharisees, knowing too much but not seeing what is around us and unwilling to understand the reality of God and this world, and knowing the letter but not the spirit?

Are we sure that it's enough to be pleased with what we know today? Are we living within a steady, immovable religious tradition, inside a box, or are we renewed by knowledge of revelation by the Spirit every day? How hard are we looking for spiritual knowledge of God? Are we knocking insistently on God's door? Jesus said to be in Him. How difficult is it to be in Him? The apostle Paul said, "Be ye followers of me, even as I also am of Christ" (1 Corinthians 11:1).

Now the question is, what is easier, to be in Christ or to be a follower in the examples of the apostle Paul in order to reach the will of God? It all depends on how deep you are in His Spirit or how much faith you have for the challenge.

A Christian believer, whose life is close to the Lord, yet not completely in the Lord, even if he has the Holy Spirit, but is not letting his own spirit be guided by the Holy Ghost, is ineffective. And if such is the case, then whatever the believer does in his life will have no positive results. The effectiveness of faith can be compared to a person who knows what he wants to write and who has the motivation (the need for spiritual understanding and guidance), and the paper (purpose and will) and a sharp pencil (a working spirit) in his hand (life), and who starts and finishes the letter (gets the job done). But a person who wants to write a letter, having the paper and pencil already on the table but refusing to reach for them, won't be able to write anything.

If the person has no will (faith) to make a commitment (in believing) to move his hands and grab what he needs with a clear understanding of what he wants to write, even if he is sitting at the table (in church), then nothing will be done. Living in faith and looking for the will of God is not a process involving emotion. It is a spiritual reality, where the soul's heart reaches the human spirit with a clear understanding of its need to have contact with the Spirit of God, who declares to our spirits what needs to be understood by our human minds through revelation.

Jesus said, "Therefore I say unto you, what things soever you desire, when ye pray, believe that ye receive them and ye shall have them" (Mark 11:24). Whatever our hearts desire, if our lives are oriented to God's glory, we will have it. Why do we have to be in Jesus, that is, in His Spirit? Because it is the only way to get the right answer from God or to do the right thing for Him.

More than two thousand years have passed in our fight with evil. Generation after generation of people have fought the adverse circumstances of their daily lives, and we have come to the point of knowing all the miseries that we'll have to live through in our lives, even when we have God and all His promises to help us.

Lately in this world, the constant reminder of the need to gradually increase our spiritual knowledge through revelation, where the Christian is encouraged to take on a higher challenge in his own personal life, is absent from the universal teaching of most Christian leaders. The words spoken by these leaders are like feathers in the wind: in the minds of most believers, they just fly by. Instead of those words heaving a weight in their hearts, making them think about, meditate on, and become interested in learning the things from above, they are falling weightless on seemingly deaf ears, not only while they are in church, but also in their daily lives.

It seems that the preaching of the gospel today involves only a reminder of all the good things involved in the Christian life. By avoiding speaking about adverse situations and many other relevant subjects, preachers are failing to move their congregations to seek a higher spiritual knowledge or to properly warn them about wrong interpretations of the Word. Keeping believers in a world of emotional warnings, spoken with great eloquence to touch the conscience, without directing them on specifically how to do the right thing in the learning of the gospel, is a travesty. It looks like a form of holy entertainment that pleases the audience but doesn't touch on or encourage spiritual growth in the personal lives of the believers, making no spiritual challenge. Leaders instead should be encouraging their congregations to continue seeking God and His will after they leave church and go home. Leaders should be first to lead by examples of their own spiritual lives and practice what they preach, in order to see their flocks rising spiritually.

If this is not true, that Christians are not growing spiritually, then why does the Word of God warn us of the loss of faith, of things going from bad to worse, and of many other unpleasant experiences in the lives of believers? Is it not because of ignorance of the Word, laziness, a lack of vision, and comfort with the secular life that many Christians know of but fail to attend to their spiritual life properly or as a priority?

It is not only the responsibility of the spiritual leaders of the church to lead the believer to seek a higher spiritual education. It is also the believer's responsibility to be interested in such spiritual learning. The responsibility belongs to both parties.

In one word, the existing mess that we are living in is a direct spiritual consequence of not knowing the meaning of the Word of Jesus when He said, "But seek ye first the kingdom of God and

His righteousness and all those things shall be added unto you" (Matthew 6:36). That is the main spiritual doorway to enter into a world where not only the believer's spiritual needs of any type are fulfilled, but the secular are too.

The gospel and the church exist, but the wound that we have, resulting in our weakness, seems never to heal. For the preaching, many churches are filled with hundreds, some with thousands, of congregants. A belief in God exists in these churches, but only the Almighty knows how many of His children are in His Spirit, challenging themselves through their faith, and which ones He can use for His victory. We need to grow our faith and knowledge spiritually, not intellectually from a point of egocentrism. The believer has to humbly challenge himself in his faith, believing in it.

"You have brains; use them," someone once said. Well, we have been using our brains and we haven't done anything worthwhile apart from trying to be better than the other brothers and sisters in our own denomination, never mind others. Being successful in your material and financial life doesn't mean you are spiritual. Some godless believers have more money than hairs on their heads. So, what is the difference between the godless believer and the so-called Christian who lives with one foot in the church and the other in the world?

If we don't wake up spiritually and start being inquisitive before the Almighty, then another couple of thousand years will pass by with humans not knowing or taking chances. We won't be breaking any of God's laws if we ask, "Lord, can I? Is it in Your will?"

A Christian should grow in his or her spiritual knowledge and not stay the same. Some Christians think that because they have belonged to a church for a long time, they are experts, when in reality they are stationed in a lack of spiritual knowledge, belief, and faith. It is like still being in high school, sitting through the same lectures over and over but not obtaining the knowledge needed to earn a college degree.

And this is all because the professor has no wisdom and no interest in learning more so as to be able to teach more. This is where the students have to understand, if they wish to reach their goals, that if they are not fed intellectually, then it's time to find another "restaurant," that is, a better way to become educated.

Spirituality is the same way; it's a growth process according to your own understanding, desire, wishes, and needs. Man can show you the way, but is up to you to get to the end of the trail.

In the spiritual life, the process of learning is the same as in the secular life. The one world, you can see; the other, you believe in. How much you believe determines how much you will learn. How high you are willing to reach is how high you will go. The amount of power you want to have is how much power you are going to get. It all depends on you. How much you want of God is how much you're going to get of Him.

Ignorance and laziness are things given by Satan, whereas wisdom and courage are things given by God. And we are right in the middle of these two poles. The removal of ignorance and the gaining of wisdom each has a learning curve. To get rid of ignorance, we have to learn how. To get wisdom, we also need to know how. It all depends on the wishes of your heart, your calling, or your willingness.

Every Christian, except for those who are new to the gospel, should have learned more than the basics throughout the years. If only Christians had an interest in learning where their places were and what their spiritual gifts were, as members of the body of Christ, then the church would not be fruitless and the body of Christ inactive, and this world wouldn't have so much evil in it.

Being a defender against evil is not enough, but if you are an attacking defender, you will make evil run, with a chance to nab the devil and place him in custody. For that you have to be in good spiritual condition. Then this world would see that something is happening. But the Christians of today are not surprising anyone, because slowly but surely, they have been dropping their spiritual guard, as has been the case for quite some time. They don't even notice or care about what is happening in the world in terms of those things the gospel has warned us about.

The secular world has no interest in what is happening in the church or with those who preach the gospel, unless someone does what is described in the Bible: "For the name of God is blasphemed among the gentiles because of you" (Romans 2:24).

If we have to be like Jesus, we have to surprise and amaze the world with our deeds in His name, for God's glory, as He did when He was among us. We think we are correct in our misunderstanding that our belief and faith are worked out in the realm of human emotion, when in reality it is those erroneous thoughts and beliefs that are holding us back. Our human emotions are confusing us in our weakness and ignorance, because we don't understand how spirituality really works.

Spirituality is a higher knowledge that comes through revelation and is accompanied by certainty, where what is predicted in the Bible, is fulfilled. A working belief and faith never have room for emptiness. If a person does feel emptiness, then it means his or her faith is not working, for different reasons. On the other hand, sometimes a "spiritual touch" in our human emotions, delivers superficial fulfillment which, after a short time, brings out emptiness in our lives.

There are emotional feelings that come about through spiritual revelation, and there are human emotions that come about through feelings, both of which have a different emotional sensitivity. One is known in advance because it is revelation of a higher knowledge, and the other is based on the feelings arising from, say, the latest news—something that the mind receives first, then the soul or heart feels the impact of. But then there are spiritual feelings arising from the soul or heart that come to us without us hearing any news, good or bad, or witnessing any developments in our secular life.

Jesus's first human spiritual feeling of fear, and maybe desperation, sadness, and emptiness, occurred when he went to pray on the Mount of Olives and had the experience of sweating blood. He knew in His Spirit, as the Son of God, for what purpose He had come to this world. But in that knowledge, as a mortal believer, as we all are, His human feeling of fear of the future, experienced in His human emotions, took over His soul. Who can say whether or not at that moment in His earthly life, it was the presence of Satan himself, the hand of death, that Jesus felt?

Uncertainty of the soul gives rise to a negative feeling when, for some reason, the human spirit becomes a neutral presence in the soul, leaving a feeling of emptiness and worry about being all alone.

But we do have spiritual experiences in our inner person, which bring about feelings of happiness and joy. Jesus also had such emotional feelings. Take for example the moment when He sent the disciples to do their first missionary work. When they returned and reported to Him the good news of their mission, Jesus, praying to the Father, thanked Him, rejoicing in the Spirit, glorifying God. That was the happiness of a man, a Teacher, about his students having passed the exam about the gospel.

For a person who has no real spiritual experience or knowledge, it is difficult to distinguish between emotional feelings and spiritual feelings. There is a difference between the two. Emotions are part of our human existence and are perfectly normal. There is nothing wrong with expressing ourselves through our feelings.

But the danger is when, in our emotional and presumed spiritual confidence, the other, unnoticed spirit takes advantage of our emotions, leading us to think that it is the Spirit of God, when it is not. That is when we need the skill of spiritual discernment.

Spiritual feelings are all personal, even if the spiritual experience is lived with many other believers together at the same time. Real spiritual experiences in a believer rarely last for only a short time, but even if they do, they leave no feeling of emptiness behind as everyday emotional experiences do. Not too many Christians can see the real work of the Spirit in themselves. They think that they have been touched by the Spirit at some given moment, when in reality they have been touched by their own emotions. And at the end, they don't understand why they have an empty feeling in their hearts.

The active presence of the Spirit of God never leaves a believer with emptiness or fear, the way it happened to Jesus and some of the apostles when the latter were in fear for their lives. To feel fear doesn't mean the Christian believer lacks the Spirit of God; it means that at certain moments, the inner sensibility is more attuned to human emotions than to the presence of the Spirit. And why does this happen? Maybe it is that the Spirit, for some reason unbeknown to us, "stays still" to see how our soul's representative, that is, the heart, reacts when it is all by itself. Will it call upon God for help, or will it, in its confusion, go its own way? Jesus's heart called for help upon the Father. That is a heart that, even when it feels alone, knows for certain to whom to direct its call for help, accepting as God's will whatever the outcome may be.

We must know ourselves and not take our spirituality too lightly or believe that everything is okay with our traditional religious way of life. When we do believe in such a way, those are the moments when we have to be very aware of our own thoughts and their propensity about negative feelings.

The Christian's spiritual life is a baby, not a rebellious emotional teenager called "believed knowledge" who ignores us when we are trying to teach him or her how to live, when it is already late for the lessons to begin. The concern we have for our baby boy or girl when he or she is defenseless is what we have to exercise when checking on our spiritual lives. If we don't approach our spiritual lives this way, then we may be cheated out of going in the right direction. Whose fault is it for not growing up spiritually in knowledge and understanding?

Being an expert in the Word doesn't mean being knowledgeable and religious, or spiritual, that is, in the right spirit. The danger for a believer is to fail to remember that there is another spirit, one that is always trying to interfere in our spiritual lives, making us believe that we are right. When we have this type of false confidence, we don't, like the Bible says, test the spirits that appear in our lives, not only the spirits that refuse to recognize the Son of man in the flesh, but also the ones that may be leading astray a believer who is not spiritually aware of Satan's tricks.

Our unchecked confidence makes us forget God's warnings. The almost invisible interference of a wrong spirit can easily confuse us and lead us away from the path of right understanding. We have to stir up our spiritual hunger and conquer ourselves first, and then we can move on to conquering this world for His glory, defeating evil systematically, not in a little way, but in a big, glorious way.

First we have to be honest about our faith before God if we are to get ready for action. We are the ones who in Jesus's name, being in Him, have to bring evil to His feet, as a church in one body, for Jesus to present this evil to God Almighty for judgment.

Now we have to transform our weaknesses and doubts into knowledge, faith, and courage by the power that God has given us to battle Satan and his evil spirits. We have to remember what the apostle Paul said about the struggle against the spirits of heaven and man (Ephesians 6:12). We have been given the right to battle Satan, not only to free any lost or possessed souls from him, but also to neutralize him according to the wishes of our hearts.

To love peace doesn't mean that we Christians have to be passive in the Spirit against Satan and his followers. But how are we going to fight him if there is no one telling us, teaching us, or guiding us to reach the spiritual knowledge that we need? If we don't take the initiative to reach for the highest of God's wisdom, then who will, when no leader will teach us how to take chances before the Almighty to conquer our enemy? The Word of God has to be branded upon our hearts and minds, and imprinted in our souls, so we can "put on the whole armor of God, that [we] may be able to stand against the wiles of the devil" (Ephesians 6:11).

CHAPTER 8

Now we'll go through some questions to try to understand why God talks about the suffering of His children and why they will go through such difficult experiences in their lives, including persecution, imprisonment, betrayal, and killing, along with all kinds of suffering and pain, not only physical but also spiritual.

Why does He allow His children to go through such painful experiences, in some cases with horrific endings? For whom is the benefit of such suffering? What is God gaining with this? Is this the ultimate test of faithful resistance until the end of the believer's life? Or did Jesus talk about our trials in life because He knew we'd fall short of faith and knowledge of His Word, leaving us unable to defend ourselves in His name against the evil of men's deeds? How can we defend ourselves against the evil of suffering, misery, and death? Can we avoid all the things He said we'll have to go through?

Do we truly understand all the promises He left for us about learning how to defend ourselves? Jesus said, "Behold, I give unto you power to treat serpents and scorpions, and over all the power of the enemy, and nothing shall by any means hurt you" (Luke 10:19). Those words are a promise of defense against evil spirits, and of any man under the influence of such evil spirits, who cause all the adverse circumstances in our secular and spiritual lives.

The problem for Christians is not what Jesus said about all the misery and tragic consequences we will have in our lives. The problem is our failure to understand how to use the power of His promises in the spiritual world. If Christians would only understand the meaning of the well-armed strong man defending his home and everything that is his, then they wouldn't have any miseries or tragedies, because they would know how to use the power of the Spirit, who will come to their defense as promised by the Lord.

The misinterpretation and contradiction among believers exists in the knowledge and understanding of the Word of God, not in the promises of the Lord for our lives. That is why He said what He said about the unpleasant things in our lives. What He said about adverse circumstances was not a promise of suffering in our lives. Suffering exists because of a lack of faith, spiritual knowledge, and understanding, otherwise revealed to teach people how to be in Him and live in the Spirit, believing and having a working spiritual weapon called faith, along with the understanding that all His promises are the bullets to be used by our faith according to our gifts or the wishes of our hearts.

Every person has the right to express their own opinion, according to their own knowledge, understanding, experience, faith, spiritual condition, and interpretation of the Word, as to how we might enable God's promises to work on our behalf through the Spirit.

We are obligated to notice in our Christian lives if our planted seed of faith is growing into a fruit tree, a bush, or a bonsai tree. Is the plant producing the expected fruits in our lives, according to the Lord's promises, or is it just growing green leaves that are pretty for the eyes to see?

What is the opinion of the leaders of today's church? Is the answer a religious, intellectual, theological, philosophical, or spiritual one?

Remember, we have to be of one mind and one spirit. Can we, according to our wishes in the will of God, not only make those evil spirits run away, but also neutralize the demonic herds in order to lay them at our Lord's feet? What is the correct answer?

If a number of Christian leaders of the same denomination or different denominations were placed into separate rooms and asked the question "Can evil demonic spirits be neutralized and sent to 'jail,' that is, the place God has set apart for them in hell, without any possibility of coming out until Judgment Day?" would they come up with the same answer? If they did, would that mean the leaders were real spiritual people to whom God has declared in revelation the correct answer as to whether or not such a thing could be done in His will. But if they come up with different answers, that means something is wrong, but not with God, because there are questions only God can answer.

As members of one church in the body of Christ, with all the modern-day churches included, we need to be connected. Not only for purposes of achieving one spiritual goal, but also, according to our knowledge and known need of any type, so that all the churches will be as one. If we do not provoke God in our faith or our beliefs, challenging our faith in His promises, He won't move a finger, never mind His hand, to do anything. That is why we need to get rid of our overwhelming knowledge of the letter of the law, our belief that we are correct, and our titles, to understand that in God's world, He is the Master and we the tools. Because if He doesn't build the foundation first, whatever we build atop the soil will come down like a sandcastle beneath a child's foot. Or if it should stand for a while, the strong wind of circumstances will bring it down.

The Bible says in Psalms 127:1, "Except the Lord builds the house, they labor in vain that build it." The foundation is already built, and atop that foundation, in His will and according to the wishes of our hearts, we can build on the promises He has left for us, with His authorization. The only thing we have to do is ask if He will allow us to build what is in our hearts for His glory.

There is no sin in asking; the sin is in not trying or not challenging our faith when we think that something like this cannot be done, according to our own interpretation of the mysteries of the Word of the Almighty. Our Lord said, "With man this is impossible, but with God all things are possible" (Matthew 19:26). Man's wish to do God's will without God being involved in everything, is impossible to achieve. And that is knowledge without a proper understanding.

If only humility and faith existed in the lives of the leaders of the church, not before other men, but before God, then they would understand the purpose of seeking His kingdom. Justice, according to the leadership of the Almighty, will be the reward for the leaders and all Christians who believe in His promises, and ultimately challenge themselves for victory. We must fight for an understanding of the unity of one mind and one spirit by fasting and praying. Then nothing will be impossible. That is the only way to challenge our faith in Him to cement His promises, through knowing Him by our close fellowship with Him. But for this to happen, Christians need to really wish for God to enter their lives. And this need must exist not in their thoughts, but in their hearts.

The spiritual unity of Christians of the world today looks not like a solid granite rock but a wheel of Swiss cheese, which looks like a rock that is full of holes. The holes are the different understandings, beliefs, and so on that make the body appear as one piece in its religious togetherness, but it is not, even if it is in God's name.

To ignore the warnings of the Word about what those holes represent weakens not only the solidity of the gospel in its religious representation, but also the spiritual lives of believers. Because of this weakness, with the exception of a few, most of the body of the church in Christ is sick. The only remedy is to recognize that the church is going down a wrong path and to repent, which will result in the correction of a wrongly directed faith. Faith, walking on the correctly directed path in the Spirit, is the only medicine that God has given since the beginning of time, and if that medicine is of no use, then no one will get healed.

How can we learn if we do not take chances, always thinking along the lines of our own doctrinal ideas, backed up by a basketful of doubts or different opinions because of the different denominations, doctrines, and interpretations, and not revelation? When we approach God with a sincere heart, looking for the knowledge of His will, He'll see the intentions of our hearts and declare His will to us. He'll give us the answer we are looking for. He always has time for us.

Jesus said, "Ask and it shall be given you. Seek and ye shall find; knocked and it shall be open unto you" (Matthew 7:7). Diligently, we have to seek, knock, and ask, insisting until we get what we desire. Many times we do not insist because, judging by the time that has elapsed, we think that God doesn't hear us. But that is not the truth. He wants us to be persistent about our needs or the wishes of our hearts. He wants to teach us how to insist to get what we need.

Jesus tells us the story of a friend who comes at midnight and for whom the host has nothing to put on the table for him to eat. Speaking to His disciples, He said the following:

> Which of you shall have a friend, and shall go
> unto him at midnight, and say unto him, Friend,

72

lend me three loaves; for a friend of mine in his journey is come to me, and I have nothing to set before him? And he from within shall answer and say, Trouble me not: the door is now shut, and my children are with me in bed; I cannot rise and give thee. I say unto you, Though he will not rise and give him, because he is his friend, yet because of his importunity he will rise and give him as many as he needeth. (Luke 11:5–8)

God will deny nothing to anyone under any circumstances if the intentions of the person's heart before Him are true. Everything, anything, all wishes and revelations, will be granted only if we have faith, courage, persistence, belief, and trust.

In Mark 11:22–24, Jesus says, "For verily I say unto you, that whatsoever shall say unto this mountain, Have faith in God. For assuredly, I say to you, whoever says to this mountain, be thou removed, and be thou cast into the sea; and shall not doubt in his heart, but shall believe that those things, which he shall saith shall come to pass."

In the spiritual sense, a mountain can be a problem. Satan, being the highest mountain overlooking the hills and dunes, which are his demons and evil spirits, is our main problem.

Satan's army of evil spirits and demons is our primary concern. It is the reason for the spiritual struggle in our lives. We need to defeat Satan and his evil army in the name of Jesus, unless the angels of heaven will do the job for us with the Lord being in front of them, not in front of us.

A general without his army is only another man with a title. As soldiers of heaven, we need to take down Satan's army and hand it over to our all-star general and Savior, Jesus Christ, leaving Satan to be handled by our commander in chief, that is, our Father in heaven.

From the devil's attack on our weaknesses to the consequences of sin in our bodies, our lives are a battlefield between good and evil. We are the only ones who decide what to do, according to our understandings, beliefs, and faith, not forgetting our boldness in the Spirit, if we have it. We can take things in our lives the way they come, by doing nothing and leaving everything to the "will" of God, or we can give in or give up, or we can fight to the end.

Nobody can say God won't fulfill His promises. If what we ask doesn't materialize, it's because we don't know how to ask, we asked wrong, we have no faith, our faith is wrongly directed, or our hearts before the Lord are not correct. How do we know which is the correct approach? There are many answers, but you will know the declared truth in your heart as revealed by the Lord God.

Many times Jesus, in order to be understood, spoke in parables, comparing the spiritual world with our daily lives on this earth. Now imagine a police department. Although some of the people working in the police department are officers and some are civilians, not all of them walk a beat on the streets for the security and safety of the citizens. It's the same with the church. Not everyone is a preacher, nor in the army, are all generals. In the spiritual world, it's the same: not everyone is doing the same thing, but as in a body, every cell has its own position and a specific task to do. The same thing goes for society.

The law gives full authoritative power to a police officer so that he may act in a situation that needs to be investigated, or stop an individual who is acting suspiciously. But first, before he even becomes a police officer, he has to know the law from top to bottom if he is to act accordingly within the framework of the law. A police officer may have information from a previously committed crime, so he may look for someone in particular, or in some cases look for someone who is creating some kind of disturbance, or stop someone about to commit a crime, or after committing a crime. The officer has the right to arrest the person and take him to jail, not prison. When a police officer is attacked, the attacker is attacking not only a person representing the law but also the law itself, going against everything involved in justice, order, and respect. And in such a case, the police officer has the right, given by the law, to use deadly force.

God is the law, and we are His representatives. A demon or evil spirit may do damage, or attack other people or us in a physical way, such as through bodily illness, sickness, or disease, or in any spiritual way, creating an imbalance in a person referred to as psychopathology. A demon or evil spirit may also cause mental illness, causing a person to react to things in an unpredictable way, and such illness may unfortunately also affect the body.

We have been authorized by God to use the power He has given us to "arrest" or spiritually neutralize any evil in the name of Jesus, by the power of the Spirit, which is working in us to hold the evil spirit. In a way, the name of the Lord is the set of handcuffs to immobilize the evil spirit. And to neutralize such a spirit is to take it to "jail," either a specific place God will make according to our wishes or a place He has already prepared for them. He is waiting for us to take a chance.

Obviously in man's world, unfortunately, the law leaves much to be desired. Nevertheless, a judge has the right to decide a case and to condemn an individual to prison or else set him free. The power of the Spirit, in the name of Jesus, is the spiritual law, and we are like spiritual police officers. The civilians working in the police department are like believers in church, and also have the same right as a citizen of heaven to make a "citizen's arrest", if that wish is in their heart. When we are casting out evil spirits in the name of Jesus, we have the right to tell them to go to the place God has prepared for them and stay there.

If we do that, the evil spirit or demon won't be able to get out, because the name of Jesus is the key that holds those beasts in jail, the place that God has designated for them to stay until the Day of Judgment. Today, any evil spirits freed by brothers in Christ, in the name of Jesus, from any people who were possessed by them are evil spirits who will sooner or later get into someone else's life later on. But if an evil spirit is sent to where it belongs, which is hell, and ordered to stay there in the name of Jesus, it won't be able to get out. The question is, will we take the chance to ask our God if we may do this in His will?

It is true that Jesus never said to a demon or evil spirit to leave the person and go to a specific place and stay there, as it is true that many of the things written in the Word of God are not detailed, and maybe even have been tampered with when it comes to discussing specific spiritual actions. The reason for this is not that the Word of God is untruthful. The problem or lack exists in man's understanding. Whether intentionally or by mistake, something was omitted or lost from the original scriptures, perhaps in the translation.

We read in Revelation 22:18–19, "For I testify unto every man that heareth the words of the prophecy of this book, if any man shall add unto these things, God shall add unto him the plagues that are written in this book: And if any man shall take away from the words of the book of this prophecy, God shall take away his part out from the book of life, and out of the holy city, and from the things which are written in this book."

That is why we need the Spirit of God, just as we do in many other spiritual cases, to know if something has been altered in the scriptures unbeknownst to us, for the Almighty to declare it. And if nothing is altered, we need from God the revelations that only He knows we need.

Remember, if for some reason the Word of God was altered, it was done by people who were not from God. And maybe these people removed from scripture the parts describing the spiritual defensive tools that believers in Christ might use against the evil spirits and partners of Satan. Whether the words in the Bible have been removed or not, we need the Spirit of the Lord no matter what. Because even when the written words of the Bible are material; by themselves, they are the spiritual essence of God.

These words are the whole reason why we Christian believers need the Spirit of God to take up first place in our lives. Some experts in the Word, in their interpretations of the gospel, base their theories on different historical documents, comparing these to the Bible itself. And even when everything is done in the spirit of the common good of religion, it lacks spiritual revelation directly from God. Whatever comes from God is in the Spirit; faith resides in the human spirit through knowledge of revelation, and God has given it to man to contact Him.

To be given a revelation to separate the truths from the lies, or to determine if something has been taken out of the Bible or added to it, is to know the unknown. No one can say for certain that in the writing of those words, someone at some later date didn't remove words or add words to his or her own condemnation. That is why today, as always in the world of the Almighty, we need His Spirit to know the truth, one of those truths being that we have a gift, according to the wishes of our hearts, to do the will of God. And even if no words have been changed in the Bible, can God really, according to the wishes of our hearts, create a place to "jail" those evil creatures? And if the place is already in existence, will He, according to His promises and the wishes of our hearts, comply and incarcerate the evil spirits?

Again, if we ask God in the name of Jesus if we may do as we wish in our hearts for His glory and He says no, we have lost nothing. But what happens when there is something that we can challenge ourselves to do but we don't do it? According to the Word, it doesn't say that we can't challenge our faith based upon the wishes of our hearts.

God wants us to know not our own interpretation or intellectual understanding of spiritual matters, what we think is correct or not in the Word of God, but revelation through the Spirit in the spiritual world, which God wants us to know, understand, and live in. He asks us not to change what is already written or add something to it, but to challenge our faith by way of the inquisitiveness of our hearts, seeking to discover what our faith can do for us as is written in the Word, for God's glory.

The Lord Himself gives us authorization to use our faith to deal with the powers of darkness and tread upon them according to our spiritual gifts or the wishes of our hearts. Again, He said, "Behold, I give unto you power to tread on serpents and scorpions, and over all the power of the enemy: and nothing shall by any means hurt you" (Luke 10:19). It sounds incredible, but challenging your faith and belief in God makes a lot of things that He promises possible, if it is His will. And how do we know if it is His will or not if we don't try and ask?

Who can say for sure that something like this is impossible when His Word says, "What is impossible for man is possible for God" (Luke 18:27)?

Believe in the power of the Spirit and all things will be given unto you. This is the spiritual challenge of our faith, that is, the challenge to go the extra mile in our believing faith for God's glory. And then we will believe that what is impossible for man to do alone is possible for God to do through man's faith.

Remember the words of Jesus in Luke 17:10 when he was

talking about the unprofitable servant. Seems to be that many Christians don't have any understanding of what it means to go the extra mile even when they should.

The apostle Paul said, "For we wrestle not against flesh and blood, but against principalities, against powers, against the rulers of darkness of this world, against spiritual hosts of weaknesses in the high places" (Ephesians 6:12). Those principalities, powers, and rulers in people's lives won't be able to do any damage if, according to our desire in the promises made to us by the Lord, we "arrest" them. We just need to ask.

Once "in jail," they cannot get loose. Think if all the crooks, from pickpockets to assassins, getting picked off one by one and put in jail in any town or city. Wouldn't the citizens feel more secure and less worried when there are no criminals on the loose? The fewer loose evil spirits, the less evil in people. The fewer "sick" people there are, the more healthy and happy people there will be.

Faith, belief, and trust are the pillars of our spiritual life. One cannot exist without the other two. Without them, we have nothing. Faith is conviction and confidence, and belief is confirmation and assurance. They are like air and water. One depends on the other, and the two become one. Trust in those two spiritual pillars and you will have victory and peace.

At the beginning there is always a price to pay. The first Christians, the ones who began spreading the gospel throughout the world, had to pay a price. They were the first fighters, who had to do what nobody else could do, but they did it according to their faith, belief, conviction, and courage. They knew, they understood, and they took their faith up in arms, and like the first pioneers, with no knowledge of what was ahead of them, but with more than just a few mustard seeds, they went into the wild spiritual world to conquer souls for heaven, believing and trusting in the One who had sent them to battle the enemy of man's souls, understanding and accepting the consequences of any outcome, always believing in the final victory.

These early Christians were attacked, beaten, put in jail, and killed, convinced to the end in their faith and ideals that they were doing the will of God. And they were. Like in the Old West, the government told the people something along the lines of, "The open country of the west is yours. As much land as you can acquire, that land will be yours to start a new life." The people knew then they might have problems on their way far into the unknown, for example, some might never reach their destination, but one way or the other, all of them paid a price in their lives for the new land.

The first pioneers of the gospel did not have the Bible. They preached and taught only what they knew and remembered from what Jesus had left them, along with the help of the Holy Spirit.

Today in the twenty-first century, we have more than what those first courageous gospel pioneers had. We have the Bible, through which we can go back one time or one million times to read and study. We gain understanding not only through the teaching of good, knowledgeable Christian brothers, but also according to our own direct interest in the will of God and the guidance and teaching of the Spirit of the Lord. It's as if the early Christians had the first color television set, whereas today we can access television from different electronic gadgets by way of the internet. Also today there are more places we can turn for Bible College, Sunday school Bible teaching, and small group Bible study in the home. But the most important thing to have is an interest in learning and the will to learn.

The first thing to understand is that man can teach you up to a certain level by telling and showing. The first step to knowing of and receiving the things God has in store for your life is to seek His wisdom, His revelation, and a knowledge and understanding of Him. These things can only be learned through the spirit, and not from a learning intellectual interpretation. Man will show you the way to learn, and you will decide if you want God to give you a diploma.

Today the Bible should be revealed in a way that is more understandable to us so that we may reach the impossible. But we are short on the courage to rise to this spiritual challenge, or short on dedication, or perhaps short on curiosity, because of a doubting belief and a shaky faith, where courage and a fighting spirit do not exist, so we are held back in our quest to conquer evil. It is our lack of spiritual knowledge and an understanding of how to beat evil that is keeping us in defeat.

If we do not learn how to use the teachings of the Lord to become victorious in every area of our lives, then we will be slapped again and again by the one who wants nothing other than our failure. Faith and belief are the only keys to open the door to the knowledge and spiritual revelation that we need to understand His Word living within us. To know His will is to have the revelation that guides us to victory in our spiritual lives and our secular lives.

Hebrews 11:6 reads, "But without faith it is impossible to please Him, for he who cometh to God must believe that He is, and that He is a rewarder of those who diligently seek Him." Today, whether we admit it or not, we have all kinds of problems in our lives, even if we are believers.

Why, when we have such an abundance of promises from our Lord, do we start questioning if God's promises are possible, necessary, or correct? No wonder evil is patting us on the back and smiling—because he is enjoying our misery. He won't be patting or smiling if he sees in us what he saw in Jesus.

Why in our secular life do we do whatever is necessary to reach whatever goal we decide to reach, even when the task is very difficult and sometimes almost impossible? Why, when we challenge ourselves in the spiritual world, does it take so much effort? Is it because faith is much more difficult to "touch" and understand than a plan for a secular project, something that we can see and visually "touch" in our minds?

There is no other way under the heavens to do God's will than to be under His direct guidance. Jesus's way of life as a mortal man is the perfect example. Whatever things we may do according to our own understanding, thinking that it's the will of God (but it's not), God in His Almighty knowledge won't miss the chance to take advantage of our spiritual need and help us. He knows that in our hearts we love Him and want to serve Him, only sometimes we do things our way, as the children that we are, thinking that we know more than our Parents.

God as a good Father looks at us and smiles when He sees the stubbornness of our light-minded attitude, thinking that we know so much that we don't need any help. He is concerned about us, just as our earthly parents were when we were little.

When we are young children, our parents guide our first steps, holding our hands. Step by step, we get stronger, bolder, and more confident. Upon reaching a certain level of confidence where we thought we no longer needed to hold our parents' hands and have them help us, we heard them saying, "You're not ready yet, my child!" But we insisted, and we got our wish. We were free to meet our first friend, the hard floor; and instead of a smile we had tears, but not of happiness.

When we were teenagers, our parents were still concerned about us, fearing we would go wild. When we grew older, our parents were still thinking about our well-being because we were theirs, no matter our age or how old they were. Even when they said nothing, deep down they still cared. God has the same concern for us. He doesn't want us to suffer in any way, so our adverse circumstances are proof that we have a problem. The difficulty is a wake-up call, as He has warned us to expect. But in our ignorance and our arrogance, we think we know better, so we keep hitting the dust of adversity.

What will it take to make us stop and cool our jets, the ability to weigh the pros and cons in our lives? How many times do we have to get hurt before we'll learn? How much heartache must we suffer before we come to our senses, gear up, push away or ignore the evil spirit in our lives, and ready ourselves for an encounter with the Spirit of the Lord, giving Him a chance to guide us to victory?

There are two ways to serve God, but only one is correct. One is our way; the other is His way.

Jesus never made any mistakes or did anything that was fruitless. He never did anything that resulted in nothing, even when He was rejected. He always said: "For I have came down from heaven, not to do my own will, but the will of Him that sent Me" (John 6:38). This is kind of like saying, *I'm not here doing what I want or think will be better. I'm doing precisely what I was told to do by the One who sent me.*

He wasn't trying to guess what His Father wanted Him to do or was trying to tell Him, as we do many times without results. To do His Father's will, He first had to be told—and He was told through revelation in prayer—and then had to be guided by the Spirit to do things right. Seems to me that most Christians haven't gotten to the point of living a life of revelation, with *revelation* meaning the opening of secrets, instructions, or information that has never been heard before and is only for your ears, that is, the things that God wants to do through you.

The lack of knowledge and understanding is why in this world, evil is still in control of the circumstances causing the inconveniences in our daily lives.

The devil knows, and we think we know everything about life. That's why there is always something missing. Otherwise things in our lives would be quite different. The Word of God is teaching us to pray and call upon Him in any time of need, for the brethren to come together as one, with the saints' anointing and laying on of hands to rid believers of whatever problems they may have, knowing that all problems are caused by evil spirits. Once these spirits are stopped and gotten rid of, the affected person is free of any further evil intervention.

Why don't we learn how to pray, not only to get rid of whatever evil spirits are already at work, but also to get rid of any evil spirits that may be waiting to cause other problems. This way, you will prevent any evil spirits from entering your life again to mess up another area of it.

The question now is, can you believe in that or not? You, according to your faith, belief, knowledge, understanding, interest, and desires, through prayer, are the only one who can get that answer directly from God, without any guesses, deductions, or mere opinions. The challenge is yours alone.

If you were given foreknowledge of an adverse situation in any area of your personal life, would you wait for it to hit you, or would you try to prevent it? It is known that nothing good can come from evil. If we know this, then why do we do nothing about evil until it is active in our lives?

CHAPTER 9

S atan's main objective in this world is to destroy every human life, for every soul to be lost. People are so spiritually blind that they don't understand that misery, pain, suffering, and death are not a direct consequence of some political misunderstanding among nations or within a single nation. The reality is that such problems are a consequence of the absence of God in people's spiritual lives. And such a situation may develop by way of a person's ignorance of God, rejection of God, or complete lack of interest in the things of God. The sort of spirituality that is not rooted in the knowledge and understanding of the Word of God is the work of an evil spirit, an evil person, or both.

Such a superficial takeover sees spirituality as irrelevant in understanding the need for God in every secular area of life, be it national, societal, or personal. It is an act that overwhelms our spiritual and secular lives. In a life of adversity, people, in their spiritual ignorance, but not in the abundance of their own intellectual understanding of life, regard such adversity as something to be expected, given to them by destiny.

The problems in this world and in our lives are spiritual, not political, intellectual, idealistic, or religious, even when these problems arise as negative spiritual consequences in our earthly lives. A spiritual person whose main objective in life is to do the will of God does not concern oneself with earthly preoccupations, but believes in the promise of being supported by God Himself. We are reminded in Matthew 6:33 "But seek ye first the kingdom of God, and his righteousness; and all these things shall be added unto you."

It is to be expected that we'll have secular responsibilities and obligations while we are in this world, but we also understand that we are not to allow such pursuits to keep us from seeking or doing the will of God. Of some people living in this world, Jesus said, "They are not of the world, even as I am not of the world" (John 17:16), meaning that one may act in the physical world but be rooted in the spiritual world.

To travel as a tourist to another country, you don't first go to that country to make money, return to your home country, and then go back to the other country again as a tourist. You make money in your own country. Jesus is letting us know that in this world we are just passing through like tourists, and because we are residents of heaven, we should have all the necessary means, that is, our blessings from Him, to survive in this "country" we are touring. That is His assurance, not that we will be given things that we don't need in this world.

If politicians were not of this world but of the Spirit, they would have a desire to put God first in their lives and in their nations. Then the results would be completely different because God Himself would be the One who would govern, giving the people the wisdom, as He did in the times of Israel through David, Solomon, and others. There were no disagreements among people, governments, or kingdoms. Instead, only peace and prosperity existed, and God took care of the real enemies of His people inside and outside the land.

People lived in their land in peace, something that is not happening today, even inside the territories of the most powerful nations. To one person, to a nation, or to the world, it seems we don't have what it takes to reach that spiritual challenge, perhaps because there is no one to remind us, guide us, and show us that the promises of God are for real.

The pride we as a nation have in our Christian life for believing what our own Pharisees are telling us, in that we are better than the rest of the world, is a trick of the devil—a trick that has been making us spiritually weak unbeknownst to us. The purpose of the trick is, and always will be, to get us to stray from the path to heaven by trusting man.

When a Christian involves himself partially or directly in politics, that is questionable. Why? Because the gospel of politics is quite different from the gospel of Christ. Even though the gospel of politics in this world is true in its own way too, we can see the misery this gospel is bringing to this world and people's lives; and all because our political representatives practice this "gospel."

In the hearts and minds of politicians, God isn't first, even when they think and say so. They say things such as, "No problem, I can handle it." That is not true, because when you begin mixing fresh water and salt water, that is, God and money, you will find it impossible to taste both spirituality and luxury. Our modern political times are no better or worse than the old ones; the temptation to do evil is the same, and the weakness of man is still the same.

From ancient times to the modern day, one can count on one hand the number of honest and decent Christian politicians there have been, that is, if any have ever existed. A politician may be spiritual but not religious, thinking that he or she is a spiritual believer in Christ. Even when politicians call themselves Christians, we know what the world of politics is like. That is why the Lord said, "No man can serve two masters: for either he will hate the one, and love the other; or else he will hold to the one, and despise the other. Ye cannot serve God and mammon" (Matthew 6:24). If you think you are able to serve both, then you are lying to yourself and being a hypocrite to others, a double standard position that deep down most politicians have in their hearts. This means that they can pass a lie off as a truth and make the truth look like a lie, for which the end will be the same for all of them. This is reminiscent of the times of Jesus with the Pharisees and their cronies, with the Pharisees always seeing someone else at fault and guilty, but not themselves. That is why so-called Christian politicians don't see the difference between the gospel of Jesus and the gospel of Satan in their service to the nation and the people.

The only way a Christian can involve himself or herself in politics 100 percent is if he or she prays constantly to the Almighty that He keep the government under His direct power so that real spiritual Christians may follow His directives to bring about the well-being of the nation and, through it, the world. And that is one heavenly challenge.

We must understand in our faith that we must give Him the chance to help us pick the right leaders, to replace the secular "religious" evil ones. This can be done by putting into practice a spiritual plead of good to God.

Do Christians have to participate in civic duties? Absolutely, as they fulfill other responsibilities in society. But if for some reason there is something you dislike going on in politics, society, your personal life, or any other situation, the best way you can be involved is to bend your knees and raise your hands before the Throne of Justice, and start making a difference.

Insist on knocking on the door, and yield if you have to, until God hears you. God says, "Call unto me, and I will answer thee and show thee great and mighty things, which thou knowest not" (Jeremiah 33:3). We are definitely not knocking, calling, looking, or insisting enough. Even in this world of evil, we can get together and make a difference. Satan works through people's greed to control the main creation on this earth, which for man is the treasures of this world, that is, material wealth.

Jesus came to this world with one purpose; He even died for that purpose. He was crucified and killed for a different reason than to amass material riches. Jesus said it Himself: "Ye cannot serve God and mammon" (Matthew 6:24). The love of money is the most dangerous love that has ever existed in man's life. Why? Because it started as a thought in the heart of the one who became eternally hungry for power, a power that his own spirit transformed into a new evil called greed, an evil that man in his weakness has accepted in his terrestrial existence.

Rarely do we remember those words of Matthew 6:24, because we don't see the connection between the spiritual reality of our secular world. Even when we are in the daily process of making a living, which we are supposed to do, we are wasting ourselves in pursuit of that goal. Instead of putting our faith in all His promises into practice and not worrying because He will provide, we keep fighting against the wind. Even when we know, we have no understanding of what deep faith means. Understanding what it is to believe and trust in something that exists but that we can't feel the weight of is one of our problems.

Maybe the problem is that we Christians know too much and, in that knowledge, even when we won't admit to it, our hidden pride and ignorance is preventing us from acknowledging that something is really wrong with our understanding of the Word or our faith. That is the reason that evil has the upper hand in some, or most, of the adverse circumstances of our lives.

One of the things that we should be attentive to is knowing who our enemy is, and the enemy per se is not man, but Satan. And if we know it is Satan controlling man, then we need to act, not react. Being alert, prepared, and ready to attack your enemy, that is, the evil in man or an evil spirit, is different from preparing yourself for when your enemy attacks you. The effort is to realize that as members of the body of Christ, like cells in a body in their proper positions, we need to get closer and be united to work as one.

All Christian leaders who believe in one continuous mission of prayer, in one special prayer against evil, should promote one rule for all Christians to follow in church and at home: pray to God, asking Him not only to protect us, but also to arrest, to neutralize, the already known evil of misery before it strikes, that is, to stop man from doing evil. This should be a spiritual law in the name of Jesus, the prayer of someone gifted by God, or a child of God with a wish in his heart, with only one objective: to immobilize the enemy of the human race and of heaven by praying unceasingly before the throne of God.

In defense of ourselves, we gird ourselves in our faith and belief in the impossible, trusting God that we will be victorious in the battle against the evil hordes. Let us sharpen our knowledge of the will of God; let's be bold, courageous, and valiant; let's get dressed for battle in the name of Jesus; and let's conquer the heavens because they belong to us as He has promised in His grace and love.

Let's have faith, belief, and trust in the One who is with us to help us take back the road that will take us back home, so we can conquer our spiritual weakness, a weakness that not only has killed our relationship with God but is also trying to destroy the last of whatever is good that we may still have in our lives. When we are dead spiritually, that is when an evil spirit will fight nonstop to destroy the flesh through that same weakness, which at different stages of life and in every generation gives rise to the same degenerate, immoral lifestyle that people live.

Satan opened the box of weakness in Eve, and now he works

in people the same way and for the same reason: to destroy. A person may be destroyed for a lack of spiritual values and morals. Satan's pride is the motive for the greatest crime committed against human beings, by insinuating the same thing, appealing to men's curiosity, that killed Adam and Eve's spiritual life. That is when sin was born in all its ramifications, with Satan having control over men's spiritual death in this world.

The second crime was the killing of the flesh, when Cain killed his brother Abel because of jealousy, again because Satan made insinuations to Cain, who was a man weak in his emotions and feelings. And third, Satan is trying to destroy man's soul completely, hoping to remove any possibility of revival of a working conscience, first through poisoning man's heart in his thoughts, and then through the abuse of his own body.

This sort of weakness blinds people and neutralizes their understanding of morality, causing their reasoning to become distorted and their bodies to become perverted and degraded. It was precisely for this reason that God destroyed the earth, first by floods and later by burning the cities of Sodom and Gomorrah. Satan's pride, jealousy, and weakness were passed to men's lives with all the possible negative ramifications.

There is no difference between one sin and another in the eyes of God. The amount of sin because of people's continuous rebellion and rejection of reason, and the acceptance of iniquities by people who see no difference and care not for morals, decency, or the rules of their Creator, will cause God's wrath to be meted out in due time. The question is, how is one to understand this?

Are the beliefs of people who think that they are right in terms of the truth, not man's truth but God's, just plain ignorant because of pride and convenience? Or are they so taken by unclean spirits that they really believe, in their spiritual blindness, that God is in favor of their degenerate, perverted, immoral lives? They must be for them to say that God loves and accepts their way of life, contradicting His own Word.

God in His love and mercy loves all His human creations, even when we were born in sin. What the Almighty doesn't love in His creation is sin, any sin that any person is living out and practicing. That is the reason He sent His only beloved Son, for the redemption of human souls. And not only for one specific sin, but for all the sins in man's life.

PART II

THE PERVERSION OF THE FLESH AND MIND IN A DEAD SOUL

PRIDE. IMMORALITY.
ARROGANCE. REJECTION.

CHAPTER 10

According to people's own convenience, understanding, and weakness, they keep their ideals open to interpretation. A man's opinions and interpretations of his own truth form a foundation for discussion with others who have a different point of view, whether the topic involves their personal, political, religious, or business lives.

Agreements and disagreements are like the daily bread of society, no matter what the subject may be. From the early time of man to the present day of structured society, many have believed in idealistic thoughts, which in turn came into being. The main essence, according to man's understanding of his own nature, is to create what he thinks is the proper way for him and his fellow citizens to live their lives.

At the beginning, when everything is put in the right place, some things work perfectly for the intended purpose. First comes the thought, then the idea, then the job of convincing other people, until finally the idea is put into motion. The same process occurs for people who disagree; they try to convince other people not to agree because their beliefs and understandings about life are different.

To be culturally cultivated is to be polite in your disagreement, listening to the arguments about whatever hot topic is being discussed. But a lack of understanding in many cases, or stubbornness, has caused this cultivated culture to hit the dust more than once. Arrogance, personal interest, and blindness because of ignorance, pride, convenience, and many other factors make many of the people in any society, old or modern, fight for an ideal that others may not agree with.

A very human reaction arises amid the disagreement because the issue involves making intellectual interpretations in the absence of morality, and morality is one of the branches of the spiritual tree in the lives of those who believe in a higher wisdom, where morality and respect are to be honored. But if that tree does not exist in the heart of a person, then moral values don't exist there either.

Spiritual blindness, religiousness, and weakness in the life of a person who believes in libertarian ideals, many of whom do so because these things represent the law, create the illusion that one is free to do wrong as a way of life. People who suffer from these things consider that to behave immorally is their human right, all the way to the skies.

Man has created his own rights according to his own understanding, and if someone else does not agree, tough luck. Disagreement entered people's lives when they lost sight of God's truth. The truth does not belong to man, but to God, because God is Truth.

But man wasn't ready to be a loser for the second time, so God said, "The truth is Mine." And just as he did at the beginning of his fall, man still blames others for his failures, pointing to people's misunderstandings of his unacknowledged weaknesses. When there is weakness in a person's heart, that person will live a life without the will to understand right from wrong, believing that he or she is right and others are wrong.

A person with a lifeless soul in a body whose will is controlled by intellectual "instincts" of survival is, without knowing it, hoping for a future that will not manifest. The heart doesn't know that without a corresponding human spirit able to be guided to redemption, there is no healthy future life. It's only the human spirit, the connecting bridge between man's soul and heart and God's Spirit, that shows the heart and soul the real truth, which belongs to God. A spirit has been given to man for his future existence through the soul and heart, allowing for the admission of wrong and subsequent repentance, which gives life in recognition of God's truth.

Spiritually, man is dead, having come to be what the Italians call "Il morto che parla," that is, "the dead man who speaks." We can compare a man's pride to a person who is so drunk that he has no control over his walking or other actions, denying his drunkenness and continuing to walk against all odds, suddenly gaining control over his movements for a moment to say "I'm okay." The same goes for the stubborn arrogance of a self-induced righteous man, holding himself higher than God's truth.

When a man is telling the truth about another person or circumstance, he has to prove it to be believed by the listener. But what happens when the idealistic believer is trying to convince you that he wants to have the same right that you have? Even if that right goes against your personal understanding of morals, decency, spiritual beliefs, honor, and respect for what God Himself has created. For example, the contemporary issues of abortion and sex-and-gender fluidity, among others, is where people may see the degradation of life on any level.

You know you are right, not because of some ideology, but because of the common sense you have regarding the rules that God has created to bring order to the human race, telling us what is wrong and right for people not to create the next Sodom and Gomorrah.

The Bible says that evil will go from bad to worse. The increasing rate of that evil means that people will practice not only one specific kind of evil but also all kinds of evil, committing an ever greater number of acts of evil with more intensity and in a shorter amount of time, continuously, without stopping to think of the physical and spiritual consequences for a neutralized conscience that must determine what is right and what is wrong.

People are the ones who cause evil to rise and become greater. A person who practices evil will spread sin, which is against God. It may start with an "innocent" white lie. If the person gets away with that lie, next time the lie will be a little bigger, and so on. The same is true for when one steals, cheats, or does something even worse. The real problem arises when one is in denial, refusing to admit that one has done wrong, perhaps saying in his or her defense, "Well, a lot of people are doing it." The denial will be stronger if the person doing wrong thinks it is within his or her rights to behave that way.

Since man was kicked out of Eden, he has been trying to establish for himself, according to his own understanding, an acceptable world in which he believes he is right. He has been seeking a position of righteousness without remembering the rules of God most of the time, if not completely ignoring them altogether. Man imposing his truth over the truth of the Almighty blinds him spiritually in his weakness and pride.

A person with wrong values and beliefs never likes the truth of God. The Word of God says that His truth is like a knife that penetrates man's soul, heart, and spirit to separate the lies from the truth, or vice versa, to clear the mind of its confused understanding. We read in Hebrews 4:12, "For the word of God is quick and powerful, and sharper than any twoedged sword, piercing even to the dividing asunder of soul and spirit, and of the joints and marrow, and is a discerner of the thoughts and intents of the heart." It causes pain and shame to be cleaned, and if we don't use the soap of our working conscience, we will die in our sinful dirty life.

Sin has no difference to it; it is dirty and wrong whether we like it or not, or accept it or reject it according to our understanding and/or personal convenience. Some people develop moral values according to their weaknesses and beliefs. In sin there is no difference, whether in quality or quantity, between wrongdoings—from a white lie, to a wish that someone would step on a banana peel, to trying to be a magician and make something or someone disappear. Some people do not want to hear that they are wrong.

Whenever God is brought up in conversation, people with questionable moral beliefs say in their own defense, "God is love!" And that is the truth: God loves sinners, but not their sin. The other indefensible excuse is: "Well, if God didn't want us to act this way, He wouldn't have created us this way!" God has never created anything wrong, whether humankind or any other thing with any kind of life, including mountains, rocks, and sand. You have to make a difference in your own understanding, not according to your own beliefs of right and wrong, but according to God's truth of what is right and wrong.

Don't want to change because another man is telling you that you are wrong? Fine, don't listen to him, but give yourself a chance to listen to what God is saying in His Word about your weakness, and determine for yourself if that is the way He wants you to be, if only you'll confess, and believe and trust in Him.

The only thing that can be said in your favor is that the person who lies is no better than you. Sin does not necessarily favor weak people. The difference between certain sinners is that one will ask God for forgiveness and the other will ignore his or her wrongdoing.

Try to be fair. Get yourself in balance, and fight within yourself what you don't like to hear of God's words from others when they tell you that you are wrong, a truth that may give you an uncomfortable feeling in your heart and thoughts. Just compare God's truth to yours.

At the beginning, there will be moments of confusion. To understand what is happening with your feelings, emotions, and thoughts, you will have to know what is happening inside of you. If you are feeling such discomfort, it means there is a battle inside of you, as the wrong spirit that is in control is preventing you from having a clear mind to reason and to accept what is wrong. This keeps you in a stubborn defensive position, also giving you a defiant attitude and a wrong understanding of righteousness. At the end, you get mad.

If you feel that you are having this sort of reaction because the truth of God and His Spirit is trying to help you in your inner being, don't fight it. Instead, stop, take a deep breath, and cool off. Get yourself in a neutral balance, and then taste the imitation "sugar" against the real sugar of God's truth to find out which one leaves a bitter taste in your mouth afterward. That is, which truth in that moment of denial makes you feel more uncomfortable and angry?

Give yourself a chance to have an open door where you can have an escape way. If you don't do that, you'll find yourself drawn to the wrong people, the wrong conversations, the wrong thoughts, and the wrong things to see or do. It is better to lose some so-called friends and bad habits than to lose your soul because of your stubborn pride. God won't come down from heaven to kick you in your sitting cheeks to wake you up to reason; His truth is more than enough. If His truth offends you, it means that your beliefs and pretenses are wrong.

It is God who is saying you're wrong, not man; man is only repeating what God is saying. Man cannot reward you, but God can.

CHAPTER 11

E very sin is the result of a moral problem in a dead soul, which has no active human spirit. But sometimes that oppressed and disregarded human spirit that is trying to help through common sense, which is the conscience, can make you feel uncomfortable with the things you do not want to accept because they do not fit in with your beliefs. An active human spirit, on the other hand, has its life through God's Spirit and brings that life to your soul. When you recognize in your heart and accept the painful truth that what you have believed is wrong before God, you'll be rewarded with a much greater freedom than what you had when fighting with your life for the wrong reasons.

In the twenty-first century, one of the greatest moral sins, which exists in the darkness in every generation, is now reappearing slowly but surely for everyone throughout the whole world to see. Many will compare this moral weakness with mass murder, yet the difference is that this kind of act does not result in a killing field where people's bodies are destroyed. With this sin, no bodies are killed; they are just corrupted to the point that the individuals' common sense is shattered beyond recognition, removing the ability to see and know what is right and what is wrong, in what is called human decency. And because their souls are dead, these people's spiritual blindness and suppressed consciences make them believe that by their rights it is time for society to recognize them. There was a time when God decided to erase people from the face of the earth during Noah's life by way of water, and later Sodom and Gomorrah by fire. Next time is for the guessing.

People of all kingdoms, governments, and empires were and are contaminated. They fail to remember the past; otherwise, they would know that time and time again, people have committed degenerate acts, poisoning their societies. These people were not savages; they were supposed to be civilized people who knew the difference between right and wrong. But they ignored both moral standards and their own common sense. And instead of doing something to correct this situation, they chose to look the other way.

That was and is the case of some civilized nations, which in their so-called democratic society of any religious belief, is accepting the understanding of a libertarian version of human rights as a normal way of life in their societies. Some countries where morally indecent behavior is prohibited in public are criticized by countries where immoral behavior is accepted as a human right. The latter condemn the former for prohibiting immoral behavior in public.

Countries professing to be Christian examples of freedom, where the flag of morality is supposed to be the standard of decency, equality, and respect for others, have long disappeared. Those standards do not exist today in most self-proclaimed democratic nations. What exists today in those countries as a normal way of life is drug use, gambling, prostitution, sex trafficking, alcohol use, pornography, and child abuse, along with low-paid workers in many industries, plus other things that may or may not be ignored by the general public. This all allows immoral "Christians" working in the government to take billions of dollars in undeclared money (in terms of taxes) and deposit it in their offshore bank accounts—all in the name of capitalism and democracy, where those on the top don't check each other for cheating, although they sure do check those people beneath them whom they represent.

This does not account for the personal contributions made to our representatives in government, which money is untraceable but known to exist. The Word of God says about these so-called Christian believers, "For the love of money is the root of all evil, which some coveted after, they have erred from the faith, and pierced themselves through with many sorrows" (1 Timothy 6:10).

Any nation that has the audacity to allow this modern version of slavery to exist, from which money can be made at every level of the sick society, and is criticizing other nations for disallowing this kind of democratic capitalistic liberalism as a law for equal opportunity in terms of so-called human rights, is a cynical, disrespectful, twisting-of-truth nation controlled by evil.

The evil spirits have not changed their tactics; they are still in control because no one is opposing these spiritual beasts in a spiritual way, in the way that it's supposed to happen. In the meantime, Christians are ignorant of or indifferent toward the matter and therefore are failing to fight those evil spirits by not getting on their knees. It is not by secular rules, regulations, or amendments to the law that this spiritual war will be won.

Throughout generations, people in high places have failed to act against immorality on all levels because they had that same immoral weakness, or they shared empathy with the weak ones. The same thing is happening today in all self-proclaimed liberal democratic countries. They are pushing to have this perverted behavior permitted as a way of life, insisting on human rights and moral equality in their immoral way of life, backed by the law. This happens even when specific immoral behavior is not part of the system, and is prohibited by law in other countries, but recently allowed in some countries by law to be taught in the schools.

Change comes about in a person not by way of the law, but by recognition of conscience. If the conscience is suppressed by any ungodly force, then a person with common sense is without any understanding of right or wrong to be able to rationalize for himself. There is no law that can change a soul; a soul can only be changed when the heart is free of evil spirits. When a man's conscience, through his common sense, allows him to see the difference between right and wrong, his human spirit is helping him to acknowledge the need to make a decision.

Any person can live in denial of whatever weakness he or she may have. A person may even deny the truth of God in his or her blindness, pride, or ignorance, but the truth of the Almighty won't change because of anyone's wrong belief. A person can get philosophical about it and put all his or her arguments and beliefs on the table, but it won't change God's truth. The degenerated moral weakness of any person is a degradation not only to the body, but also to the dead soul, which is enslaved by a powerful evil spirit that has neutralized the human spirit and its common sense, without allowing the possibility of reason to help the heart to think, thereby preventing the person from seeing and understanding his or her own spiritual condition.

The denial of wrongdoing is the first solid base that keeps the person in a position of an attacking-defensive edge of self-protection against their rights and their own spiritual misunderstanding of their cause. Scientists, through genes, and psychologists and sociologists in their studies of the brain, have established that whatever abnormality exists in a person is hereditary; or the person is lacking some kind of inner "something".

How difficult is it for people with a degree to admit that the root of any problem in a human life is not something in accordance with their own findings, is not the result of life circumstances, and is not a matter of the body's malfunctioning because of some weak inherited genes? No, it is a spiritual abnormality reflected in the human race through the consequences of sin, the result of people's spiritual hearts being disconnected from God's life. Instead, people are living in the intellect.

What can those knowledgeable people say about their own wicked ways, known only by God and maybe someone else? Can they say that they have inherited a genetic imbalance from their ancestors or that they have a spiritual problem just like their ancestors?

Worms eat dead flesh. In a soul disconnected from God, the worm of evil is what is eating man's soul, and this is reflected in the life, body, and lifestyle of the sinner. The same can be seen in a person who uses drugs, drinks alcohol, smokes, and eats more than he or she needs, along with engaging in other "needed," and perhaps contaminated, pleasures. In time, the abuser ends up seeing a doctor in an emergency room, if he or she is lucky to get there on time.

In this world where people and other creations are under the influence of evil, confusion leads to a state of chaos in the spiritual life of every person who does not understand, or does not want, the chance to be clean and clear of sin. Many times the dependency of our feelings in our emotions is worse as a result than the rationalization of our brain.

Feelings alone are a one-way street, for or against, but those feelings can also place a person in a state of confusion without the possibility to react. Confusion arising from emotional feelings creates turmoil in the mind, touching those emotions in such a way that the person may go either way, with unpredictable consequences. If the heart and mind is not given a chance to rationalize and understand the chaotic confusion of the moment, the person will have no way out of this predicament.

If there is confusion in feelings, or a blackout in the brain or mind, whichever is preferred, the brain or mind will be slow to react. Even though the brain is an independent working machine, in a moment of disconnection with reality, it is always in need of help. Only our human spirit can help us through our understanding and reasoning so they work correctly with our minds and feelings, according to our need at the moment. Otherwise the nonreasoning mind by itself, controlled by confused emotions, is like a monkey with a gun.

It will remain that way if, in our moment of need, we refuse to fight to understand our present state of mind as we try to make the right decision. It all depends on how strong we stand in our understanding of the adverse circumstances we are experiencing, with confusing emotions and without our human spirit helping. Thoughts, feelings, reason, all have to be given a chance to work correctly with God's help, without any extreme uncontrolled emotions. We are the only ones who have direct authority to make, or refuse to make, any decision. Reacting in accordance to whatever the situation is in our minds is the right thing to do if we are to give ourselves a chance to balance the circumstances without going to extremes. The point should be to refrain from concentrating on the confusing emotional feelings at the moment, where loud thoughts cannot be controlled.

The concentration should be in fighting, against all odds, for the inner understanding of those boiling emotional feelings of the heart's mind. Such a moment is needed as a chance to climb up over the troubling gravity of those feelings in order to find a solid peace. A solid moment of peace will allow for the chance to calmly analyze the uncontrollable thoughts of desperation, giving a person the ability to reason and to understand that a spirit that is not from God is in control of his or her disturbed emotions. That is a wrong spirit working in the person's inner senses.

Evil is a power that works through the heart's mind, that is, in a person's thoughts, and in some cases through his or her eyes. God is a power that works through our human spirit. And conscience is the voice of our spirit that helps us to recognize what is right and wrong in our thoughts. We do this by way of reasoning and using our common sense—that is, if we are not standing in the corner of stubbornness, rejecting what is right because of our arrogance, pride, or ignorance. If evil is in control of our human senses, then it means God is not, and the sign of this is confusion, desperation, rebellion, and anger, along with emptiness and poorly understood emotions, which are what causes the person's inability to reason, always thinking that he is right and that those who stand against his position are wrong.

When God is allowed to be in control, none of the previously said exists. The reason is that God is not a God of confusion, but of a clear understanding of right and wrong, which leads to inner peace. All things within human nature that go against God's established rules are wrong and immoral. And none of them are excusable, although there are people who believe that their way of life is normal and it has to be accepted.

It is known as a moral degradation for a person to use his or her body for the pleasure of the flesh with another person of the same sex. Even when that immorality is prohibited by God's law, it is known to exist anyway in different nations of different religions, and it is in practice in secluded places within different societies. In the past, it was shameful to practice that immorality openly, but today people have defied the taboo and have brought their immorality out into the open, where they are proud of it, having determined that it is not indecent to be immoral, as it is for them a normal way of life. Those people do not understand that as humans of the same gender, they will not be able to create a family because such a union is unable to bear fruits. And what is more important is that that kind of union is prohibited by God.

Today, nothing of this is a secret, and most of the people in this world know about its existence. This immorality has incrementally increased in every generation, slowly making its presence known. More than anywhere else, this happens in so-called democratic countries, where people believe in equal human rights and therefore legally permit this immorality in and by man's law.

Even in very religious countries around the world, this immorality exists, and it doesn't matter how strongly their leaders criticize it in public, people still practice it. The source of any immoral behavior is an evil spirit that no man's strict law, stiff punishment, or extreme religion has the ability to conquer. Slowly but surely, through time, this weakness has spread throughout the world like a spider web and is no longer taboo. Today the ideology is in favor of human rights. It is no longer an issue of morality, but a right that those people think they are supposed to have universally, because according to them, God created them that way.

Now, in some of the so-called civilized societies of "cultured" minds, some spiritual leaders and people of religious denominations, in their advanced understanding of civilization and human rights, have called to invoke the tolerance, love, and understanding that God has for the sinful world. These people, ignorant of the Word of God in their spiritual blindness, are calling in favor of recognizing and accepting their rights as equals of their spiritually immoral iniquities as a way of life in society.

What is sad about this situation is that some of the so-called servants of God are the ones who are speaking out in their favor to be accepted. In some denominations, the heads of local churches are guiding other souls to the same tragic end, something the Bible calls "the blind guiding the blind." How can these people not see that what they are teaching is wrong, not according to man, but according to the Word of God?

It is easy to understand that this sort of "religious spirituality" has nothing to do with the spirit of the gospel. God Himself, through His servant the apostle Paul, tells us why this sin is an abomination to Him. We read the following in Romans 1:18–32:

> For the wrath of God is revealed from heaven against all ungodliness and unrighteousness of men, who hold the truth in unrighteousness; because that which may be known of God is manifest in them; for God hath shewed it unto them. For the invisible things of him from the creation of the world are clearly seen, being understood by the things that are made, even his eternal power and Godhead; so that they are without excuse: Because that, when they knew God, they glorified him not as God, neither were thankful; but became vain in their imaginations, and their foolish heart was darkened. Professing themselves to be wise, they became fools, and changed the glory of the incorruptible God into an image made like to corruptible man, and to birds, and four footed beasts, and creeping things. Wherefore God also gave them up to uncleanness through the lusts of their own hearts, to dishonor their own bodies between themselves: who changed the truth of God into a lie, and worshipped and served the creature more than the Creator, who is blessed forever. Amen. For this cause God gave them up unto vile affections: for even their women did change the natural use into that which is against nature: and likewise also the men, leaving the natural use of the woman, burned in their lust one toward another; men with men working that

which is unseemly, and receiving in themselves that recompence of their error which was meet. And even as they did not like to retain God in their knowledge, God gave them over to a reprobate mind, to do those things which are not convenient; being filled with all unrighteousness, fornication, wickedness, covetousness, maliciousness; full of envy, murder, debate, deceit, malignity; whisperers, backbiters, haters of God, despiteful, proud, boasters, inventors of evil things, disobedient to parents, without understanding, covenant breakers, without natural affection, implacable, unmerciful: who knowing the judgment of God, that they which commit such things are worthy of death, not only do the same, but have pleasure in them that do them.

For these people to say that what God is saying about them is untrue, in their religious beliefs in favor of their immorality, is to be under the complete control of an unclean spirit of deception. Such people do not know in their spiritual blindness, that within them they are rejecting God Himself, when His truth, not man's, is telling them that they are wrong, making them angry.

And this is also something that is easy to understand. For such people, it is much easier to live by their religious rituals, according to their own understanding of the gospel, than to accept the truth about their way of life. Is their angry reaction not a sign that something is wrong with their beliefs or their way of life when they are told this? Seems to be they don't see the sign.

Now the question is, who is the one who may judge any man's life when all men have been born in sin? The Bible says there is not even one person who is free of sin if he does not come to repentance. Jesus said in John 8:7, "He that is without sin among you, let him first cast a stone."

We people have the problem of always seeing something stuck in someone else's eye without noticing that we have something in our own eye. That is human nature, and sometimes we forget about it even being Christians. Sometimes in our secularity, we don't see the spirit of weakness in the life of any person. We don't always have in mind the weak spirits of the air that the apostle Paul speaks about. But as spiritual Christians, who according to the gospel know the difference between wrong and right, we have the right to speak the gospel, and because of this, we cannot be judged for telling God's truth.

Warning a person, any person, is not judging. When a doctor says to his patient to stop using drugs, or stop drinking, or stop living in some other problem, he is not judging his patient; he is warning him of the future consequences. In John 7:24 we read, "Judge not according to the appearance [that is, what you may think, because of what something looks like]. But judge righteous judgment"—that is, having full knowledge, and not to condemn, but to warn.

The difference between one person and another, when both have committed the same immoral act or succumbed to any other weakness, is that one has recognized his sin before God, repenting and accepting Christ as his Savior, while the other fights for his or her rights, according to their own misinterpretation of decency, self-respect, and honor as a so-called Christian. Being rebellious and confused, unrepentant sinners reject everything that God says about their sinful way of life. But they do not reject God's love and mercy. What they are rejecting is the part where He is telling them about their weakness.

They say God is love, and this is true. God loves the sinner, any sinner. What He does not love is their sin, their weakness, their confused weak heart. Like the Word of God says, "For by Grace are ye saved through faith, and that not of yourselves; it is the gift of God, not of works lest any man should boast" (Ephesians 2:8–9). This verse is speaking about a faith that is overpowered by a spirit with a different understanding in the heart of man, a heart that is afraid to lose what is wrong without knowing and understanding what is right. People still have a chance to understand the difference and accept what God is offering in His gift of life.

We have a chance to be saved and to change, not by our own works, trying to show how good we are, but by understanding, believing, and accepting the truth of our incorrect way of life before the Almighty, and repenting to be saved. Some have taken advantage of the opportunity that God has given us as a present, not as a reward. The reward will come later, when you persevere to the end of the present life you have accepted from Him. At the end of your life in the flesh, when you are in the heavens, for the rest of your existence, you will be crowned with a golden crown and rewarded with eternal life. You will be accepted in the heavens, not rejected.

If for some reason in our Christian belief any malicious or misunderstood criticism rears its head, that is because we have mixed feelings about the subject at hand. Perhaps we lack the knowledge to approach the popular saying, "God loves the sinner but hates sin." In reality, it should be said, "God loves the sinner who repents, but He hates the sinner who rejects or ignores His love, mercy, and offer of salvation"—just like He hates the ones who, after salvation, for some reason reject the gift of eternal life, disregarding Jesus's sacrifice on the cross when the Father sent His Only begotten Son for the salvation of man's soul.

Even before Jesus came to this world, God said that He hated Esau for what he had done with the birthright that God had given to him. God doesn't hate just because. God loved Jacob not because he tricked Esau, but because in his heart he held deep regret and sorrowful repentance for what he had done before the Almighty. For that repentance, God loved him (Malachi 1:2–3). That is the way God loves us when we repent, recognizing our sin before Him.

God despises sin and the sinner who doesn't repent, but He loves the sinner who repents. When we cannot see through a person to the evil spirit that is causing him or her to sin, separating the person from the spiritual wrong within, we are not seeing or understanding with God's eyes and mind.

If we can't accept other people for what they are, because of their weaknesses, then, following Christ's teaching, we have a problem with understanding why God loves us when we are sinners. But if we understand, then we will have much more reason to intercede for others still in sin. The same chance that someone else took with us in the past is the chance that we have to take with others. If the planted seed falls upon good soil, we will see the result, but if we plant the seed and the soil does not receive the gift of life, then we are neither responsible nor guilty. We must not criticize or condemn that person who has any evil of any perversion in his or her life, but instead seek understanding of what is happening within him or her. So at the end, the responsibility of repentance is in the hands of the person who must make the decision about his or her own future course. But for those who have an evil which does not let them rationalize for themselves, it is in our interest to understand the spirits of Jesus's words about fasting and praying.

Even if we as Christians don't have the same weakness, our own particular weakness is no better before God. And if God has used someone to open our eyes, showing us the way to forgiveness and salvation, that is repentance, today we have to be of the same sort of use to others. Not with confrontational words or attitude, but with the knowledge and guidance of the Spirit, understanding that we are not fighting against a person, but helping the person to see the weak and evil spirit within him.

On one occasion, Jesus says, "Howbeit this kind goeth not out by prayer and fasting?" (Matthew 17:21). We should practice prayer and fasting as Jesus did. There is no law, government decree, human rights movements, church, denomination, or legal institution that will change a sinner's ways. Only by faith do those who in their hearts believe in the promises of the Lord change.

Our job is to do more than the best we can, fasting and praying without poking out anybody's eyes. Other people's salvation or condemnation is in their own hands, after we do our jobs. Our responsibility is to save souls from hell, with God's help and blessing. If for their cause such people come out into the open and fight for their rights for which they are united, then we Christians, with much more reason, have to be united in fasting and prayer for the deliverance of such people from evil.

Church leaders of today are not doing enough to reach out to each other, become united, and pray for a specific need, leaving aside denomination-specific guesses, deductions, doctrines, and interpretations. There are those who understand the need for a spiritually united force to fight, in the same mind and spirit, for all the different spiritual needs found in people, society, governments, institutions, and nations.

A solid, spiritually unified force is what will win. Individually, most of the leaders are busy with their own obligations to their churches. Nothing is wrong with that, but there is a need for spiritual unity and expansion, not only at the city or state level, but also across the whole country and, if possible, the world, something that today is possible with the technology enabling contact with the rest of the world.

The hope is for one wish, one desire, one understanding, one body, one church, one mind, and one spirit, to being connected to the other living members of the body of Christ. The stubborn evil, fighting for the rights of immorality, has led to being officially recognized and accepted in thirty-two countries so far in the 21st century. And it won't stop there because it keeps moving forward.

In these so-called democratic civilized countries, the highly educated people are trying to bring this evil to schools, to be understood by children and young adults. Even some government officials are proclaiming their right to be accepted in society as equals, a right demanded as the air needed to breathe.

In every high school, without exception, there are students already contaminated by this spiritual "virus." Unfortunately, this is happening not only in secondary schools, but also in colleges, universities, the government, sports, the armed forces, the entertainment industry, and every other level of society. We can see how that evil spirit grows and takes its place slowly but surely, with almost no opposition whatsoever from the Christian world. And when there is such opposition, it consists only of commentary in sermons or personal conversations, and that is only because evil begins screaming publicly for its rights. We don't have to wait for anyone to do something before we get into action; we have to be active 24/7, all year round, in every church around the world—to get rid of not only this wicked spirit of immorality, but also the other wicked spirits that are creating in people's lives all the tragedies predicted by the Lord.

We need to fight that evil and to do this we need only two inseparable realities: one is to make a difference in the spiritual world and second is that this secular world will also see the difference. The Lord said, "Therefore I say unto you, what things soever ye desire, when ye pray, believe that ye receive them, and ye shall have them" (Mark 11:24). And what is the result of the promises of the Lord in our lives? A lack of faith in the lives of believers, or maybe a lack of wisdom, or vision, or courage, is why the Word says that the world will go from bad to worse. And what is sadder than anything is that too many church leaders think that uniting to engage in such a spiritual fight is impossible.

The leaders of the church around this globe, whether they know each other or not, need to take a chance. They must try to be in contact and create a system of communication where the doctrines of all participating members are unified in one mind and one spirit. Church leaders need to go, according to the Word, wild against all odds, and create a culture of voluntary fasting and prayer in the church, in the hopes of cultivating Christians who believe in God and are willing to present themselves to Him.

Christians can pray to God the Father, in the name of His Son Jesus, to get rid of the evil spirits that are in control of this world and people's lives, no matter what denomination the people belong to. We should believe and have faith in the promises of the Lord, so we can challenge our own beliefs according to our faith before the Almighty.

If for unbelievers the preaching of the gospel is unhinged, how much more should it challenge us believers to achieve the impossible? But that challenge is in the hands of the real spiritual leaders of the church who understand against whom it is we struggle. Under their direction and guidance, we should go against all human understanding, in the faith of our wild belief, for the glory of the Highest One.

Without faith, belief, understanding, courage, and a defiant attitude against evil, there will be no victory, but maybe a lot of questions to answer someday. Asking God if something is possible is not a sin; not asking is a sin. "Therefore to him that knoweth to do good, and doeth it not, to him it is sin" (James 14:17).

The day when the secular media publish, show, or talk about some "strange goodness" that is happening in the world, will be the day when we know that we really have the devil on the run. With God's gift in our lives, and with our hearts oriented to all His promises and to our faith in Him, He will move his hand to intercede in this world. He promises, "If my people, which are called by my name, shall humble themselves, and pray, and seek my face, and turn from their wicked ways; then will I hear from heaven, and will forgive their sins, and will heal their land" (2 Chronicles 7:14).

Even though these words were spoken to the people of Israel, we Gentiles may still follow them. We need to stand firm on our feet first if we are to be able to help others. It won't matter what the evil spirit is when we are standing strong for the truth and for the freedom of an oppressed soul.

CHAPTER 12

Obviously, today we are not even close to achieving the vision discussed in the previous chapter; otherwise, things would be different. For the real spiritual Christians, not the so-called religious ones, the time has come to think big, not locally, but nationally and worldwide. And not for just a short time, but through constant communication with others to achieve unity of mind and spirit in the will of God for the purpose of victory over evil, an evil that cannot be conquered by guns, blood, and the loss of lives, but by the power of the One whom the Almighty brought back to life from death, Jesus Christ. Because, "For the kingdom of God is not in word but in power" (1 Corinthians 4:20). And that power is His Spirit, given to us in our lives to do His will and fulfill the wishes of our hearts, if we believe and have faith.

For people of this world, criticism offers an entrée of disagreement served with a salad of right and wrong and a dessert of dissolution, where stubbornness, misunderstandings, arrogance, pride, resentment, anger, protest, threats, hate, and many other sour gifts given to people by the lord of this world serve as entertainment on the way to hell.

It is very sad to see today's so-called Christians playing religion and not even noticing it. To some extent it is not their fault, but the fault of the leaders, who are in a state of working the conscience of the believers in their ignorance of the Spirit. Like the Bible says, it is a case of "the blind guiding the blind", who believe in a man who is making them feel guilty or entertaining them every time the church doors are open. That is not even religiousness.

The problem with most Christians, in their faith, is their lack of interest in looking deeper into the Word of God. This is their job in prayer, to be able to distinguish between the Spirit of God and the evil spirit. Not all preachers behind a church pulpit are preaching or teaching the gospel in the Spirit. Some leaders want to avoid making any waves by splashing anyone with the raw truth, meaning they're more concerned about offending people than they are about preaching God's truth. An unnoticed and unrecognized spirit of arrogance in the lives of those who know the Word from cover to cover, in their position as leaders, are blind to the real spiritual knowledge of the will of God.

In this time of gospel-religious-political correctness, most church leaders are not taking a chance to go the extra mile, nor are they good officers in the heavenly army. They are failing to take the initiative to accomplish the mission in the will of God.

God is not a spirit with origins in the human intellect, where theories are born. He gives us spiritual knowledge of Him and reveals Himself to our hearts, as He is the Spirit of wisdom. People without the Spirit are unable to effectively learn or teach the Word of God. People who do have the Spirit but who, because of pride and arrogance, put their faith in their own knowledge, prevent the Spirit from leading the way in the will of the Almighty. An absence of faith in the Spirit is what has halted the spiritual progress of many church leaders and everyday Christians in their quest for spiritual wisdom, vision, and revelation of His will.

Today, the teaching of the gospel has been replaced by a human-devised spiritual ideology. Many church leaders don't even notice that they are stuck in philosophical religiousness, where they are unable to reach real spirituality. A lack of a real spiritual interest in both the person who is ignorant of the Spirit and the person who "knows too much" to learn and teach the gospel has been catastrophic to the Christian world. But it is no surprise that this is happening, because the gospel says that this world will go from bad to worse.

The proof that this prediction is coming true is the chaotic spiritual condition of the world. It is evidently seen by the rising levels of violence and immorality in all facets of people's lives, through people who do not care, do not notice, or else ignore what their own consciences dictate. This is something aligned with the irrefutable truth expressed by the apostle Luke in the lives of the believers, that one is an unworthy servant of God if one fails to transform one's life for the glory of God, to wit: "So likewise ye, when ye shall have done all those things which are commanded you, say, we are unprofitable servants. We have done that which was our duty to do" (Luke 17:10). Here we need to understand the meaning of going the extra mile in taking chances, which is to seek to do God's will for His glory.

No wonder the Word of God reminds us, encourages us, and hints to us about the promises of the Lord fulfilling the wishes of our hearts. How can we challenge ourselves, how can we put our faith to work, if we don't put forth the effort to understand what it means to go the extra mile? If you don't learn how to build your own house first, how can you teach others to build houses for themselves?

The foundation (the promises of the Lord) has already been built, but we haven't yet been told what kind of materials (acting in the Lord's promises) we need to build the house. One of those materials is the courage before the Almighty to turn the wishes of our hearts into reality.

Although both church leaders and churchgoers are at fault,

the former, who have the responsibility to open people's eyes to God's grace, will suffer consequences that are much more severe than those suffered by the latter, who are under their spiritual guidance, to whom God has said, "My people are perishing for lack of knowledge, because thou hast rejected knowledge, I will also reject thee, that thou shall be no priest to me: seeing thou hast forgotten the law of thy God, I will also forget thy children" (Hosea 4:6). Those words were spoken not only for the spiritual leaders of Israel at that time but also for the know-it-all spiritual leaders of today.

Satan doesn't know what it is to take a break or go on vacation; he works 24/7/365, with no weekends off. He is a very greedy individual, wanting his payoff to be not just big, but immensely huge. That's why he works so hard: to get the most he can. He looks for weak souls to conquer and seeks to confuse those who are living in the right way. His goal is to destroy them.

Meanwhile, Christians complain about their difficulties, the harshness of life, and the misery of people under evil control. In this world, there is a saying that goes, "If you want to cry, go to the chapel." That doesn't even help though. Only real spiritual Christians, those who are guided by the Spirit of God and seek His will, will get results from their God-given gifts, or will see the wishes of their hearts fulfilled, if they come to recognize and acknowledge the promises of God. Every Christian needs to find out for himself where in his faith he stands.

If we find ourselves having to intercede on behalf of another person who is under an evil threat, whether or not he or she knows this is so or is able to react appropriately to it, this doesn't mean that God is deaf to our prayers, or has no time for us, or would be offended if we were to call on Him. We take courage in what God says in the Bible: "If my people which are called by my name, shall humble themselves, and pray, and seek my face, and turn from their wicked ways; them will I hear from heaven, and will forgive their sins, and will heal their land" (2 Chronicles 7:14). What more do we need to move God's hand, having such a promise?

We need to do exactly what He wants us to do: humble ourselves, recognize our sin, admit it, and repent of it from the bottom of our hearts. Can we do that? If we can do it, then we may have whatever we wish in our hearts to act for God's glory by saving a soul or fulfilling any other need. God will be pleased, and we'll have our needs and wishes fulfilled. It is simply up to us. But if we know we are able to do this and we don't do it, for whatever reason, we better take a moment to come up with an excuse for the day when we will stand before God and submit to His judgment.

We know that a person under evil control is incapable of rationalization. There are cases where the person is so far under a particularly oppressive type of control, in a state of denial and rejection of the truth, that he or she is incapable of any understanding. This is where we, if unified and of one mind and one spirit, with one wish before the throne of God, could cast the evil spirit out of the person, or persons, no matter the distance between us.

Jesus said, "Verily, verily I say unto you, he that believeth on me, the works that I do shall he do also; and greater [works] then those shall he do; because I go unto My Father. And whatsoever ye shall ask in my name, that will I do, that the Father will be glorified in the Son. If ye shall ask anything in my name I will do it" (John 14:12–14).

Jesus says, "*Whenever* you ask for *anything* in my name, I will do it" (emphasis added). The apostle John said, "And this is the confidence that we have in him, that, if we ask any thing according to His will, He heareth us" (1 John 5:14).

How do we know that we have the ability to do such things if we don't ever take the chance and try? Surely in the twenty-first century, the images of man, and birds, and four-footed beasts, and creeping things haven't disappeared. Today, spiritual degeneration, moral erosion, and indecency exist in the form of freedom of choice, such as through television, the world of fashion, the fight for equal rights, fake news, politics, explicit or violent movies and art, and human law, which is full of holes—not forgetting the love of money, that is, greed, the main reason people pursue any of those things.

The evil weakness described in the previous paragraph has attacked people with such force that it continues to destroy the moral values of all those who are influenced by them in the name of equal rights. If immorality is given the right, humanity will stop to exist, because sooner or later without any wars, but with a lot of wrong love, there will be less and less people in this world. The concept of decency will disappear altogether with the natural way of male and female procreation. But it won't disappear as a business, because the business of renting one human body to create another human body will cause more dead souls to be brought to "life". The creature has given to people the superficial pleasures of this world to keep them, in their weaknesses, in a state of false happiness, where they are spiritually blind and confused, while someone else is making money off them.

God offers the chance of salvation, by the sacrifice of Jesus, to any wicked sinner who recognizes his or her own faults. Because such people have been enslaved by the spirit of sin, our duty before God is to intercede for them, whether they understand their spiritual condition, recognize their sin, and admit it, or else deny their condition, rejecting the idea that they are sinners, or ignore the matter entirely. Our Christian job before God Almighty is to bring such people into His presence through prayer. Let's plant the seed of our faith, like the four friends who believed that if they could only get their friend through the roof, Jesus would heal him. That story appears in Luke 5:19–20.

In the spirit of our faith, let's take these people in our prayers through the roof of our believing, wishing hearts and put those souls at Jesus's feet. We have to take the initiative praying for these people, whether such people know we are doing so or not, whether they like it or not, or whether they approve of it or not. The fact is, they are under a wrong spirit that they are unaware of or else deny. We need to plant the seed of our faith for God to give the increase (1 Corinthians 3:6).

Always remember, we are not fighting with any man, but against the evil spirit in the man. Let our prayers for men's lives bring about a miracle, with God enlightening their hearts so they may understand His truth regarding the salvation of their souls.

Before God and in the name of Jesus, we need to pray for the souls of the people who do not know Christ, even those who say they know Him but do not. We bring them before God the Father according to our faith and the desire of our hearts. He won't let our prayers go unanswered. In time, because of your prayers, the lives of those you pray for will change for the better.

It is impossible for us to have the love and mercy of God if we are not in His Spirit. But when we are in His kingdom and we understand the apostle Paul's words about our struggle with spirits, then He will miraculously perform everything that is impossible for us to do. In faith we have to plant the seed; God will do the rest. That is a solid promise from the Savior Himself.

Our spiritual duty and responsibility is to conquer the enemy of the human soul. If we don't try to do that because of our doubt, misunderstanding, or misinterpretation of the revealed Word of God, then we should check our spiritual priorities.

Speaking on whether one should talk to the person or just pray on his or her behalf, the Word of God says, "And the prayer of faith shall save the sick, and the Lord shall raise him up. And if he has committed sins, he shall be forgiven him" (James 5:15).

So if we ask God if it His will to heal someone and He says no, we are free of responsibility. But if we think that we are going to get our hands on something bigger, and then we let our doubts, personal misinterpretations of the Bible, or other inaccurate spiritual conclusions prevent us from getting busy, we had better get on our knees and pray about our own condition, or else we'll have to answer for our failure to act. The Word of God says, "Therefore, to him who knows to do well and does not do it, to him it is sin" (James 4:17).

CHAPTER 13

The devil has done such a good job of confusing people that the one who is wrong believes he is right, and the one who believes he is right doesn't want to think or hear that he is wrong. That is very human, and we admit we behave this way, but rarely do we accept it in our inner beings. As people with some degree of intelligence, we like to think that we are always right, and when we are right, we are. But we also have to be honest about it when we are wrong. Like the old saying goes, "If it ain't broke, don't fix it." But what happens if something with a person is broken and he or she doesn't want to admit it? Who can say who is right and who is not? Well, to a small degree, our intellect is right if it has the ability to reason and if it submits to an honest examination of itself to determine if it is certain in its beliefs. Unless a person is completely blind and can't see the difference, is ignorant, or flat-out rejects any notion that he can be wrong, he will never admit that what is white is white and what is black is black.

In the spiritual world, what comes first is the honesty of a man's heart before God. An honest person, with God's help, will be able to see whatever is wrong in his reasoning process and, after recognizing this, make the decision to be saved by Christ.

If we recognize our sin before God, we are moving in the right direction, and when we accept salvation, we leave behind our human intellect, because otherwise it could get in our way as we seek to possess God's wisdom. We are ordered not to live by our own intelligence alone because God's wisdom, given to us, is much higher than our human intelligence.

The wisdom of God in our lives is what allows us to see and understand His world, which also helps us to understand the secular world. God gave us the intellect so we could choose between right and wrong, but if we allow God's Spirit to supplement our human wisdom, then we'll always take the right steps in both the secular world and the spiritual world.

In one word, we have our human wisdom topped with God's wisdom. We are covered all around because we are in God's Spirit and not in our own selves. Even when we are in this messy world surrounded by a very fierce and ungodly force, understanding in whom we have our lives, we are protected by His promise. That means that even when we are like everybody else on this earth, mortal, our spiritual lives in this world cause our souls to become residents of heaven. Because of God's love and mercy through the sacrifice of Jesus Christ, we have been given a heavenly celestial passport (faith) that gives us a chance to get a visa (salvation) for our residency (citizenship) in heaven. And that is the understanding that we have accepted as the conditions of this life in order to have a forever better eternal life.

Whoever fails to understand or refuses to admit, recognize, and accept what the Almighty, through His Son, has done for the people of this world is doomed for eternity. A person who rejects the offer of salvation will forever be a resident of Satan's burning kingdom.

Don't let your stubbornness, ignorance, pride, arrogance, or religion cause your soul to be lost forever by failing to give yourself just one real chance to really know the difference between hell and heaven. Help yourself while you are still breathing.

Some people find it hard to understand the difference between heaven and hell. As the Word of God says, "Which things also we speak, not in words which man's wisdom teacheth, but which the Holy Ghost teacheth; comparing spiritual things with spiritual. But the natural man receiveth not the things of the Spirit of God, for they are foolishness unto him: nighter can he know them, because they are spiritually discerned" (1 Corinthians 2:13–14). To be capable of spiritual discernment, we need not only faith and belief in God but also, more importantly, His revelations to understand His Word, which give us a chance to know the meaning of those words. For the natural man to be able to understand those words, he has to give himself a chance to believe in what Jesus did for him when He died in exchange for the salvation of man's soul.

Faith is a spiritual gift from God to men, and besides bringing salvation, its purpose is to allow people to acquire spiritual wisdom so they may understand what human wisdom through the intellect cannot conceive. At the same time, spiritual discernment helps us better understand the things of the world. Sometimes we sense in good-hearted Christians a sort of laziness or a lack of real interest that is preventing them from seeing the reality of this dark world under evil control, which otherwise would lead them to reach for the wisdom of God in their lives and seek the salvation of others. We see every day, everywhere, the disgusting things done by men, for whom this is a normal way of life. But we know how sinful all that is, not according to our own understanding, but according to what the Word of God declares is wrong in man's life.

For some people, the things they like in this secular world represent a misleading way of life. Other religious people may consider such a way of life correct given their erroneous spiritual beliefs based in their wrong knowledge of the Bible.

If we are not responding by praying forcefully, then maybe we think that whatever we are currently doing is enough. This is not a matter of becoming religious or too spiritual, excusing ourselves so we do not have to get involved in something provocative and spiritually unknown. Our job as Christians is not to provoke anyone who has been misled, accusing them of something personally, but to tell the truth of God without any confrontation, followed by fasting and prayer. If we don't try before the Almighty Throne to look for His Will in this matter or in any others, which can be our God's gift or heartfelt wish because of some kind of personal conclusion in our own belief, that means we have a problem of our own.

Satan is taking all kinds of chances through the people he controls. People not guided by the Spirit of God do not see the truth of God. But spiritual believers should. And what is it that we are doing? Whatever it is, it is not enough.

The devil is running us over, and we are just saying what a bad boy he is. Maybe that is why God predicts the end of the world, because of our lack of faith and failure to challenge ourselves in the promises of God.

God is with us, not any two-bit strongman of any land with his army. We do not need to make an appointment. Let's agree on something, let's get together and bend our knees before our God, let's knock on His heavenly door, and let's plead in our faith and believe for His intervention. Let's pour our hearts out before the Father in the name of Jesus. Let's keep calling, asking, knocking, and insisting until we get the answer. Our persistence according to the Word of God will get results.

If we understand what sin is, it is time for us, as the old saying goes, to be "sick and tired" and do something about it, not cry over it. This is not a deal with the devil; this is the great deal of our own believing faith as a challenge, within all the promises our Almighty God has made to us, against the rulers of this world.

The leaders of the church are talking about spiritual revival, something that is supposed to happen only once in a while, but that is wrong, as revival is not for regular churchgoing Christians. Revival is for people who don't know Christ. For the ones who attend church, they are not dead and in need of revival if they are in Jesus. Revival is for the sinners of this world whose souls are dead to God. But for any sleeping Christians, an awakening is needed.

The church needs to live in a spiritual awakening, not only once in a while, but every day, all the time, as a way of life and not as a spiritual project. We need to practice in this world what we will be doing in the heavens at the feet of our Lord, before the throne of God. We are to be in the Spirit in Jesus, to be in the life and world of God Himself as Adam and Eve were in the Garden of Eden.

We have to get out of the religious "spiritual" box; we must understand what is at stake in this world full of evil. We have to walk the talk, and keep walking and talking. To be a churchgoing conformist who thinks that everybody is out of line but oneself, trying to save what is already saved, is to be a very selfish servant of God and quite ignorant too.

We have to like and love the person, not the sin, which definitely is the unclean evil spirit in the person. We need to learn how to fight the evil of sin, not the sinner, and any spirits that are opposed to the salvation of the human soul. That is why we need to understand the spiritual meaning of the apostle Paul's words when he said, "For wrestle not against flesh and blood, but against principalities, against powers, against the rulers of the darkness of this world, against spiritual wickedness in high places" (Ephesians 6:12).

Today's believers are very touchy in their feelings and very quick to be offended. Why? Maybe it has something to do with their wrong knowledge and spirituality, or maybe it is just that their latent pride jumps up when touched by emotion?

Be honest with yourself; fight sin on your knees; and win in Jesus's name. Then you can pray for any soul that doesn't know better. Speak the truth. It is better to have twelve real spiritual Christians in church than twelve hundred so-called religious "sleeping" Christians who may say they care for the things from above, but who in reality don't.

Don't feel bad. No one is better than anyone else in this world. The difference is that some have recognized their weakness and accepted that they have wrongly understood truth and salvation, while others keep walking against the wind.

Criticism coming from any so-called Christian who does not see the difference between the man and the spirit within him, and the effect of his reasoning, is a sign that the Christian's inner spiritual world is impoverished.

Give God a chance in your faith. Start from any little need or wish that you may have and grow up in the Lord. You won't be sorry or disappointed, because you have to know that the "sweet" excellences of sin are a bitter-sour death at the end that pride and arrogance carries within.

This world offers freedom according to its own understanding, and that is in every country. People have freedom or liberty of expression according to each nations' unique idealistic system, culture, religious beliefs, and so on. Conservatives, liberals, socialists, Democrats, political or military dictators, radicals, nationalists, or monarchs make no difference. None of them as political or spiritual leaders guide their own people without extremism, even when they may say that they believe in God or their constitution. To believe is one thing; to respect and follow is another.

The rules that these entities create for the people to follow are rules of control with a false idea of absolute freedom. In some cases, there are too many or not enough rules, because there is not even one leader, including those who call themselves religious, who accept God's rules as a way of living everyday life. The results of this sort of spiritual and secular mess can be seen every single day.

Even if a leader may preach religious rules, he doesn't live by them. The proof of this is not only the sorry spiritual condition of every country today, but also the tragedy created by the leaders in the suffering of the people under their democratic, dictatorial, or any other oppressive system, whether religious or constitutional. The wrong spirits have taken control over the slowly disappearing goodness, kindness, respect, mercy, and a real understanding people have of humanity.

Now more than ever, the evil forces in man's life, falsely operating in the name of God, are spreading their "truth" in such a way that even Christians believe these lies. That is something the Bible has warned us about, telling us to be careful, because Satan will come as a sheep to destroy us. And if we are so easy to convince, accepting things we have no clear understanding of, then we definitely need to stop and review the Word of God, asking God Himself to help us.

We cannot do our jobs as Christ's followers if we are not under the guidance of the Holy Ghost. We cannot do our jobs if we do not fast, and we cannot do our jobs if we do not pray constantly. The power of a Christian is not only in his faith, but also in his believing prayer. Faith is the base, and what we build atop it will be according to how well we believe.

Today, some democratic governments criticize other governments for an excessive use of force against peaceful demonstrators, who in their immorality and weakness, not because of any political need, are taking to the streets in their own countries for their immoral rights. And the criticized governments, unwilling to tolerate such immoral propagandistic acts, forbid the public acceptance of such an immoral way of life. While the accused reject any blame, the accusers in their high government positions want immorality to be accepted and codified in law as a way of life for their people, as they seek for themselves.

The church in its teaching of the gospel, and some governments, according to their laws, their system of morality, and their respect for cultural traditions, are working to defend sane and healthy morals for the sake of their citizens and to promote their cultural values. Some leaders of the Western world, while defending immorality and granting freedom to practice it, are trying to protect their own perverted moral and spiritual sickness by changing the laws and seeking the church's approval.

Such actions should be prohibited as they contaminate the minds and souls of those who believe that God created man and woman for each other, not for man-on-man or woman-on-woman relationships.

No law against such a perversion will prevent people from engaging in such acts, but the intersection of faith and prayer will bring about the change. Laws or religious beliefs for or against have nothing to do with solving what is a spiritual problem. The people who criticize others are blind to the immorality of their own nation, which is in jeopardy of a spiritual catastrophe.

Freedom is not to be taken as libertinism in any case, because if the borders of freedom are trespassed, it will be a deviation of justice and reason. Where the people go astray, becoming faulty and corrupt and acquiring bad habits, which is happening today in many free democratic countries, evil is at work. And as the children of God who are free in the Spirit of God, it is our obligation to defend the borders of that freedom. No man with an evil spirit should escape our watchful eye.

CHAPTER 14

Well-meaning Christians who are in the fight against evil have a hard task ahead of them. Although it is right to have laws, it is impossible to prevent a person from engaging in a morally wrong act that is permitted by law.

It is true that the law can be used to prevent some secular behavior, even when the problem is a spiritual one, with the law not touching that spiritual problem. But if a man intends to plant a tree and we see this as a spiritual wrong, we have a fifty-fifty chance of winning if we bring a lawsuit against him.

Regular citizens are accountable to the law, but the representatives of the law can go any which way they want. Even when a judge, say, is against a certain immorality, he or she cannot go against the law in his or her rulings. The loopholes in the law, along with a person's constitutional rights, causes the outcome to be a mystery, as it will be in accordance with the understanding at that moment. Even if the judge weighs in favor of morality and decency, it won't stop Satan from poisoning man in his weakness.

We may not see advertising of any kind, but the evil spirit will keep working. So, a win in the law is a half-way victory, and a loss takes us again to "round one" spiritually speaking. Satan may suggest that Christians may even begin exterminating immoral people, which obviously would be a lie. Killing a person who is under an evil spell won't kill the evil within, because it is impossible for a spirit to be killed materially.

An evil spirit can only be neutralized or immobilized spiritually, without the taking of life in the flesh. Anyone who implies anything contrary to this is an evil person.

Christians sometimes forge to separate the secular world from the spiritual, trying to fight the one that is closer. Perhaps they think in good faith that they can make a spiritual difference when they fight certain beliefs or work to change the law.

The correct approach to immorality has to be a spiritual one with the effective tools of fasting and praying, not to bring the case before a court of law. Because the latter approach is limited, whether one wins or loses. At the same time, anything that can be done by law to restrain people from advertising immoral things or performing degenerate acts in public, or any other place where children, older people, or people of a different opinion on the matter could be offended by such a display, would be excellent, at least for a while.

The effort of every Christian is to understand and convince himself that the fight against any spiritual weakness has to be fought with faith and a knowledge of different evils. Let us always remember what the apostle Paul said: "For we wrestle not against flesh and blood, but against principalities, against powers, against the rulers of darkness of this age, against spiritual hosts of wickedness in high places" (Ephesians 6:12).

Negative powerful spirits suppress people's reasoning, understanding, and common sense, preventing them from seeing what is right and what is wrong. A spirit that corrupts and destroys not only a material body in a dead soul, but also the mind, without any regard for race or intellectual belief, is a power impossible to be defeated by man's law.

Every Christian must always remember that every problem

in people's lives is spiritual in nature, not intellectual or material. The spiritual problem reflects in people's intellectual and material lives all secular inconveniences and miseries. And with that goes a moral imbalance, which has nothing to do with the intellect. Even though we live in a secular world, the problem will always be spiritual, and only spiritually can we fight it. The law will not be able to open anyone's eyes to their spiritual problem in a person. Only God's mercy upon the person in his or her determination to accept or reject His offer of salvation is able to do that.

Christians need to understand that an evil man is a man with no spiritual understanding, a man who is blind to reasoning and incapable of admitting wrongdoing or guilt. He regards himself as a victim of a lack of understanding by the people who are telling him that he is wrong to practice such a way of life. That is why we need to pray to unlock the common sense of any person with a spiritual imbalance that blinds him to the truth.

We can get philosophical about all human beliefs and try to engender a different understanding, but that is an intellectual approach. Even when we mean well, any solution we come up with here will be merely superficial if the individual in question agrees. The point of convincing a person that he is wrong is not to help him change his mind; the point is to change his heart. We want such a person to understand the difference that a healthy and solid spiritual foundation can make, which will allow him to see what is right and what is wrong in life, something made possible by an irreproachable conscience before God.

If a person of doubtful morals and values does not change at the root, meaning in his or her heart, then his or her spiritual life will always be empty, dead. And even if the person's life seems full, he will experience moments of emptiness brought about by misunderstood feelings. For such a person, his heart needs his spirit to be its guide to God, with a deep understanding of a clean and clear life based in a conscience empty of remorse and full of happiness in the life of His Spirit.

The people who serve God by living an immoral life are people completely blinded by an evil spirit, a spirit that is preventing them from seeing what the Word of God is saying about them but, at the same time, making them believe that they are correct and right. The Word of God reads, "Professing themselves to be wise, they became fools" (Romans 1:22). Those people are using their own deductible understanding of the love of God as an excuse to preach to others a theory based not on the truth of God, but on their own convenient interpretation of that love. According to what the apostle Paul wrote on this topic, those people are rejecting the Word that reads, "For this cause God gave them up unto vile affections: for even their women did change the natural use into that which is against nature: And likewise also the man, leaving the natural use of the woman, burn in their lust one toward another; man with man working that which is unseemly, and receiving in themselves that recompense of their error which was meet" (Romans 1:26–27).

In their spiritual ignorance, those people try to convince others to accept their way of life as if it were a right given to them by God in their weakness. People today who think this way don't read in the Bible the things that are abominable to God. Why? Because evil is in control of their lives, not God. Because if they were to read what God finds abominable about their way of life, they would be condemned by the same God they are serving.

These are the kind of God's servants who will stand before Him on Judgment Day and hear Him say, "I never knew you: depart from me, ye that work iniquity" (Matthew 7:23). Before, they excused themselves, saying, "Lord, Lord have we not prophesied in thy name? And in thy name have we cast devils? And in thy name done many wonderful works?" (Matthew 7:22). It will be a terrible moment for those who, in their egocentrism, believed in the righteousness and arrogance of their own hearts, when they hear from the Almighty, "Not everyone that saith unto me, Lord, Lord, shall enter into the Kingdom of heaven; but he that doeth the will of my Father which is in heaven" (Matthew 7:21).

How many so-called spiritual leaders have stopped and thought about the Lord's words of warning?

No man is excused of any stubbornness, pride, or arrogance before God when he does not give himself the chance to find the truth, thinking more of his own understanding and righteousness before the world than of trying to humble himself and learn with God's help. That is why many times the question is asked not only of secular people who may say they know God when in reality they don't, but also of the ones who are involved in so-called service to God. Such people, from ancient times to the present day, really don't know that the veil of their arrogance blinds them so they are unable to see their own lack of humbleness. Their numb human wisdom and their icy hearts cannot feel the warmth and mercy in the Spirit of the real God whom they say they know.

While such people reject God's truth, others who believe in God are killing other believers, calling them blasphemers and heretics or just enemies. Is this not the devil's strategy to bind them in their stubborn pride, spiritual blindness, and temporary glory? If so, all such things will end the day they stop breathing air.

The people of this world become fanatics of their own beliefs, and many of them do not understand that in their attitude they are rejecting reason, which otherwise would enable them to understand the difference between right and wrong in their lives.

Anyone who has chosen a wrong path may now have a chance to choose a better way, without any fanaticism, seeking God's truth instead of man's. This chance is given by a man who came to this world but, as He said Himself, was not from this world—a holy man who came to sacrifice His life for all our wrongs, a heavenly earthly man who accomplished a task on earth that no regular man would ever have been able to accomplish. And because of that sacrifice, we do not have the right to reject His gift of life; otherwise our stubborn, fanatical self-righteousness will be our condemnation. That is why the Son of man came to this world in the flesh, to become the spiritual salvation of humanity, an act that most people the world over, in their belief, could never imagine, leading them to question if Jesus, as a man, was afraid to die.

PART III

WAS JESUS AFRAID TO DIE?

FEAR. DOUBT. INSECURITY. COMMITMENT. FAITH. SACRIFICE. VICTORY.

Many things have been said, preached, and taught about Jesus's life and death, and some people with right, honest intentions have tried to explain the circumstances of His existence. The existence of a holy man, as the spiritual Savior of the human race, who is known by the world as Jesus Christ, the Son of God, the first spiritual holy man to come in the flesh to a world where sin has its kingdom.

All explanations are accepted according to those who are in agreement with the story of any writer who is trying to shed new light upon the death and resurrection of Jesus according to the Bible. Some with differing points of view may disagree, meaning well when describing Jesus as a simple holy man. The ones who believe it is their duty to tell the truth always direct the message of salvation to people so they may understand the sacrifice and suffering of Christ. A message to save the people of this world from eternal condemnation is delivered with the hope that all will be in the will of God.

The story of Jesus' death is a truthful undeniable reality in its biblical details of the material suffering of his body in its spiritual meanings. Perhaps you have never before heard of the spiritual experience Jesus as a man went through, as he was in spiritual agony within His soul.

In this story, there will be some repetition of words and phrases that may look like mistakes, but they are not. What this is, is the effort to help you, with God's blessing Spirit of discernment, to understand how the spiritual-secular world works within us. It is important for us to know ourselves in the work of our human spirit, along with our rebellious heart and intellect.

For those who wish to see the difference between their own believed spirituality, in the knowledge of themselves and the world of the Almighty in their lives, this is a challenge to understand. The wisdom of God in our lives is the one thing, the only thing that through His Spirit will give us the knowledge, enlightenment, vision, and revelation of His truth alone.

CHAPTER 15

Sometime after God Almighty looked down from the heavens and saw the spiritual condition of men, and after He had flooded the world once, He decided for the second time to do something about it. The first time only a handful of people were saved; the rest were lost. Most every person in existence died, together with every creature that walked, flew, swam, or crawled.

God gave to His people, through Moses, the first rule of law in the Ten Commandments—which presents rules to follow for purposes of a clean conscience, order, and respect. For the future world, Moses's law would be the basis for the creation of secular laws for different nations and societies according to their cultures, beliefs, and traditions.

The law given by God to Moses for the people of Israel, according to the Word of God, was the first set of spiritual rules for people of any nation, to engender an understanding of ethics and of the difference between right and wrong for the chosen ones. The Ten Commandments present laws of understanding for the human conscience, where morals, respect, honesty, and humbleness must be the base and the pillars of decency and obedience.

But that law of understanding and obedience did not prevail in men's hearts, according to God's will and warnings. So, many years later, another law, not one of understanding and obedience, was given to men. It was a new law with the same understanding of God, but it was meant to overpower the first law. This time, man was given the opportunity to eschew following any rule to the letter and to explore the spiritual reality of the law. God this time has given man the same understanding, with the difference that man will determine his own future by either accepting or rejecting the will of God in the spirit of His love, grace, and mercy. With such an understanding, man's heart is given the flexibility to work in his conscience and common sense. It provides him with the chance, according to his heart's will, to have spiritual victory in the future given by the Father through His Son's sacrifice to save the souls of humankind, to live eternally in heaven or hell.

The first law was meant to implant ethical knowledge through an understanding of the letter of the law, urging man's conscience to obey and follow. The second law was to love through faith and belief. One was to be obeyed by dictate, proclamation, or decree, whereas the other was to be self-determined, that is, accepted or rejected by the individual. In a way, both have spiritual endings because both have a spiritual beginning, seeking to work in the sometimes numb conscience of humankind, as man is the only one who can choose at his own end.

According to scholars, the second-known law is the Code of Hammurabi, proclaimed by the Babylonian king of the same name, who ruled Mesopotamia from 1792 BC to 1750 BC. Others say that the Egyptians, three thousand years before Christ, had a rule of law for their nation, but none of those laws spoke of the salvation of man's soul.

As is always the case when one attempts to distinguish between the facts and the guesses of good-intentioned historians, one may assume that nothing is 100 percent certain except for the Word of our Creator.

In ancient times, laws were established for the people of many nations, but many of those people didn't follow the rules. Was this because they were ignorant of the law, or because they rebelled against any kind of order, obedience, or respect? God has given people the right of self-determination, which they have in their will. But for some reason, many of the Israelites disrespected or chose not to practice the law of Moses, maybe because they had no clear understanding of heaven and hell or, life and death. Or maybe their spiritual leaders were doing a poor job of teaching their people.

Maybe the people knew the laws but ignored them most of the time. The problem, as in all other nations, was in people's hearts—an unknown spiritual rebellion against their own consciences, and confusion over what is right and what is wrong.

Evil makes people in their hearts rebellious against not only God's rules but also everything that is good and sane, which corrupts their lives and cripples their common sense so they do not see or understand His love and blessing. We mustn't forget that the same evil today is working hard interfering in people's lives so as to claim their souls, no matter who they are, killing in most of their hearts their reason and common sense, making them unable to know of God's care for them. For that rebellious attitude, God has hardened their hearts and rejected them.

A person who lives by his instincts and intellect alone, a person who exults in self-determination without recognizing what is right and what is wrong in his life, which leads to self-righteousness, is doomed to failure. It is impossible for a secular human mind to understand spirituality or holiness. Even many Christians don't know the essence of such a way of life in a world that is often spoken about but never experienced.

All we know about spirituality or holiness is what the Word of God tells us, which is that it is not something from this materialistic secular intellectual world, but from the Good Book, in this case,

God's life and God's world. God's world is impossible to explain in human words. To try to explain it is like trying to explain what air is made of, besides giving the scientific explanation of nitrogen and oxygen, and their components, and the components of those components. In the end, everything material that exists was spiritually created, and it was God who made it. Science cannot explain how things came to exist at the beginning of creation. It is the Creator who has created all material things.

We must understand that this material earth, over which Satan is the landlord, has spiritual life. For the ones who know the difference, an evil act could intervene directly or through someone else to affect our secular and spiritual lives.

When we experience in our soul's heart an unpleasant emotional feeling of emptiness, loneliness, sadness, or some inexplicable inner pain, our fear and desperation shields our mind from any understanding or reasoning. We remain uneasy, as the experience has its own spiritual dimensions because the sensation of an overwhelming power creates a not understood state of confusion.

Even when a person by his own understanding comes up with a clear explanation of what is happening to him spiritually, sometimes such a moment is entirely inexplicable. It just happens. The reason and the understanding come later, but how it happens in the spirit is another story. The apostle Paul went through such a spiritual experience. He said, "I know a man in Christ above fourteen years ago, whether in the body, I cannot tell, or whether out of the body, I cannot tell: God knoweth; such an one cougth up to the third heaven" (2 Corinthians 12:2). When Paul was traveling from city to city to persecute Christian believers, Jesus appeared to him, blinding him. The story is in Acts 9:1–19. Paul accepted the experience as an act of God that changed his life, with results that would have been impossible to achieve by way of human knowledge or power.

It is man's self-surrender in his faith and belief in God that his "I will" becomes part of God's will. Such a person in God's will, will be used in supernatural acts or chosen to live through unexpected experiences allowed by God. Such actions will become a tool for strengthening a man spiritually for the glory of the Almighty. Jesus's "I will" was unconditional to the Father, even when He was in heaven as His Son. The Son of man's complete surrender to God's will on earth caused a separation in Him between the birth of a man by and in the Spirit, who is from God but in God, being Himself God as a mortal man among men.

That separation of the earthly person and the celestial person was caused not by earthly means, but by spiritual means. It was suited to the first creation, which was a holy body, holy soul, and holy heart in a holy human spirit in the life of God's Holy Spirit, that is, the birth of God in the flesh in the person of Jesus as a man. This is the Trinity of the heavens, as one God Almighty put Himself on earth and was in heaven at the same time, being the Father, the Son, and the Holy Ghost, and at the same time the Savior of the human race.

Jesus the earthly man was a human being who never took for Himself the right to be the Almighty God that He was in His Trinity in the heavens, and he did not take for granted the power that He had as the Creator in the Spirit as a human. He was an earthly mortal with the right to be God on this earth if He wanted to be, but He left that right in heaven with all His Trinity so he could be part of the human race as a regular mortal, but also a holy and spiritual man.

A man who believed and trusted in God with all his heart and soul, who had a heart, a mind, and emotions in his soul—that is, a person with all the characteristics of what is called a human being—is what Jesus was in the flesh.

Jesus teaches and preaches about the salvation of men's souls, which was and is His goal as Christ the Messiah. This was a new revelation of good news for the world called the gospel, which was planted within the living soul that He became. His heart in obedience to His human spirit was what kept Him constantly connected to the Father through the Holy Spirit.

The human spirit that God has given to man is more than a soul, just as the soul is more than the flesh. The soul, not the material body, is the beginning of a spiritual life, but because the soul itself is spiritual just like the heart, it is invisible to the human eye. That is why the soul of a person needs a material body, so that the person can be identified and recognized by different fixtures in the secular world. In time, after the soul separates from the flesh in death, the identified image of a person in the flesh will be transformed to a celestial unknown, a "material body" that makes the individual recognizable in heaven or hell, as was the case on earth. It was "material" that Jesus had when He transformed His body of flesh into a celestial body in front of His disciples (Luke 9:28–36). A spiritual, holy, earthly dust in the new life of the souls and spirits of Adam and Eve, which became unspiritual material when they lost their holiness to sin and became what we know as secular.

We mustn't forget that God is a spiritual being and that everything He has created, even though it is material, is also spiritual, pure, and holy. When He created earth and man, the holiness of His creation and presence made the world a spiritual place, and every material creation became spiritually pure because earth at that time was pure. The day Adam and Eve sinned, holy spirituality disappeared to become contaminated material, called secular, for its lack of purity.

Sometimes we would like to think that by God's will, we are able to see spiritual beings with our human eyes. A real spiritual Christian can tell if a presumed miracle or vision is from God or from some other spiritual being. It is impossible for the unaided mind to understand this if it is not revealed by God. For religious believers, any supernatural appearance is seen to be from God, when maybe it is not.

There are two kinds of supernatural acts that God, according to His will, will perform. First is a sign of warning, which can come through dreams, visions, or prophecies, to alert the person's heart or cause them distress depending on the spiritual message. Second is a supernatural act to be seen by His child's human eyes—or spiritual eyes when, in His will, He opens them. And that child will know for sure, deep in his heart, through his spirit's revelation and confirmation of the vision, dream, or other message, that it is undoubtedly an act of His doing. It is not merely a vivid dream or vision, or any other message manipulated by another spirit in the so-called subconscious, taken as a spiritual revelation from God.

An evil spirit may take advantage of person with a naive or ignorant heart whose lack of knowledge of the Word makes him an easy target to confuse and cause to deviate from the truth. A person with faith may be wrongly directed for lack of knowledge of the Word and lack of spiritual discernment. A heart should live in accordance with the human spirit to warn us, guide us, and reveal to us the difference between right and wrong. But because of its spiritual blindness, such a heart rejects any understanding for reasons of ignorance, arrogance, or plain lack of interest arising from pride in one's own wrong belief.

The lifeless condition of the soul is the result of a heart that has disconnected itself from God. Consider a person who has no culture, no respect, no education, no understanding of manners, no self-respect, and no obedience and who is dirty, loud, inconsiderate, cruel, savage, unpredictable, uncivilized, wild, and many other things that a normal person, contrary to all that, is not.

No person who considers himself to be opposed to all that will accept such an individual as a close friend. A person like that is considered to be death to a normal relationship or friendship because he lacks respect and an understanding of right and wrong. The civilized souls in the Garden of Eden, whose hearts followed God in their human spirits, obeyed the Spirit of God. But after dying and being kicked out of Eden, the human spirit came to be ignored by the human heart.

The education of the soul's heart is accomplished through the understanding of right and wrong, through the obedience of one's conscience or common sense, a common sense that is given to the heart by the human spirit to see the difference between good and bad so that one may repent and be accepted again by God.

In a spiritual sense, to be "revived" or "resuscitated" is to repent with an understanding and admission of one's guilt. That is when a soul is resurrected and comes alive again. Such a soul is considered a living soul with a regenerated heart, accepted by the Spirit as part of God's life in the unity of the heart, which is in constant communication with the spirit—a human spirit that becomes active as soon as man's heart has God's life in it again.

Before understanding, knowledge, and reason entered into the equation, the soul's heart was living by its instincts and intuitions. Is this not like the knowledge, understanding, and reasoning of the human spirit? Even when the soul determines its own course according to the heart, it is not capable of understanding higher spiritual knowledge by itself. Unless the spirit declares itself to the heart, it becomes "terrestrial", and the reason for that is the consequence of sin. The soul's heart has a reaction of its own, which is to either accept or reject the gift of salvation through its deductible instinct.

The heart by itself does not understand all of what is wrong or right because it is like a child. Now, after the Garden of Eden, we become God's children by submitting to the process of rebirth. And as spiritual children, we need to be guided by the human spirit, which teaches the heart how to discern between right and wrong, which before, in the Garden of Eden, was not necessary for the soul and the heart because they were one in God. But when, according to God's gift of self-determination, the heart decided on its own to let instinct or intuition separate it from the human spirit, is when man separated himself from the existing spirituality in God, losing his eternal life with his Creator. That is when the heart, led by its own curiosity, decided to ignore or put aside the warning of the voice of reason.

Now we need to learn what to do or not do, because the child that is our soul is incapable of knowing the difference between good and bad, right and wrong. We need to be taught how to discern between right and wrong, good and bad, and to know what this difference means, namely that one is the spirit of good and the other is the spirit of evil. To learn how to follow the directives of the human spirit, which is our reasoning conscience, which follows God's Spirit, teaching and guiding us, is the way to the perfect harmony that we humans should have with God and His Spirit, and not with any other spirit.

Because the soul is dead, with the human spirit ignored by the heart, it is separated from God, and the person is someone who is not religious or spiritual. The heart reflects the conscience. And these reflections help the instinct to distinguish, at any given moment, what is convenient or not, if the heart seeks to take some sort of action.

When the spirit within a person is weak, it is because the soul's heart refuses to cooperate. Or the spirit is just pushed to inactivity; that is, the heart ignores the presence of the spirit completely. The so-called inner voice of the conscience is not heard when the heart in its understanding fails to stop to consider whether its acts are right or wrong, convenient or not, even when within itself it has the instinct to make a choice.

If the heart rejects the reflections of the conscience, the soul has no chance of salvation. But if the heart allows itself to understand its own reflection and see its own instincts in its moment of need, that reflection will allow the human spirit to intervene on its own behalf to get in contact with God's Spirit. That will create a chance for the recognition of wrongdoing, repentance, and acceptance of salvation. Even when we are dead to God because of our empty spiritual lives, the bridge of direct spiritual communication between God's Spirit, our own pushed-away or ignored human spirits, and our hearts still exists. And God always keeps that bridge open for us. But it will continue to be closed if there is "something" that is not letting us use it.

Consider the situation between two countries when, for some reason, one of them breaks an agreement or does something severe. As a result, the other breaks off relations and cancels all contracts. The bridge of communication and relation is always there. If those who are guilty recognize their mistake and apologize, then the restored relationship will cause that bridge to open and become ready to be used again.

The heart is vulnerable just as an unknowing child is. The process of saving our souls begins when we make the decision to acknowledge our wrongdoings. We assess our feelings, desires, wishes, and so on to discover which are good and which are evil. And let us not forget that at the same time Satan is trying to distract us and draw our attention to unrealistic and dangerous things. Satan is against the protection and salvation of the human soul. Satan is the one who will always interfere in the education of our real spiritual selves.

That evil spirit has the power to tempt the human heart in its weakness, innocence, ignorance, confusion, and naiveté, and to completely separate a person from his conscience (human spirit) and understanding (heart), leaving no chance for the heart to stand strong by way of real spiritual knowledge for the benefit of the soul. This is like presenting to the soul, as to a baby, a choice among a bunch of candies, all of which are poisonous, even when they look good and we imagine they taste delicious. But the baby doesn't know the candies are poisoned, because in his "understanding" he can't see the difference between good and evil.

The education of the human heart for the benefit of the soul and its spiritual life can be compared to the teaching of a child from kindergarten to university. The child has many different lessons, experiences, difficulties, and goals, and at the end receives the long-awaited diploma if he puts in the effort. How many Christians are going to or went to the spiritual learning school of life and through all the attendant difficulties to receive the desired PhD in wisdom, revelation, knowledge, understanding, and vision from the heavenly university? The knowledge gained from such an experience makes a man stand strong and confident in his spiritual and secular life. The "diploma" designates him as a man strong enough to protect his spiritual household.

The church leaders are spiritual guides responsible for directing others in the Spirit to the Word of God. They are the "parents" of their "children" in church. The parents, in the interest of the future of their child, are on top of the child's education both at home and in school. If the child is obedient to the parents, he won't deviate in his walk by listening to the voices of certain so-called friends. Even when the child is tempted, he will fight the temptation from his friend, understanding that it is not the voice of the right sort of friend but the voice of the wrong sort, about whom he has already been warned.

He'll remember and be obedient, knowing of his parents' advice and warnings about the adverse consequences. But if the parents don't do a good job of instructing the child, helping him see the difference, the child won't grow up to be strong in his decisions. So he will be knocked over in his attempt to do the right thing, for the lack of understanding the difference between right and wrong. But if the child, after the parents have done a conscious job of educating him, for some unknown reason deviates from the teaching of his parents, the parents are free of guilt before God and the child will have to endure his adverse life circumstances and, all by himself, fix his own life, whether secular or spiritual.

If our "adult" heart knowingly takes a chance and disobeys its Parent (i.e., God), ignoring whether or not its decision is right or wrong, it will pay the consequences, either in the flesh or before the Almighty. Growing up to have an understanding of right and wrong, the "student" is responsible for his actions. It is not the school or teacher's responsibility for the student's lack of interest, or the "parents" in the church. Our soul is who we are, the child. Our heart is the will of our brain. Our human spirit is our mother conscience, who advises, helps, and prevents. And our soul's heart, our Father, is the Spirit, who is our Teacher, Guide, and Protector. We need to undergo all this learning because we were born in sin, but Jesus from birth was a holy Son of man, and even He had to learn and understand obedience.

CHAPTER 16

To understand Jesus's life and death, not just the story we read in the Bible, we have to walk a mile in His sandals, as the saying goes. There are two ways to do that, either through the intellect or through the spirit. And then we will come to only a partial understanding of what He suffered in His body for our sake. The suffering of His body is one thing, but the spiritual pain He felt in His soul is quite another, something impossible for us to understand in its full spiritual magnitude by way of words.

When we see someone hit their own finger with a hammer or has some other kind of wound, we say, "Oh my goodness! That must have been painful!" In a way we can relate, but we never actually feel the pain. It doesn't matter what kind of face we make when we feel a chill go through us while looking at that hammered finger or any other wound.

There is more than one kind of pain, not only physical but also psychological, spiritual, and so on, and all of them are of a different quality. All the human emotions and feelings that a person has, Jesus had too. No other human soul in human history, before or after Jesus, has had such an experience of spiritual grief.

We'll never be able to put into words the experience of Jesus's sacrifice, because words do not exist to describe the spiritual, psychological, and physical suffering and agony of His body, mind, and soul. He endured physical pain, but the worst was the pain in His soul because of the uncertainty of His own heart when He took upon His shoulders the sins of the whole world. That effect is just impossible for us to comprehend.

The pain of uncertainty that His soul experienced in that spiritual world is unexplainable. To imagine His soul in Hades being accused of sin by Satan is impossible. We read in Matthew 26:38, "Then he saith unto them, 'My soul is exceeding sorrowful, even unto death.'" Why was His soul worried, anguished to the point of perhaps desperation? Because His heart was the one who had to show "face" in Satan's court.

In our little brains, we may think that because of the feelings He had, He wasn't sure of His own heart. Otherwise how do we understand the feelings that He had?

Any physical or psychological torture any person has had to endure does not compare under any circumstances to Jesus's suffering. Often the agony of a tortured person ends with his or her physical death, including death of the physical heart, which in the spiritual realm stops being active. But Jesus's heart continued to function in a spiritual world as He was alive in His body for the purpose of His mission to carry the consequences of the world's sin. This was a reality which was like a contaminated open wound, along with a feeling of unbearable pain brought about by sin, without knowing if the wound could be healed.

He had, for all His spirituality, in the life of His own soul, to face the challenge of appearing in front of Satan with a heart carrying every person's sin. He had to pass the test of purity and holiness of a sinless heart to save His soul, still carrying the sins of humanity on His shoulders. It was in anticipation of this horrible trial when Jesus experienced the agony of the incertitude of His soul, which passed into His heart, awaiting the final test before Satan in his own domain. That is why Jesus prayed by saying, "Father, if thou be willing, take this cup away from me: nevertheless not my will, but thine, be done" (Luke 22:42).

He would have no one by His side when that moment came, and He knew that. The mere thought that His soul had to go through that ordeal, in His promise and obedience to the Father, as a man, caused Him to fear for the unknown outcome for His soul, not for His flesh. Because He knew He would have to endure the physical punishment up to the moment of His physical death, for His spiritual heart to stand trial to prove Him guilty or innocent in Satan's court.

As a man, His thoughts about how His soul would fare on that heavenly mission ahead of Him would not leave Him alone. Thinking as a human, He wondered how His heart would stand up before the enemy of the human soul. His concern caused His soul to tremble as His internal body system reacted with growing anxiety toward the unknown. More human than that cannot be. "And being in an agony he prayed more earnestly, and his sweat was as if there were great drops of blood falling down to the ground" (Luke 22:44).

This is one of the times in Jesus's life where He, as a man, had the experience of a real feeling of fear or panic, coming from the depths of, not His spirit, but His soul, in need of God. He knew for what reason He had come to this world. He knew He had to suffer. He knew that He was going to be punished and His body would be an open wound. He knew that parts of His flesh would be hanging from His body. He knew that His body would be torn almost apart, but for that He was not afraid. As a man, He did not fear to die in His body. He knew His body wasn't His life. There was nothing that He couldn't know in His Spirit in terms of what would soon happen to Him. But the human within Him, the person in the flesh, had a grip on His soul in fear of the unknown.

That is why when He went with His disciples to the Mount

of Olives, He told them, "My soul is exceedingly sorrowful, unto death" (Mark 14:34).

A holy man with a mission, who in a moment of distress and perhaps desperation, hoping for a way out, asked as a son, believing that he could be helped, "Abba, Father, all things are possible unto thee. Take away this cup from me; nevertheless not what I will, but what thou wilt" (Mark 14:36). He expressed his willingness to accept any outcome when He said, "Nevertheless not what I will, but what thou wilt," speaking of His Father.

Jesus knew that the fight He had ahead of Him wasn't physical but spiritual. He felt that the peace He had had up to that moment left Him, and in its place was an extreme emptiness, along with an unknown feeling of worry about death in His soul, squeezing away in a never before felt fearful anxiety. In His soul He was really afraid. For the first time in His life as just a man, He was having the spiritual experience of His death in the flesh. Never before or after has any other human felt in his or her soul the reality of the unknown life and death of the human soul.

There was a spiritual power and an aura of greatness between Father and Son, one spiritual, one human, in such a way that each had His own borders, even when the human son was in reality the Son of man in the Spirit.

Jesus's soul knew that the future of His spiritual person depended on His heart. At that moment as a man, He had not only the normal fear that any person would have but also His own doubts about this mission. He would have to go through the experience of descending into hell as a holy person, even though He was the Son of God. And as the Son of God, but in His human form, He accomplished His mission.

What is very interesting is that Jesus as a human was not, at that specific moment, sure of the outcome of His mission. But as the Son of God, He positively knew that everything He had to go through would be accomplished. But as a human with all the knowledge, revelations, faith, and beliefs that He had, He still faced an unknown, even being in the Spirit as the Son of man. So even with Him knowing that He would rise from the dead, what was it that made Him be so worried? Was it a moment of weakness or what? As He said in Mark 9:31, "The Son of Man is delivered into the hands of men, and they shall kill him; and after he is killed, he shall rise the third day." Was He speaking as the human He was, or as the Son of man in the Spirit, or as the Son of God?

In one person there were two individual beings; one very human with the normal feelings and reactions of happiness and fear, and the other being Spirit and therefore spiritual. How does one understand why Jesus told His disciples about His soul being worried to death, if the Son of God, *not man*, knew everything ahead of time about being victorious? That is the knowledge that we have today as humans. In the knowledge of our spirits, we know and accept the will of God for whatever outcome materializes in the end. In that same spirit, as humans, through our feelings and emotions, we are in a different dimension from Jesus.

When a person, any person, is condemned to die and waiting for the moment of execution, they feel the fear of death in their heart, which oppresses their soul and gives rise to feelings of emptiness in relation to the unknown, which perhaps causes them to become desperate in their very confused heart. The feeling of fear about death reaches a certain level of agony because the person doesn't know what will happen after death, meaning what is on the other side of life. The only thing the person knows is that he or she is going to be killed.

If the person thinks about that, he or she might guess where they will end up, hoping for it to be heaven, even if they never cared about heaven and hell. At such a moment, close to the end of life, most people are uncertain of the other side, or maybe do not even think about it. But they do think about whether the moment of death will be peaceful, violent, or painful for them. The sorrow, worry, and pain are present in a state of mind that is maybe confused in a desperate soul, hoping for a last minute miracle. That was the condition of Jesus as a man with His feelings before the Father, but on a scale one billion times more excruciating for Him in His soul.

Jesus's suffering on the cross ended in the moment when, upon His physical death, the person of his soul took the world's guilt upon His own heart and went off to the gates of Hades. As He entered and stood before Satan himself, Satan could find nothing to accuse Him of. Jesus then rebuked Satan, took all the enslaved souls from the time of Cain up to that present moment, and freed them. Then He left Satan's kingdom.

The sins of the world that Jesus took with Him to Satan's kingdom were like a dirty bag He carried, but not His own. That is why Satan found no sin at all *in* Jesus, and because of this, he had no rights over Jesus's soul; Jesus's heart was pure of any sin or guilt. And because of that, Jesus had the right to "confiscate" the souls that Satan had under his authority.

Jesus simply volunteered to wash with His own blood, through the sacrifice of His life, not only the sin of the ones He had gathered from the bottom of the pit, but also the ones who currently believed and, in the future, would believe in Him, waiting for redemption in paradise. With His sacrifice, He accomplished the cleansing act, washing the sins of men with the running blood of His wounds from the purity of His heart. Satan found nothing to accuse Jesus of because nothing was in Him. About His own "dirty bag," He never had one. That was one thing Satan hadn't ever known about Jesus's spiritual heart, even when he knew that Jesus was the Son of God.

Jesus as the human Son of His heavenly Father didn't know

everything. He Himself said when His disciples asked Him about the end of the time, "But of that day and that hour, knoweth no man, no, not the angels which are in heaven, neither the Son, but the Father" (Mark 13:32).

The date of the Messiah's return is not written in the Bible. Maybe, just maybe, the Father, from the beginning of His holy Son's earthly life, had planned without His Son's knowledge, another epic spiritual event, one whose outcome is known only to the Almighty in the "future" of His eternity, when He will screen the condemned souls who undergo purification by fire.

Are we to understand that there is yet another chance for salvation, for those who initially rejected the offer of salvation of their souls after a horrific eternity of suffering and pain in God's thousand years? Maybe those souls will be the ones purified by fire? Having said this, I recall what the apostle Paul wrote: "For who hath known the mind of the Lord [God the Father] that he may instruct Him? But we have the mind of Christ" (1 Corinthians 2:16).

God the Father knows everything, but Jesus, the Son of God, as the human He was, was not given the knowledge of certain things. And that is our position: we know what God allows us to know in His will. He is the Lord God and we are His children, and because in this world we don't know everything that is needed, it is declared to us according to God's will—that is, if we are standing in the Spirit of God and not by His side. And even if we are standing in the Spirit, there are things we won't be given knowledge of, for God the Father, to test our faith and our belief and trust in Him, for whatever outcome is to occur in our lives that is known only to Him. That is why when Jesus prayed to God, He said, "Abba, Father, all things are possible unto thee; take away this cup from me; nevertheless, not what I will, but what thou wilt" (Mark 14:36). Knowing that, Jesus was faithful to God the Father to the end.

God, the Father, will never allow His only begotten Son to perish at the hands of Satan. Because even when His Son was a human, His spirituality and holiness were part of the Trinity.

Jesus as God, one of the Trinity, didn't have to sacrifice Himself for humankind, but His love for His perishing creation was so intense that He decided to become one of us. It is His immense love, grace, and mercy, shown by His sacrifice on the cross, that gives us a chance for the salvation of our souls. To any person who rejects God's love and the offer of redemption made possible by His Son Jesus Christ, God Almighty says, "Vengeance is mine; I will repay. And again, the Lord will judge His people" (Hebrews 10:30). He will judge not only His people, but also the Gentiles, who, like the Israelites, rejected the Son of God, walking away from salvation. Can we imagine what the wrath of God would be like for those who reject Christ's redemption through his sacrifice on the cross?

In Jesus's life there were two times when Satan lost to Him. The first was when Satan tempted Jesus in the flesh on the mountaintop after Jesus's forty days of fasting. The second was when Jesus descended into hell and Satan tried to find any sin in His heart to accuse Him of, but because of Jesus's clean, clear, and pure heart, Satan failed this time too.

Hades was empty after Jesus claimed the souls of the ones who lived before and after Moses's law, bringing to them the gospel of salvation. The Word says, "By which also he went and preached unto the spirits [souls in Hades] in prison" (1 Peter 3:19). Those souls accepted Christ and were saved. Jesus took those souls to paradise before His soul and Spirit returned to His body for His resurrection.

We must always remember one thing: it doesn't matter how

much we desire or wish to do something for God's glory, and it doesn't matter how much love and heart we put into our effort, if we are not in the Spirit, seeking the things of the Spirit, then our effort, even when well intended, will bring no unified understanding and no results to our lives, for lack of spiritual knowledge and revelation. So do not expect to be given a better chance or a second opportunity when you are dead.

According to Luke 16:19–26, there are two places where people's souls end up after death. One is Sheol, hell, Hades, and the other is Abraham's bosom. Before Jesus's time, those places existed, and after His death, the place of the afterlife came to be known as paradise. Paradise is a place of peace and joy in the heavens, close to the kingdom of the Almighty. At the end of times, the souls in paradise will go on to the kingdom of God with Jesus to celebrate victory. The Bible mentions different places, like heaven and hell, where people's souls will go to experience different consequences according to whatever they have done in life. I believe we are told of these two places for a reason. Many people have different beliefs about hell and heaven, just as they do about life after death. Many of them will be more than sorry to find out that they were wrong, because by then, it will be too late as they will have rejected salvation for being "too smart".

Trying to describe the places where souls await justification or condemnation is not simple. Intellectually we can approach the subject, even though it is a spiritual one, in a philosophical way, as has been done before. We may be correct in our attempt, but not correct in terms of true spiritual precision. What is called Hell, Hades, Sheol, and the lake of fire existed before Jesus's death. That was and is a waiting room and the final "residence" for all generations who in one way or another rejected God while they were alive.

The Almighty knows of what we don't even have a clue.

Abraham's bosom was a specific waiting place of peace in the heavens for the people of the Old Testament—prophets and other saints, both before and after Moses brought the law down from the mountaintop—who understood what it was to have respect for the things of God in humbleness, reverence, and obedience with a sincere, faithful, and believing heart before the Almighty, up to the time of Jesus's resurrection.

People who believed in God or had a humble, honest, and sincere heart, which the Almighty in His knowledge saw in them, have a chance for salvation in the future that only He knows they deserve. And they will be rewarded for having in their hearts the presence of their Creator in their faith.

We have to remember one thing: everything that is impossible for us to even comprehend or accept is possible for God to do. And just because we think that something is not right because we don't see the light at the end of the tunnel, does not mean the light is not there. We are far from understanding God's thoughts and will, and the things we don't know or don't need to know. The righteousness and blessings of God in man's life at all times depends on the level of faith in man's heart.

Today we do not live under the law of Moses; we live under the law of God's grace and His love for us through Jesus's sacrifice, which is a spiritual law of a new agreement.

Abraham's bosom may no longer exist. But if it does exist, it is also a resting place in the heavens for the ones who believe in God, not according to the gospel, but according to their hearts. In their faith, such people believe and trust in the one Creator, and their hearts are known only by Him, who will be the Judge of all, whether we are wrong or right in our assumptions.

Paradise, after Jesus's death, is the resting place of the souls who have passed away believing in their Savior. Those are the souls who are waiting for the great celebration promised to them by their Savior, together with the ones who were in Abraham's bosom after Jesus's resurrection. That, along with the ones Jesus took from hell after He was found by Satan to have a clean and righteous heart, with the right and the power to free the souls under Satan's dominion. Unfortunately for individuals of all beliefs, who in the iciness of their arrogant pride reject their own guilt without repentance, hell has been filling up again.

So now is the time to repent, because later, on the other side, when that pride will no longer help, it will be too late to say, "Oops, I was wrong." From that place after judgment, those souls will be sent to their second and final residence in the eternal lake of fire, a place where they will remember how wrong they were in their stubborn know-it-all arrogance. That is where Satan will end up too.

The Bible reads, "And the sea gave up the dead which were in it; and Death, and hell delivered up the dead which were in them; and they were judged every man according to their works" (Revelation 20:13). And the sea gave up its dead (that is, people's bodies), and Death (that is, Satan himself) and Hades (hell) gave up their dead (that is, all the people's souls held by Satan and the evil spirits and demons) and they were then let go from hell, so that all the souls reunite with their bodies to be judged according to their deeds. After God condemns all the evil spirits, demons, and other creatures to the eternal lake of fire, Satan, which God called Death, will be the last one to be judged.

Our future heaven is part of the three levels of the heavenly kingdom of God, where the Father has His throne. There will be a new heaven and a new earth at the end of time, a newly transformed heavenly, spiritual, earthly world, which will be our home forevermore. Right after everything is finished, at the moment of celebration in the heavenly kingdom for the Lord's victory against evil, Jesus will give that victory to the glory of the

Father. That is why Jesus said to His disciples, "But I say unto you, I will not drink [celebrate] henceforth of this fruit [that which has been conquered] of the vine [victory] until that day when I drink [celebrate] with you in my Father's Kingdom" (Matthew 26:29).

There is one thing that needs to be explained, and that is the resurrection after death. When the Word says that all those dead will come to life for judgment or justification, it means that the bodies of the people in their original creation—not in the flesh, but transformed—will come alive. For the souls in hell and those in paradise, they will again be in the human image or form in which they were created. As we know, every soul that has a human body will be separated from it at the time of death. The soul, in due time, will be reunited in the resurrection with the new transformed body, whether the soul ends up in heaven or hell.

We will each be resurrected to life with a transformed body from another spiritual dimension, but first, the ones alive will be transformed directly into their celestial bodies. Christians must have the knowledge of spiritual revelation and vision, and the understanding of the real spiritual teaching of the soul's heart. We need to understand that it is our spiritual heart, in the intellect of our mind, that needs to learn for the sake of our soul.

The Bible says that from our hearts come weak thoughts, wrong desires, poor wishes, wrong decisions, greed, immorality, and too many other things to mention.

In Jeremiah 17:9–10, God says, "The heart is deceitful above all things and desperately wicked: who can know it? I the Lord search the heart, I try the reins, even to give every man according to his ways, and according to the fruit of his doings." The difference between our human wisdom and our spiritual wisdom is in our hearts. The learning, understanding, and accepting or rejecting is done according to the heart's own will, in its reasoning through the understanding given by its human wisdom.

The heart will be either rewarded or punished for what it has convinced itself to accept, reject, or ignore, what it believes is more convenient for the future of its soul, and what it has chosen, either right and wrong.

Our spirit helps us understand our heart, which is in the will of God, teaching our heart not to learn through deductions, feelings, and emotions, but through spiritual revelation, which brings knowledge and reason. Spiritual revelation translated to our human brains allows us to know, see, and understand the difference between right and wrong.

Transformation translates what is spiritual to our intellects so we may have a secular understanding. We need to understand that the spiritual heart, being part of the inner spiritual being, that is, the soul, needs spiritual education, which comes from the Spirit teaching our spirit and then our heart, which is the "inner lawyer" that "represents" our soul.

The knowledge in our hearts comes through the teaching of the human spirit, which gives to our minds the knowledge that we call intelligence. Such intelligence represents life, according to its knowledge and will, and the heart will determines whether the soul will remain free or be sent to prison for eternity. That is why Jesus said, "And thou shalt love the Lord thy God with all your heart [knowledge and will], and with all thy soul [life], and all your mind [reason and understanding], and with all thy strength [passion]: this is the first commandment" (Mark 12:30).

The knowledge we have developed in specific fields is what we called human wisdom, which is the bridge between ignorance and intelligence that helps us to develop secular know-how in our world, which is a field of opportunity. Spiritual knowledge begins in the heart and leads to the road that can light the way to God's wisdom, if only one will seek it. The sensibility and understanding within our intellects, that is, our minds, depends on the dedication and discipline of our hearts.

Pushing toward the goal to reach spiritual knowledge without an understanding of the Word and without revelation, the intellect and/or intelligence may take us to the wrong spiritual path, which is the way of confusion. Not everything that comes from above is from heaven.

To be in His will and know God's spiritual world is an accomplishment through spiritual revelations, a method of spiritual education that does not depend on mental imaginings, deductions, guesses, thoughts, and so on. The spiritual education of the "intellectual heart" is the most difficult and important to accomplish if one is to be in the Spirit of God for the sake of the soul. The heart is weak and in need of spiritual knowledge gained through revelation. For this reason, the soul desires that the heart submit to spiritual education with the help of the Spirit for its salvation. It is our hearts that need to change, not our intellects. Our intellects will change when the thoughts of our hearts become pure, not double-minded.

How was Jesus holy without any blemish of guilt even when He was born in the flesh? Because He was born of the Spirit and in the Spirit. And if He was without sin, it means that His soul's heart, that is, His spiritual person and flesh, was clean of sin. His mind had no impure thoughts of any type because He surrendered His heart and His thoughts to the will of God's Spirit. And that was because His heart was in continuous communion with His human spirit, in the Spirit of God. Even though Jesus was born from a woman, from His mother's womb, the Spirit of God protected Him—His flesh, soul, and heart—from sin while he was a person.

Even though Mary, Jesus's mother, was pure in the eyes of God, that is, untouched by man, she was, like any other person, born in sin. But because Jesus was created in the flesh by the Spirit of God, her body, heart, and soul were cleansed and purified for the occasion of His birth, protecting her from original sin. In short, her inner spiritual life and her material body, we could say, were in a state of "holy quarantine" for nine months till the time of His coming to the world.

It could be said that this is an example of, as it says in the Bible, something being impossible for man to understand, perceive, discern, or comprehend but possible for God Almighty to do.

A perfect order of holiness comes about when a person is in the Spirit of God, allowing the Spirit to guide his or her own human spirit and teach his or her heart. In our mental awareness, through our intellectual knowledge and understanding conscience, the heart works in fellowship with the spirit, together as one in communion and fellowship with the Spirit of God.

That spiritual connection makes us holy in the discipline to pursue our goal of His presence and will in our life with perseverance. His presence covers our spiritual lives and our bodies, guarding us against any evil attack, whether physical or spiritual, whether known to us or unbeknown to us. He will give us this protection if we really are in continuous fellowship with the Spirit.

It says in 2 Thessalonians 3:3, "But the Lord is faithful, who shall stablish you, and keep you from evil." If Jesus had any unknown weaknesses as a human, we don't know about them, as the Bible says nothing about it. If he had any, perhaps He had them under control because of His strong spiritual unity in the Spirit. Because of His strong spiritual contact with God, He always rejected temptation, having a solid understanding in His heart of right and wrong. Such rejection was strong because of Him being in the Spirit with God the Father in an unbreakable union.

Jesus was always aware of the spiritual protection, strength, and revelation available to Him in this world where He had to fight in the flesh. That is why when Satan tempted Him in an effort to destroy His spiritual life, Satan failed.

Being believers in Christ, in God's Spirit, doesn't mean we are superhumans. But being strong spiritual believers totally immersed in the Spirit of the Almighty makes us in our spiritual lives impervious to weakness. The knowledge of God's promised protection over our spiritual lives is not a problem. The problem is that we are weak in our spiritual dedication, in our faith, and in our belief in the things of God, even when we consider ourselves spiritual. Each person before the Lord knows how strong he or she is standing in faith or if he or she is lacking in something.

Any spiritual awareness that we may have is not strong enough to deal with the feelings, wishes, desires, and emotions of our weak hearts. There are times when our senses have the upper hand over our hearts, which are spiritual in nature. Even when we may think that we are strong or confident in the Spirit, heretofore we may have a moment of unnoticed weakness in our spirits.

At times such as these, we have the sense that God the Father is letting us be, leaving us alone, because He wants to see how we react to things we can't control, because even though we may feel things through our senses, the unpleasant experience is spiritual in nature. It's as if the Father is testing us in our hearts and spirits to see if our souls will call upon Him for help or just give up. Perhaps our hearts will be distracted or for some reason become disconnected from God for a few moments because of something that takes our attention. Only God knows why this happens. It could be what happened to Jesus during His experience on the Mount of Olives.

Jesus was helping us to understand that we are each two people in one—one in the flesh, the other in the spirit—when He said, "You are in this world, but you are not from this world." To gain a better understanding of these words, imagine that you are a tourist in another country, where something is attracting you and seemingly wants you to stay there. Knowing that you belong to another place where you have your home, you realize that you are temporarily elsewhere.

That is why Jesus was always praying, and why the apostle Paul recommends that one be in prayer all the time. Why? Because prayer is the action between man and God that tightens the relationship, leaving no open gaps in the spiritual world that could be usurped by an evil spirit. Jesus said, "If ye keep my commandments, ye shall abide in my love, even as I kept my Father's commandments, and abide in His love" (John 15:10). Spiritual communion and fellowship makes the individual understandings of unity and love in everything that is individual come together to form one strengthened, unbreakable union. When we unexpectedly feel empty or troubled, it is because God is allowing us to undergo some spiritual learning to make us stronger or more aware. What we need to do at that moment is, as Jesus did, to go directly to the Source of our help, our heavenly Father.

We must understand only one thing: we need prayer like we need air to breathe. Our hearts, minds, and souls are educated through the discipline of prayer, with the constant presence of God's Spirit teaching us everything we need to know to be spiritually strong and effective so we may be guided in His will, even when we feel we are all by ourselves. As someone once said, "Hard and painful in the learning, strong and confident in the fight."

CHAPTER 17

Jesus as a man, as the Bible tells us, was in spiritual contact with His Father at all times. He needed His Father's spiritual presence for strength and guidance, and He needed His godly presence to cover Him with an unbreakable, solid form of all-around spiritual protection. And that is our need in Jesus.

As a regular mortal man, Jesus had no knowledge of some future events, and the things He did know ahead of time were things He was given knowledge of because of His close contact with the Father through revelation. The knowledge given by God's Spirit was what helped Him in the most difficult time of His life. And in the fear He felt, He knew He was spiritually strong with God, even when as a man He felt a moment of weakness and emptiness in His soul, unsure whether He could accomplish His mission. This is an absolutely normal reaction when one is facing the unknown. He had one moment in His life when He, as a spiritual man, had a desperate need for His Father, not as a heavenly Son to His heavenly Father, but as an earthly spiritual man in need of God, calling to that God, the Father, on the Mount of Olives.

The other incident was when He felt helpless and called out to God on the cross like a desperate man, saying, "My God, My God, why hast thou forsaken me?" (Matthew 27:46). Understanding

172

that the end was about to come, He said, "Father into thy hands I commend my spirit" (Matthew 23:46). His words at that last moment were those of the Son of God giving His human spirit to God, His Father.

A person who doesn't know himself in God doesn't know how the human spirit functions in a human being's life. The only part of a man that returns to God at the moment death is the human spirit, which is subject to no scrutiny by anyone because it is the only holy thing within a person, whether it is allowed to be active or is ignored by man. The human spirit is the life of God that was breathed into our natural bodies, causing them to come alive in God's life, in perfect unity with the Spirit of the Creator, allowing us to become one in Him.

Man has the power of self-determination to let the Spirit lead or else to push Him aside, that is, ignore His presence and refuse his help. A spirit that lives in a person and follows the Holy Spirit's warnings and advice is a working spirit. This occurs when man is resurrected in Christ, by the understanding of his heart, and follows the will of God's Spirit by way of his own human spirit.

A spiritually dead person is a person who has no working human spirit to be taught and guided by the Spirit of God. The heart lives by its intellect and instincts, not by the knowledge of spiritual revelation. People have to remember that everything that is about God has to be processed in and through the human spirit, not through the intellect. This doesn't mean that human wisdom is unnecessary; it means that a person's spirit has to be spiritually oriented first if it is to translate to the intellect an understanding of what God wants from the person. That is why the Word says, "But the natural man receiveth not the things of the Spirit of God: for they are foolishness unto him: neither he can know them because they are spiritually discerned" (1 Corinthians 2:14).

The human mind in its own wisdom cannot conceive of or

comprehend what is spiritual, unless it is revealed by the Spirit to the human mind.

Many people believe that the human spirit died when Adam and Eve sinned, but that is a wrong belief. It was neutralized, pushed away, and in one word, rejected, which separated the spiritual man from God's life, but it didn't die. It just went back to God.

Nothing that is a part of God's life can die. The holiness of the human spirit is something that God has given to man, and that spirit is God's "property," because it does not have the choice to be self-determined as the human heart does. The human spirit always follows God's will in men's life though his love, grace and mercy. If the will of God through man spirit is not accepted, by the heart of man, then man's spirit will be unable to help, prevent, or warn. If a man should sin, then he is ignoring his spirit, and because the human spirit and God's Spirit are unified, whatever man does that God considers to be sin is a not only a grievance to the Holy Spirit but also an offense to our own human spirit.

The spiritual death of a person occurs when the soul doesn't hold the life of the human spirit in the Spirit to be one in God, that is, have God's life. And the person who has not been born again in Jesus lives in a spiritual state of only natural instincts. Believing in his or her own intuition is the person who doesn't see or understand spiritual consequences or the afterlife, even when they may say they know of such things.

A person may believe, according to his or her own understanding, that to have knowledge of religion or to be religious is to have a spiritual life. It could be possible, but only God can tell what is in man's heart.

Any life not guided by the Spirit of God through a person's own spirit, in real spiritual knowledge of the Word, is someone whose spirituality can be determined only by God Almighty. The knowledge of how the Spirit works in a person, revealing the will of God in a believer's life, is received only through the person's own God-given spirit.

The human spirit was and is the only bridge of communication and unity between man and his Creator, who lives in His Spirit and makes him one in God. Jesus was one in God the Father because His human spirit was in unity with God's Spirit, believing in God and doing His will. The Word says, "God is a Spirit, and they that worship him, must worship him in spirit and in truth" (John 4:24).

Jesus was a spiritual man on earth who, in the last second of His earthly life, spoke to His heavenly Father as the Son of man, telling Him, "It is finished" (John 19:30). Giving up His Spirit to the Father, as the Son of God, He fulfilled the promise that He had made to His Father in heaven. And as His Son, He turned to His Father at that last second of His earthly life. It was for this reason that God, on the Mount of Olives, sent His angel to comfort Jesus, assuring Jesus that His heavenly Father would be with Him all the way to the end. And the end, with Jesus's sacrifice of His life for us, began with the brutal punishment of His body, followed by the abuse and suffering of His body on the cross. Last to come was what the enemy of heaven and of man's soul never expected: victory over Satan himself in his own kingdom.

Jesus in His heart had one goal always, and that was to do His Father's will. What is interesting is that He, being an earthly human, practiced strict discipline in His everyday life, looking to do His Father's will, instead of distracting Himself with His secular surroundings—which, by the way, were not something that He avoided. When He participated in social events, He did so gladly, enjoying the time as a human person with the feelings of a regular human being.

He laughed, smiled, joked, and drank some wine, and at

weddings maybe he danced. Who knows? He was a man who at any given moment enjoyed his secular life, living the way regular people lived. He knew that those moments were times when people rejoiced and were able to distract themselves from the harsh lives they lived. Those moments were not times of separation between man and God, but times for the human heart and soul to relax with a perfect understanding of the communion that keeps people united in the flesh with God's Spirit.

Jesus was a man like any other individual, absolutely the same. The only thing the Bible tells us of His physical condition is that He got tired and hungry, but about Him being ill or physically hurt, nothing is said. We can assume that because He wore sandals, as everyone did in those days, he had scratches on his feet at times because of the sand and rocks.

The secular part of Jesus was never involved in His spiritual contact with God. Being God Himself but rarely exercising the rights this gave Him, and having the knowledge and power given to Him through the Holy Ghost, He knew every person's heart and thoughts through the revelation of the Spirit of God in Him. That is why as the Son of man, being the image of the spiritual human as Adam was in paradise, Jesus understood the need for salvation of people's souls. And as the Son of man in the Spirit, but in a human body like Adam after paradise, He was ignorant of one or two things about the future. He knew for what purpose He had come to this world, and whatever He knew in certain needful moments about people or future circumstances had been declared to Him by the Spirit. That is why He said, "I and My Father are one" (John 10:30), meaning, "Be in Me as I am in My Father"—that is, in God's Spirit—so we may be one with Him in the heavenly Trinity. That is why the Word of God tells us, "Be of one mind and one spirit."

Jesus's life was like that of any ordinary man in terms of

His earthly intellect and spiritual knowledge. The difference was His unbreakable constant contact with the Father for spiritual knowledge, superior to His intellect, and the revelations that He needed to do His Father's will. For the rest of His secular needs, He was not worried, as we are, about tomorrow. That was the advantage of being more preoccupied with God's work and will than with His personal secular life. His life was a living example of His Words when He said, "But seek ye first the kingdom of God and His righteousness and all those things shall be added unto you" (Matthew 6:33). What He was saying is, *Look for the will of God and His justice and He will supply your needs, and everything you need to do His will.* That is, keep your life free from secular worries, do what is needed, but don't fill your days with going after your material needs, for He has said, "I will never leave thee; nor forsake thee" (Hebrews 13:5). He will not forsake you in terms of your personal material needs, your spiritual goals, or any difficult moment of your life.

Jesus, being submerged in God's Spirit, could see the spiritual side of secular life. If we are not living in the Spirit, we are not in God's world and are not seeing the spiritual secular world the way Jesus saw it. And we won't have the upper hand to avoid evil, defend ourselves against it, or do what God's Spirit is directing us to do. Human instinct is to react according to one's thoughts, which are not spiritual revelations.

Spiritual revelation is inwardly received information understood by our spirits, which translates to our brains as intellectual information that gives us the knowledge to name a feeling, action, warning, or any other need, positive or negative. Make no mistake, this information is given by the Spirit. The Bible gives us examples of a spiritual power that, sometimes unexpectedly, gives us the knowledge of what is happening or will happen. That is the type of spiritual experience Jesus had in terms of His inner feelings.

One such instance of spiritual insight into His feelings was when He was surrounded by a multitude pulling and pushing Him, and a woman who had suffered a bleeding disorder for twelve years touched not Him but his robe. He stopped and said, "Who touched me?" When everyone around Him denied doing it, the apostle Peter said, "Master, the multitude throng thee and press thee, and sayest thou, 'Who touched me?' And Jesus said, 'Somebody hath touched me. For I perceive that virtue is gone out of me'" (Luke 8:45–46).

How did He know specifically that He had been touched not on His body, but on His garment? He wasn't guessing or using His human instinct to figure it out. It was the Spirit giving Him knowledge through the woman's faith. Faith is the key for the Spirit to move God's hand, as in this case and others. Because when faith is working, God's hands are moving.

That was Jesus, the human spiritual man, living in the sensibility of His Spirit. Jesus knew that He had to go through a terrifying ordeal, and who can say He wasn't thinking, as a man might, if there might be another way to fix this problem. Maybe He came up with an alternative but did not take advantage of it, knowing for what purpose He had come to this world. He knew that He would have to take the entire heavy burden of people's sin upon Himself, a task that under any circumstances would be neither easy nor pleasant to accomplish.

I ask the question: was Jesus afraid to die? The answer to that question, or whether we ignore it or reject it to please our own egos, makes no difference whatsoever; it is completely irrelevant. He said, "It's done," right before he died for us in his sacrificial offering.

Jesus, in one of His teachings, spoke about Himself as the Messiah from His divided but unified position of being both an earthly being and a heavenly Being. In John 6:31, Jesus tells the people that they may eat of the bread of heaven and no longer be hungry. People did not understand what He was saying. It developed into an interesting conversation about salvation, using God's creation, specifically, the giving to people of things of the natural world.

Jesus, knowing the people's hopes of another day of food on the table, was speaking in terms of His person being the food from above when He said to them that He is the bread that comes from heaven. But the people did not understand the spiritual meaning of His words and asked Him for a sign.

They told Him that their fathers had had manna from heaven to eat in the desert. As it is written, He gave them bread from heaven to eat. Then Jesus said unto them, "'Verily, verily I say unto you, Moses gave you not that bread from heaven; but is My Father giveth you the true bread from heaven. For the bread of God is he which cometh down from heaven and giveth life unto the world.' Then said they unto Him, 'Lord, evermore give us this bread.' And Jesus said unto them, 'I am the bread of life. He that comes to Me shall never hunger, and he that believeth on me shall never thirst'" (John 6:31–35).

"Verily, verily, I say unto you, He that believes on me hath everlasting life. I am that bread of life. You fathers did eat the manna in the wilderness, and are dead. This is the bread which cometh down from heaven, that a man may eat thereof, and not die. I am the living bread which came down from heaven: If any man eat of this bread, he shall live for ever: and the bread that I will give is my flesh, which I will give for the life of the world" (John 6:47–51).

Then Jesus said to them, "Verily, verily, I say unto you, except ye eat the flesh of the Son of man, and drinketh my blood, ye have no life in you. Whoso eateth my flesh, and drinks my blood has eternal life, and I will raise him up on the last day. For My flesh is meat indeed, and my blood is drink indeed. He that eateth my flesh, and drinketh my blood dwelleth in me, and I in him" (John 6:53–56).

For many generations, people reading these Bible passages were impressed by the words of Jesus. Even in His time, people were kind of shocked by the way He was talking about the salvation of the soul and the eating of the Lord's flesh and the drinking of His blood.

Often Jesus spoke to people in parables. Sometimes they understood, and other times they hadn't the foggiest clue of what He was talking about. Even His disciples from time to time ended up scratching their heads, not getting what He was saying to them, asking Him to explain it to them clearly.

In our day, there are a lot of symbolic explanations about eating His flesh and drinking his blood, but nothing concrete is said of the meaning of the words *flesh*, *blood*, *bread*, and *eat*. With God's blessing, I'll try reveal the meanings of those words. These words are *only* applied to these spiritual meanings when Jesus mentions them allegorically:

- *Vine* means "victory."
- *Fruit* means "conquered."
- *Remission* means "forgiveness."
- *Shed* means "promise."
- *Take* means "this."
- *Ate* means "had" or "accepted."
- *Flesh* and *body* both mean "sacrifice."
- *Drink* means "believe" or "celebrate."
- *Blood* means "words."
- *Abides* means "is."
- *Bread* and *food* both mean "salvation."
- *Feeds on* means "lives in."

- *Life* means "existence."
- *World* means "human soul."
- *Manna* means "for a time."
- *Hunger* means "perish."
- *Thirst* means "die."
- *Believe* means "live."
- *Son of man* means "image of God" or "God's life."

Why "image of God"? God created man in His image. That means man has God's life in him because He breathed His life into man's nostrils. That life was the human spirit given by God, which became the bridge connecting man's lifeless body in the created world with the spirit, which is man's soul. God has given to that soul the heart, which has its own individuality and self-determination. The "person" of the soul, through the heart's decisions, may independently choose to accept or reject or to obey or not.

Man became alive in the Spirit to be one in God. With a soul and heart, even though these are one in God, man has been given his own will. Jesus said in John 10:30, "I and My Father are One." That means to be in the same Spirit, having the same life, because God is life. Jesus was the first earthly spiritual being who came to this sinful world as the first *holy* man, just like the first spiritual being created in Paradise, called Adam, meaning Man. The creation of both was from the God of life, which is in the spirit of man as a reflection of God Himself, who is a Spirit.

Metaphorically speaking, when Jesus was telling the people how things in the spiritual world worked, He used the reality of everyday life. That is why He used in His parables stories the people could relate to from their daily lives in order for them to be able to compare and understand their spiritual lives.

CHAPTER 18

The following are verses annotated with word substitutions as mentioned in the previous chapter. In John 6:35, it would be, "I am the bread [salvation] of life. He that cometh to me, shall never hunger [perish], and He that believeth [lives] on me shall never thirst [die]." John goes on to write the following:

"This is the bread [salvation] which cometh down from heaven that a man may eat [accept] thereof, and not die.

"I [Jesus] am the living bread [salvation] which came down from heaven. If any man eats [accepts] of this bread [salvation], he shall live forever; and the bread [salvation] that I will give is my flesh [sacrifice], which I will give for the life [existence] of the world [human soul]."

The Jews therefore strove among themselves, saying, "How can this man give us His flesh to eat?"

Then Jesus said unto them, "Verily, verily, I say unto you, except ye eat [accept] the flesh [sacrifice] of the Son of man [God's life] [because Jesus Himself is God in the Trinity] and drink [believe] His blood [Word], ye have no life in you.

"Whoso eateth [accept] my flesh [sacrifice] and drinketh [believed] my blood [Word] hath eternal life, and I will raise him up at the last day.

"For my flesh [sacrifice] is meat [salvation] indeed, and My blood [Word] is drink [to believe] indeed.

"He that eateth [accepts] my flesh [sacrifice] and drinketh [believes] my blood [Word] dwells [is] in me, and I in him.

"As the living Father hath sent me, and I live by the Father, so he that eateth [lives in] me, even he shall live by me.

"This is the bread [salvation] which came down from heaven, not as your fathers did eat [had] manna [for a time], and are dead: he that eateth [accepts] of this bread [salvation] shall live forever."

(John 6:50–58)

Jesus spoke sometimes according to the way He was, man and Spirit, and of a human reality with a spiritual meaning. The last time He spoke this way was when He was instituting the Last Supper. As they were eating, Jesus took bread, blessed it, broke it, gave it to the disciples, and said, "Take [this], eat [accept]; this is my body [sacrifice]" (Matthew 26:26).

When He took the bread, blessed it, and broke it, He was performing a symbolic act of the separation of His body from this world and its entrance into the heavenly spiritual one. He did this so that His apostles would remember in the future what it means to break the bread to practice the Last Supper. This is a practice that may occur the last time for us on this earth, after which we can be "lifted" through death or actually be transformed with the coming of the Lord. Let us not forget that we are in the Spirit's heavenly world even when we are on this earth.

> And He took the cup, and gave thanks, and gave it to them, saying, "Drink [believe] ye all of it.
> "For this is my blood [Word] of the new testament [agreement], which is shed [promised] for many [all] for the remission [forgiveness] of sins.
> "But I say unto you, I will not drink [celebrate] of this fruit [that which has been conquered] of the vine [victory] from now on until that day when I drink it [celebrate it] new with you in My Father's Kingdom."

(Matthew 26:26–29)

Might this represent the future of what the Lord anticipated with His presence in the beginning of His ministry at the wedding in Cana? The transformation from water to wine is a spiritual victory of a new life in the Spirit. It is a celebration of unity and communion for Himself and His bride, the church. A celebration which will be in His Father's kingdom, in the holy city of Jerusalem, in the new spiritual land of Israel—the Israel of God, where the future living quarters of the Groom and bride will be.

"Took the bread and broke it." The breaking of the bread was a symbolic act of separation that will come to be a real spiritual event in His life, in exactly the same circumstances in the near future as after His resurrection, when He'll be lifted to the heavens.

Meanwhile, the disciples were discussing the event about which the brothers and sisters had told them, when they saw Jesus after His resurrection.

Now as they said those things, Jesus Himself stood in the midst of them, and said to them, "Peace be unto you."

But they were startled and affrighted, and suppose that they had seen a spirit. And he said unto them, "Why are ye troubled? And why do thoughts arise in your hearts?

"Behold my hands and my feet. That it is myself: handle me, and see; for a spirit hath no flesh and bones, as ye see me have."

And when he had thus spoken, he shewed them his hands and his feet.

And while they yet believed not for joy, and wondered, he said unto them, "Have ye here any meat?"

And they gave Him a piece of broiled fish and He took it, and did eat before them.

(Luke 24:36–43)

After all the expectation and the shocking experience lived by the disciples after Jesus's resurrection, they remembered the symbolic act in the reality of the Last Supper. That was the last earthly communion of the physical–spiritual union before His death.

Now the spiritual reality of separating (breaking bread) from the material body and moving into the eternal spiritual realm, with Him appearing from "nowhere" and then disappearing again, had happened. We read in Luke 24:30–31: "And it came to pass, as he sat at meat with them, he took bread, and blessed, and brake, and gave to them. And their eyes were opened and they knew him; and he vanished out their sight." Later on, the final transformation from the physical body in which He had resurrected to the spiritual, happened at the moment when He stood in front of them and a cloud covered Him, lifting Him up to the heavens (Acts 1:9).

That was the actual reality of the previous symbolic breaking of the bread, of Him leaving earth to ascend to heaven.

Throughout His life of preaching and teaching, nothing of what Jesus said was without any spiritual meaning. Back then as it is today, many people do not understand many of the things that the Word of God is telling us. This is because people are approaching their study of the Word not through God's wisdom and revelation, but with their human intuition, emotional interpretations, and sensations, which cause them to think that it is a spiritual revelation. That is a common mistake made by the good-intentioned hearts of those who want to serve God even when they know that everything that is about God is spiritual.

Taking the initiative for oneself based on one's love for Him, hoping to do His will without first giving God a chance to show the way, is a mistake. Knowing the Bible from cover to cover by memory is excellent. But when you follow the old saying of "You have brains; use them," you better be sure that you are not trying to help God with your knowledge. He does not need our help; we need His.

The danger of reading the Word with the intellect alone is that a person might confuse such an interpretation with a spiritual interpretation; the person's interpretation could be wrong even when well intended and direct, giving people a feeling of self-sufficiency, thinking that they are having a spiritually revelatory moment.

One must always carefully examine any conclusion deduced from an intuitive thought or feeling before reaching a final decision. Without making a real effort to achieve spiritual revelation, one is taking a wrong approach to God's Word. Anybody with good intentions can say something about the Word of God with the purpose of increasing spiritual understanding and thereby guide people away from the intended spiritual goal without them noticing. Senses, wishes, and emotions, plus many other wrongly understood human feelings that we assign spiritual weight to, although many don't want to admit it, are products of a person's own spiritual conclusions.

No one is exempt from this. The correct approach is one that brings positive spiritual results to a person's life, wherein God's Spirit is very much noticed.

Besides, we shouldn't forget that other spirits will try to interfere in our good intentions, confusing us—that is, if we do not check which spirit at that moment is with us, not in us. An evil spirit lives in the life of a person who does not have the Spirit of God within. Yet a person who has the Spirit of God but does not notice his or her own spirit for some reason is not in control of his or her own spiritual state, thinking that everything is the way they see it, not noticing that a wrong spirit is always close by, looking for a weak moment so it may interfere. Sometimes, in a moment of being confident in ourselves, evil spirits find an open place where they may interfere without us noticing, thinking that everything is okay—even when the voice of our own spirit is trying to warn us.

Confidence in ourselves can be deceiving, but being aware and alert is not our only spiritual responsibility. Also required is our assurance of being right in the Spirit as God wants us to be.

The Word of God warns us to be vigilant because, without our noticing, we can, in our spiritual efforts, prevent our human spirits from being directed or guided by the Spirit of God. This is what tended to happen when Jesus was trying to impart something spiritual to people such as the Pharisees and others who knew the law of Moses: they never took the time to analyze and pray to arrive at the correct spiritual understanding.

Humbleness and faith are the key to open the door to God's wisdom in our lives. Arrogance and intellectual pride will cause us to be ignored and kicked out of the heavenly realm. When Jesus said to be in Him, He meant to be in the Spirit of God, not to have some mental or spiritual feeling of, knowledge about, or emotional impression of Him.

The way to get God's attention is not through the mind, but through the intentions of our hearts and spirits. When the life of Jesus was coming to an end, the goal He had brought with Him from heaven for the salvation of the world was drawing to a close. He knew that perfectly well.

As a man, He had to control all assumptions, feelings, fears, and so on. After praying at the Mount of Olives and living through great spiritual agony, He came to face the reality of what He would have to go through. From that moment on He was all by Himself, even when He was surrounded by many people. The worst feeling a person can have is knowing the end is coming and that nothing can be done to change the situation, but He knew ahead of time that He would be all by Himself, and He accepted it. The moment He was arrested, the abuse of His person began: He was slapped, punched, spit on, pushed, and insulted. The road to hell started that night, and it was only the beginning.

Only God the Father knew what His beloved human Son felt at that moment in His heart. We can only imagine Jesus, as a human being, leaving everything in the hands of His heavenly Father, God.

Jesus endured what no other person since the creation of the world has ever endured in the spiritual sense. First, His body was beaten almost beyond recognition. Second, any man beaten like that would faint and be unable to carry not only the cross, but also his own body. Even though at a certain moment He had help, His physical condition, for some reason, was stronger than that of any other beaten man.

We can say that up to that moment, God the Father was aligning Jesus's body with His Spirit. We shouldn't forget, either, that Satan himself was involved in Jesus's punishment to break Him. Satan knew for certain that Jesus really was the Son of the Almighty in the flesh, and he had to unleash his hate against Him. Satan never knew or imagined that the person of Jesus could not be killed. He just thought that if He were human, he could kill Him, without understanding that with a righteous, pure, and holy heart in God, the soul cannot be destroyed.

The difference in the life of the body and the soul is the heart. If a heart hasn't repented, the soul is not saved, so both of them will be destroyed. But if someone is saved, meaning repented or is holy like Jesus, then his or her body can be destroyed, but not his or her soul. If the heart is without blame, then the soul is innocent and clean.

To understand this spiritual process in the life of a secular person, consider when a person is able to comprehend that he or she has a choice in whether his or her body is healthy or sick. The understanding of the mind regarding what is good or bad for the body leads the heart to make a spiritual decision. The spiritual decision of the heart is something the intellect can translate so that one may understand and choose. First comes the thought of the heart, then the reasoning of the mind, and finally the decision. The soul is our spiritual person, and the heart is our spiritual brain. Our body is our secular existence, and our secular intellect is the province of the brain, where resides our wisdom, knowledge, and common sense. These are the decision makers, spiritual and secular.

If we do the best we can to get exercise and eat healthy,

understanding that this is correct way for us, then our bodies, because of our daily discipline, will be healthy and strong.

Our intellectual understanding makes us responsible, whether we care or not, for our own health. Our well-being and the health of our bodies is in our hands. The way we understand the body is the same way we understand the spiritual heart. It has been said that from the heart comes thoughts both right and wrong, so whatever the mind decides for the body, the responsibility for it lies in the heart's will. We need to have the same responsibility in our hearts for the health of our own souls.

As we do with the physical body, we need to do the same with the spiritual heart, that is, be responsible for the future lives of our souls in eternity. If we don't care, we'll be lost. If we care, we need to follow the same process for our hearts that we follow for our bodies. We need spiritual discipline and sacrifice.

It is the intellect that is responsible for the body. The heart, with its spiritual knowledge, is responsible for the soul. Our human understanding, guided by instinct or an intellectual understanding of good and bad, right and wrong, is in the hands of our common sense. We have common sense to decide whether our lives will be lost or saved. Every individual should never forget to see in their own decisions and actions the sometimes unnoticeable intervention of the devil.

In people's lives there are two spirits, and these are at war against each other. One is the human spirit, which is on a mission to warn, save, and protect, and the other is the evil spirit of destruction and death. Our hearts are right in the middle, and it is for us to determine which way we will direct our souls in the future, either to hell or to heaven.

Satan knew that Jesus was a holy person, just as he knew that Eve was holy. Satan knew that he could not destroy holiness, because holiness is God Himself, but he knew that after Eden he could destroy, or attempt to destroy, those who are holy.

Satan knew that Jesus was the Son of God, but he was not 100 percent sure, which is why when he tempted Jesus, he said, "*If you are the Son of God!*" What Satan never knew about Jesus, as the human He was, was that Jesus, in the Spirit of the Trinity, was in reality God Himself.

But because Jesus was in the body of a human with a pure and holy heart, Satan wrongly assumed that it didn't matter how holy He was. Like Adam and Eve, His death would separate Him from His holy life so He could lose His soul. Even when Satan knew who Jesus was with His presence in this world, he never had precise knowledge of Jesus's plan for the salvation of the human soul. Satan never knew that Jesus had come to this world to save humanity. Otherwise he would never have thought to kill Jesus, knowing that by doing so he would condemn himself.

On the other hand, in his distorted mind where sin long ago took the place of reason in his blind hatred, which led him to despise and detest God, the heavens, and all of His creation, Satan cared not for his own end.

The evil spirits, recognizing Jesus when they saw Him, said in Mark 3:11, "Thou art the Son of God." On another occasion, in Mark 4:34, the evil spirit says, "I know thee who thy art, the Holy One of God." Satan definitely knew who Jesus was. Sadly, some people who have that same knowledge are numb to the reality of evil and its consequences during life.

Just as God was using His Son for the salvation of humanity, Satan was using people, such as the rebellious Jews and Romans, to do evil in the hopes of losing humankind through the killing of Jesus. It was not a battle among humans, but a fight between good and evil in their lives, with a huge difference between the fighting forces: one holy heart against the hordes of Hades and

Satan himself, all the way to the cross and then to the kingdom of Satan.

Today we the people have what God has given us since the time of our creation, which is the power to decide which way to go, whether up or down. The price paid for our salvation is so great that there are no words to describe it or sacrifices to be made to approximate it. If only we believe in our hearts through the gift of faith given to us by God, we will save our souls from eternal condemnation. No human and nothing else of this world can help us to understand the spiritual suffering of Jesus in His heart and soul before victory. A man in the flesh, having offered up His soul, not His body, in one eternal sacrifice through the actions of His heart in life, in a world where only spirits live, requires us to believe in Him according to the faith that God Almighty has given us. The only chance we have to save our souls with everything that the devil is throwing at us is the gift of faith given by the One whose life was given up as a sacrificial offering so that we may live eternally, not in hell but heaven, depending on which way we choose to walk.

CHAPTER 19

On Jesus's way to Golgotha, the cross that He carried with His almost mutilated body was heavy. But it wasn't as heavy as the weight of the sins of the world that spiritually He was about to take upon His soul. Jesus as a mortal was concerned, worried, and maybe afraid and unsure of the outcome of His mission in the garden of Gethsemane.

At what moment did Jesus take the sins of the world upon Him? Was it from the beginning when He was arrested in the garden of Gethsemane? Or was it when He stood before Pilate to be judged? If the Spirit of the Father left Him because of the sin on Him from the moment of His arrest, could it be that God was not within Him, but by His side, with His face turned away from all that sin Jesus was carrying? And Jesus, not feeling in His own spirit His Father's Spirit, yelled from His soul, "My God, My God, why hast thou forsaken Me?" (Matthew 27:46).

If Jesus was without sin up to the moment of the cross, exactly at what moment did He take the sins of the world upon Himself?

Was it right at that moment when, noticing the Spirit of the Father departing from Him and feeling His soul empty, He said, "My God, My God, why hast thou forsaken Me?"

Or was it right before, when He said, "It is finished"?

Or maybe it happened right before He cried out loud as in Luke 23:46, saying, "Father, into thy hands I commend my spirit"?

That was Jesus, a holy man calling upon God at the end of His life. He surrendered to the Almighty on the cross, getting ready for His mission. As a holy man, He took with Him his faith, believing and trusting in His heavenly Father, to the other side of this material life. He left in His Father's hands His human spirit, which was with Him to comfort His soul to the last second of His earthly life while He was getting ready for the big battle.

At the moment when Jesus cried out with a loud voice, saying, "Father, into thy hands I commend my spirit" (Luke 23:46), did He call upon God His Father as the human believer He was, or did He say that as the Son of the Almighty? Today, it is normal for a believer in Jesus to call upon God the Father. The Lord gave that right with His sacrifice to those who have faith and believe in Him. Glory to the Almighty for His love, grace, and mercy.

Jesus, in His holiness, was the only One at that moment who was in a right position before the Father without any intercessor, because His human spirit and God's Spirit were one with a holy heart and soul. It was a case of direct communication between the holy image of man and God the Father, with the holy human coming in that same spirit before God.

And when the moment came, His spiritual soul and heart were separated from His physical body, along with the interceding human spirit between Himself and the Spirit of God. It was the beginning of the greatest journey for justice and justification ever, ending in His sacrifice to save the human soul. After His bodily death, at the foot of the cross, the people who had taken His life, because of the sudden change in the skies, were in fear of what they had done and what had just happened. One of the soldiers acknowledged, "Truly He was the Son of God" (Matthew 27:54), recognizing Him in the body of a human being.

That was the moment in human history when, before God, the rights of Satan to the souls of people were rescinded. From that moment on, men had no excuse for choosing their own path to heaven or hell.

Jesus's death and resurrection has opened a door to salvation in people's lives. That salvation is in man's hands; he has the ability to choose his own end before his last breath of air. The moment for guessing, having expectations, and deducing is over. Evil's deceiving lies and the truth of God has given people the reality that humanity lives in a world where Satan is the landlord. Now, being the temporary residents that we are, we have a chance to decide if we want to live in heaven or Satan's kingdom.

After Jesus's departure, the world would change in such a way that the future would be like never before, a state of savage spiritual warfare in men's lives. Satan has become more hideous than ever before in his attacks against created humankind, gathering up and preparing the ones whose souls are of this world and therefore slated to be lost. Satan has the same greed on earth that he had in the heavens, but this time he offers to harness the wealth of this world, along with that greed, pride, power, and glory, for his own diabolical plan against men's lives.

The world, and mainly the Jews, are, now more than ever, in his sights for destruction. Satan is playing a game between the Jews and those who hate them at the same time, trying to destroy the rest of the world. The question is, who are the ones who are preparing for the beginning of the end of humanity with Satan's help?

From the first crime in this world to the killing of the Savior of the human race, and up to this day, Satan, through his disciples, is using any excuse to try to bring an end to humanity through the hands of the wealthiest and most powerful of this world, the ones who have accepted what Jesus has rejected. These are the ones with the money and the power to make decisions in the service of Satan's gospel—the so-called religious leaders of different political denominations that offer man false hope in their promises. This religion is one of wishful thinkers who sermonize and promise, in exchange for people's faithfulness, a future of security and abundance with a golden cup full of empty hopes.

Satan's overpowering of men in their weakness is not only intended to control godless people, but is also messing up the lives of Christians who are having a hard time getting in line behind Christ's teachings. For this, there is only one question to be asked: what is wrong with Christianity?

PART IV

WHAT IS WRONG WITH CHRISTIANITY?

FAITH. GOSPEL. RELIGION. POLITICS. LAW.

CHAPTER 20

In reality, nothing is wrong with Christianity, because Christianity comes from the gospel of Christ as a gift with the essence of faith in men's lives given by God. But for most Christians, that essence over time has become incrementally weaker and problematic. The problem arose because Christianity was transformed into a "spiritual" religion, where the fire of a fighting spirit in the new life was gradually and seemingly unnoticeably replaced by a growing secularism under a spiritual umbrella, where faith in God disappeared and hope in man was given first place. That is when men's hearts began to ignore the Spirit of God and His teachings and guidance. Also, the unperceived deceptive spirit began to play a bigger role, showing to man the good realities of the day and hiding or lying about the consequences that are to be paid by his life tomorrow. That is why Jesus asked, "Nevertheless when the Son of Man cometh, shall He find faith on the earth?" (Luke 18:8).

Some people's histories are like Pandora's box. Anything might come out about people—the secrets about their pasts and/or the secrets they carry in the present—and surprise even the most unsurprisable person.

Most people who act to serve society or religion have two faces, one being real and the other being fake. That is what we see from the outside. But we don't know which of the two faces is fake and which is real. This is a problem that shows that most believers have no spiritual discernment or knowledge. And this is something that happens in every generation, even among so-called spiritual Christians.

The guessing and prejudgment arises from a lack of spiritual wisdom and revelation. Being like such people, we may have our own portion of hypocrisy, and we can even cheat on ourselves, whether consciously or not.

What will happen to our "I" in the future is a mystery. Spiritually, God knows. Secularly, whether we have done good or bad is for future generations to study and come to their own conclusions. That is, if we end up being remembered by history.

If not, we'll be saved from man's judgment. At least this way, according to what we have in our hearts, when we go to the other side, we may have a better chance before the Almighty.

Knowing what is wrong and what is right, we can be our own judges, that is, if we care to be decent and honest. The one who judges himself in favor of what is right in the eyes of God and against what is wrong pleases God. God judges us not according to whatever face we put on, but by the intentions of our hearts and our thoughts as seen through our actions. Jesus said, "Wherefore by their fruits ye shall know them" (Matthew 7:20).

Our human hearts will die with our bodies, but the spiritual consequences of the intentions of our hearts for the benefit or not of our soul, will live forever in heaven or hell. Whatever thoughts our hearts follow, will be our act and our autograph in the Book of life. By those actions and the "signature" of our "fruits," we'll decide where we shall live out eternity, either above the stars or within the core of hell, wherever it is located.

Any story from any man's life can be understood in the light of biblical truth, historical information, imagination, deduction, and revelation. There are also many ways to interpret the facts of history. So, readers can, in their knowledge and understanding, help themselves to learn of the unknown truth. This can only be done if the seeker of truth gets down on his or her knees and prays; it cannot be through our human intellect or interpretations, but through God's revelation, because not all history books are truthful. And because the truth belongs to God and not to man, let the Spirit of God enlighten our understanding, not to judge or excuse anyone, but to see how clean the intentions of our hearts are before God and man.

Let's not get too intellectual or philosophical about life and history, but be realistic about the truth. And the truth is not philosophy, but a real spiritual knife that separates a man's good deeds from his evil deeds, and his ignorance from his knowledge—a raw reality that can be very uncomfortable for us. And denying or excusing our weaknesses, in the traditional humanistic way, won't justify us.

Our actions toward other human beings, in whatever position of power we may have, will be meaningful until the time we part from this world. And after, whether we believe in heaven or hell or not, we'll either pay the consequences or be rewarded for our actions at the end of this earthly life.

With this world being divided in two, it is hard to say who is right and who is wrong within their hearts. Since the first crime committed on earth, man has excused himself of any guilt. Is it the evil in people that is making us throw the first stone and then hide our hands? "It wasn't me. I didn't do it. What are you talking about? I don't know anything."

People come up with a whole book of excuses for their bad behavior and wrongly oriented hearts. Some people know the real truth, together with God, while the innocents may find themselves in a limbo of life's uncertainties, in the hands of the ones who are "always right."

When looking at humankind across the globe, we see concern in most people's faces as they are anxious for survival in their struggle for life. Obviously, they are doing the best they can to have normal lives. It is true that some so-called Christians, never mind religious believers, allow their secular worries and materialistic concerns take center stage, instead of exercising faith and thereby receiving what the Lord has promised us.

Because of their beliefs and creeds, and for living in a very materialistic world, people may have to pay the consequences. We have known this from the beginning. Man came from a spiritual world to an unknown world of secularity, a world of new learning. Now he is trying to create his own happiness, sometimes amid difficult circumstances, and many times is crushed by the rude and raw reality of life's uncertainties. Jesus said, "For ye have the poor always with you, but me ye have not always" (Matthew 26:11). We may take these words not only in their real meaning about wealth, but also in their meaning about spiritual poverty. These words are a challenge to our own understanding.

The un-understood spiritual life, for lack of faith and/or curiosity about all of God's promises in the Word of God, is the first step on the wrong path of success. When faith is ignored and hope is put into practice, the concomitant lack of spiritual knowledge brings all kinds of uncertainty into people's lives because of their naiveté, ignorance, or laziness.

To know the Word of God is to know Jesus; to know and be in Jesus is to know and be in His Spirit; and to be in His Spirit is to be in God. And if you are in God, are one in Him, then you won't be poor, unhappy, or in the limbo of life's uncertainty.

Having His mind, His eyes, and the needed spiritual knowledge through revelation, you won't need any man to tell you about the expected good future world or about people. About a spiritual person, not a religious one, the Bible says, "For in Him dwells all the fullness of the Godhead bodily; and you are complete in Him, who is the head of all principality and power" (Colossians 2:9–10).

Jesus knew people's hearts, the poor and innocent, the rich and powerful. That is why He left for us His promises, which allow us not only to reach what is necessary to be happy in this secular world but also to have everything here on earth as it is in heaven. Jesus said, "But seek ye the kingdom of God and his righteousness, and all the rest will be added unto you" (Matthew 6:33).

This world, this earth, is, among the heavens, unlike any other planet in God's heavenly creation. Being His kingdom, the third heaven where He has His throne, this earth is where His Holiness reigns over the endless universe. The only problem is that the space where this world exists has been usurped for a short time by another lord.

CHAPTER 21

C hristians, since the beginning with Jesus and after His ascension to heaven, from the times of the apostles, went in the way of the right spiritual gospel, up to the time the Roman Empire created a so-called universal religion. This marked the first creation of a universal faith in God, which has been taken by man as his own religion and has molded Christ's gospel according to a new form of understanding. Catholicism, in short, is a religious faith that is according to man's idealistic interpretation, with a gospel that confuses goodness for spirituality, and where God and His will is handled by man according to the newly created doctrines, which in time would lead to future denominations of the Christian church.

Through exercised imagination, there may be a part of history that is unknown to the world, a history between the Jews, Romans, and Christians that was never documented, and if it was, it is kept in secret somewhere for some reason.

The time of Roman intervention was during the pioneering stage of spreading the gospel throughout the world, the time after Jesus's death. This is when a new Christianity was born, which in the future would be called the Roman Church, which later was officially called the Roman Universal Catholic Church, known today as the Roman Catholic Church.

Obviously the Romans felt secure enough in their pride to call the church "universal," thinking that the Roman Empire would last forever. In one word, not all stories that have become history may have a convincing ending.

When something is created for good, the creators are the only ones who know the truth of the intention. If men later interpret a fake truth from it, this will bring dissolution. What is more tragic than that is the spill of innocent blood.

Man doesn't notice the horde of evil and demonic spirits that live in this world, interfering in his own life, even if he is doing good in the name of God. This is why man needs to be *aware* under what spirit he is doing good for humanity.

The first universal religion, the Roman Catholic Church, declared, as Jesus did, that the apostle Peter was to be the rock of this new church. That declaration is taken as one of the foundations of the Roman Catholic Church, which, according to different historians, is short of details in the history of the creation of the new church.

But the question is, who precisely came up with the idea for a new way of interpreting the gospel? And when? Was it during Jesus's life or after?

If it was during Jesus's life on earth, then why was it deemed necessary? Was His doctrinal gospel of one mind and one spirit, that is, one understanding and one agreement with only one way to believe, insufficient?

And if it was after His death, who decided that there needed to be a new approach to the gospel of salvation?

Where in the Bible does it say that we believers in Christ have to be united under different denominations' doctrines, where the interpretation of the Word of God and of God's will is understood by many in different ways? Where was the idea born for an ideology with a mix of philosophy and intellectual interpretation, where spirituality is known and understood but not practiced in the spirit? We must not forget that God gave us two knees to kneel upon so we could look for the truth as declared by the Spirit, a truth that we proclaim and believe no matter our denomination through the knowledge and understanding of our brains and our believed spirituality.

The pagans have practiced the killing of Christians for three hundred years, and no one knows exactly when it stopped. The story goes that the emperor Constantine was the one who legalized Christianity. But when did he legalize it, and why? Was it because Constantine the Great and others became believers, or was it after the killing stopped? (And who stopped it—and for what reason?) Or was it that Constantine saw what was happening with the Christians and decided to do something about it?

About those killings and the apostles, Bruno Bartoloni wrote the following, more than one thousand years later, about the new Roman apostolic church: "No Pope had ever permitted an exhaustive study, partly because a 1,000-year-old curse attested by secret and apocalyptic documents, threatened anyone who disturbed the peace of Peter's tomb with the worst possible misfortune."

As with many other things of the past, words were spoken about some of these occurrences, with presumptions, accusations, conspiracies, and excuses on tap. And because no one can confirm or deny with any certainty that any words written in history books are true, or whether any story lived by man is a lie or the truth, such words remain hanging in the air of history.

Each one of us is to believe according to what our human wisdom or the Spirit declares to us. And that is according to what kind of heart we have when approaching the subject, which sometimes, given our intellectual interpretations and guesses about what the Word says, presents us with no spiritual advantage. It is just a belief in the mind, but the religious person takes it as a spiritual revelation.

Either way, it is impossible to deny that the Roman Catholic Church was created by men to cover up their own lies and occlude the real truth, meaning the honest man may never have the chance to know the real truth. That is man, but from God nothing can be hidden. Man has to remember this whether he believes in God or not.

What was said about the death of the apostle Peter is just the tip of the iceberg. We'll never know whether or not there was a satanic curse over the lives of the people who participated willingly in the killing of not only the apostle Peter, but also of other believers during and after the time of the Roman Empire, in agreement with the Jews. Or maybe those words were written for any person in the future who may try to open Peter's tomb, to scare them so no one will ever know for what reason Peter was killed—even when Jesus said what would happen to him (John 21:18–19). As with every area of people's lives, theories and conspiracies exist in the secrets of the unknown.

We should remember that when action is taken against a person, a people, a nation, an institution, or an idea, there is most always a secret motive behind said actions.

For some reason, some people are trying to rewrite history, where epic acts of unbelievable cruelty toward one person, a race, a nation, or the whole of humanity were performed, and hide such things. This gives rise to blame and excuses, depending on who has rewritten whatever specific story, and most of the time, the truth is disguised with a lie, and the lie presents itself as the truth. This causes trouble for those who don't have the knowledge or wisdom to separate right from wrong, truth from lies. And the ones who can see the difference between the truth and a lie are hated and called evildoers by the deceivers, for being discovered.

For the person who lets their life be run by emotions, which is sometimes normal in this secular world, the realities are hard to accept. Justice is something that cannot please everyone alike, for understandable reasons. And because of that, there will always be someone dissatisfied with the results. The outcome is always a divide between those who are pleased and those who are disappointed. That is why it doesn't matter if truth is from a well-intended explanation, which could be understood either way by the people: as a verdict to be accepted or rejected, whether justice is done or not.

Accusing or excusing someone is not a final ruling, but a chance to look deeper and investigate for the elusive truth of man. In the end for the citizen who obediently follows the system, someone will always be innocent or guilty of the collateral damage done to people—either one or many—by any system or person.

The damage caused by one person, institution, or government with power over the lives of those who cannot defend themselves, may be hidden from man, but it is not hidden from the One who created man. That is why in a world where the living God wasn't known, idols were the gods of many nations. People believed and trusted in these idols, placing their hopes for the future and for justice in them. It is true even in modern times, when God is known, that the same type of false hope in man and in man's justice is still in practice, with the same spirit of dishonesty and corruption, whether in politics or religion.

For people of all different intellectual beliefs and occupations, the apostles and disciples came and testified of the new faith of the love, mercy, righteousness, and justice of the living God. With the preaching and witnessing of that same love and justice, the people had a chance to hear the good news with interest and admiration. They had a chance to find out that God's law and righteous justice is delivered according to the intentions of a man's heart, and not by man's interpretations of the rule of law, punishing people for their mistakes, presuming or prefabricating their guilt, and condemning them just because of a hearsay, without any proof.

People of a high social status, together with the rest of the population, had a chance, in their ignorance of the living God, to hear and see how the adoption of this unknown faith of love and justice was possible for them too. It promised a different world of justice from the one wherein no man may forgive them for their mistakes or guilt, even if they were to repent.

Many were driven by an eager curiosity to find out what was all this new talk of the new God, interested to hear about Jesus and His promises of eternal life, promises for which the people slowly changed their lives, accepting Christ as their Savior.

They gave themselves a chance in their new faith when they believed in the future promises of the gospel. But some people, for some reason, could gain no clear understanding of this new faith in a God they could not see or touch. They considered it a deviation from their belief in the gods made by human hands.

The important people at the head of the Roman Empire had, for some time, been hearing about this new sect, about which they had some idea, but in general they were not interested in it, at least not at the moment. Three hundred years passed in the life of the Roman Empire before the Romans saw this so-called sect as their first concern. Almost at the end of Jesus's life and after His death, from all the commotion that the Pharisees made because of Pilate's attempt to free Jesus, the Romans insisted that their prefects in different regions keep them informed of this dangerous sect called Christianity. But more than any other place, the information was coming from Jerusalem, where Pontius Pilate had to deal directly with the Jews over the Jesus case.

Pilate informed Rome of the ongoing situation with the Jewish people, answering their questions about the Jewish religion and mentioning the incredible hate the Jewish leaders held against the sect, something that was prolonged when Paul, Peter, and other apostles got in trouble with the Romans, thanks to the Jews.

Pilate wrote to Rome the truth of what happened in Jerusalem, not only to save his career and maybe his life, but also to prevent any misunderstanding about his actions that the Jews might propose to his superiors in Rome in regard to the case of Jesus. He did this just to clear himself should the Jews accuse him before the emperor of attempting to place himself higher than Caesar when trying to administer justice to the Son of God.

Another possibility is, given what historians say about the cruelty of Pontius Pilate, perhaps he had a twinge of conscience upon seeing the Jews' unjust, cruel, vengeful, hateful, and almost demoniacal attitude toward Jesus and, therefore, had a change of heart.

Other Roman prefects, not having had to experience the trial and crucifixion of Jesus, were more inclined toward the side of the Jewish leaders. Even when the Romans disliked the Jews, they sometimes found it in their best interests to please the Pharisees. For example, Felix the governor, grateful for the presents the Pharisees had given him, agreed to keep the apostle Paul in prison, knowing he was innocent.

That is an act performed by someone called "a good evildoer." Because the greedy governors were always well remunerated for their services to the Jews, they didn't care about truth or justice—same as today. The Word expresses a truth when it says, "The love of money is the root of all evil" (1 Timothy 6:10).

Nothing has changed, as the devil never lets an opportunity to destroy the truth slip away. He continued to exert his diabolical influence in the lives of other Romans, giving the Jews a chance to get rid of the Christians by the brutal way of the Roman system, which presented a way to finish the job without the Pharisees having to get their hands dirty. Influenced by the devil, the Jews, who made false accusations of heresy against the Christians, worked together with the Romans to persecute and kill the children of God.

About the persecution and killing of Christians, historians, whether Jewish or Gentile, have written many different narratives. One of these narratives claims that the New Testament's story of the Jews accusing Jesus before Pilate, asking that he be executed, and calling Christians heretics, is anti-Semitic.

According to their own deductible understanding of history, excusing, accusing, and favoring one side over the other about who the guilty ones were and what was the reason for the persecution and killing of the Christians, is something that will always present a chance to agree to disagree. The Bible undeniably attests that Jesus was accused by the Jews of, and that the Christians were persecuted and killed by the Romans for, heresy, which created a revolt. But the official story by the Jews is that they had nothing to do with what happened between the Christians and the Romans. It has been said that the Christians and Romans were in conflict over so-called religious beliefs, with the Roman Empire, a pagan nation, afraid of being converted to what the Romans called Christianity.

The real reason the Pharisees brought charges of sedition against Jesus was twofold: as retribution for what He told them in the Temple about their Jewish beliefs and their own evil way of life, and to make the Romans wary of the teachings of this man, saying it was a security concern for the Roman Empire. The Pharisees feared it was entirely possible for Jesus and His followers to convert the Roman Empire to the Christian faith, having in mind the fall of the Roman Empire.

And finally at the end when Jesus was arrested, He was accused of having referred to Himself as the Son of God. For the evil-minded Pharisees, that was the providential last straw they needed to have a case against Him.

Satan was not on vacation at the time; he was using the Jews and Romans to manifest his own will. Whether this is true or not, according to some historians, Nero blamed the Christians for burning Rome, for which Christians began being persecuted with even more intensity, whereas others say that Nero was the one who burned the city, then blamed the Christians for it. The writers of history never mention the spiritual consequences of the burning of Rome, an act with no visible spiritual connection, but nevertheless spiritual in deed.

We'll never know what would have happened if the leaders of the church hadn't made an agreement with the Roman Empire, but it is what happened. The Romans saw that the persecution and the killing of Christians for nearly three hundred years resulted in the boundless growth of the church, with more believers, even among Roman citizens. Because of this state of affairs, the Romans decided in their common sense to do something about it.

The time had come for a change of tactics. "Though beheaded, and crucified, and thrown to wild beasts, and chains, and fire, and all other kinds of torture, we do not give up our confession; but the more such things happen, the more do others and in larger numbers become faithful", Justin Martyr wrote.

At this point, perhaps because of common sense, or political strategy, or the visible injustice within their midst, or the whispers of conscience, action to resolve the long-standing problem was taken. The Romans, seeking not to look bad before the eyes of the world—as opposed to leaders today, who seemingly do not care what others may say or think about them—made a change of plan. They made this plan for their own convenience, not knowing of Satan's involvement. An armistice was called to put an end to the bloody campaign against the believers. At that point, the leaders of the Roman Empire contacted the leaders of the church, showing their goodwill and concern for the future well-being of the Christians.

It is possible that the Roman leaders, Jewish leaders, and persecuted Christian leaders came to a three-way agreement of convenience for peace. If so, the agreement would have been financially convenient for the Pharisees in that they would no longer have to pay bribes, in the form of donations and contributions, to the Romans. The agreement would have been politically convenient for the Roman Empire, helping them get out of a situation that really had nothing to do with the security of their empire. Only God knows the real situation.

Being right in the middle, and maybe with no chance to state their own opinions or set any conditions, the Christian leaders took a chance for peace.

Another aspect of the story is that Constantine the Great and Licinius legalized Christianity three hundred years after Christ's death, but it is not clear if it was done before the creation of the Catholic Church or after. Again, only the Almighty knows the whole story.

The Catholic Church believes it was founded by Peter after he and the other eleven apostles were sent out into the world by Jesus to continue the preaching of the gospel. The leaders of the Roman Catholic Church, whoever they were, took the gospel of Christ as the basis for their faith in the new Christianity, creating for themselves the only official church in the world. It is ironic that Romans were the creators of the new universal church when they were the ones to persecute Christians.

The newly created church established a new way of teaching the gospel, which many believe is not the way of the Almighty, according to the Word.

It was the first of many divisions to come in the future; the wrong interpretation of the Word would lead to different ways of believing and having faith in God, Christ, and the gospel. In this new manifestation of religion, the will of God and the understanding of being in one mind and one spirit would both be ignored because of the spiritual blindness of those at the head of the church. These church leaders spread their newly created doctrines, claiming these had come by way of spiritual knowledge conveyed to them by the Word. They accepted intellectualized interpretations as spiritual revelations, whether they did so knowingly or not.

So, the Catholic Church created a mirror of the gospel. It became the first church created by man to codify faith into religion, basing its interpretation of Christianity on human understanding. A spirit of the Catholics' own "righteousness" led them to accept these interpretations as truth. They replaced the Spirit of Truth, the will of God, revelation, and the concept of being of one mind and one spirit, all of which had come from the Almighty, with their own spiritual beliefs, "revealed" interpretations, deductions, and so on.

In this new ritualistic faith, everyone who believed in God were the saints of the new doctrine and had respect for those whose life's work was to preach the gospel or do good deeds for others. It is a mystery known only to God why new and upcoming religions felt that they had to take the gospel of Christ as personal property for their own doctrinal righteousness.

As in any other history, there are hundreds or thousands of little unknown historical details, which are impossible to provide for reasons of secrecy, lack of truthfulness, or maybe other reasons. Some things are left for the imagination of an investigative mind.

The truth of the matter is that religion on its own does not teach anyone to know the spiritual difference between right and wrong, as written in the gospel, for unity of mind and spirit. The gospel is not based on any human doctrine because it is a new spiritual covenant. It is not a mix of directives and rules concerning how to come to God and serve Him, as described in the Old Testament. You simply have to approach the Almighty Savior from the bottom of your heart. The only images that should exist in our hearts are the one of Him on the cross and the one of the known, but not always remembered, place of victory: the open empty tomb.

CHAPTER 22

————————◆————————

Time went by, and the leaders of the church saw that the Romans were serious about wanting peace, so they contacted them. That was the beginning of the end of what is unknown to us from God in His plans to perhaps willing do something different and greater in this world through His children, if the leaders of the church at that time wouldn't agree to the Romans' plan for peace.

Who can confirm or deny that this was or wasn't the moment when the Roman Empire made known to the Jews that it had created the Roman Church? Was or wasn't this the moment when they conceived the creation of a new faith in the near future, a future where Christians would accept an imitation of the gospel almost impossible to distinguish from the original? Such Christians, ignorant of the spiritual meaning of the gospel, having good faithful hearts, stood to be misdirected in their faith by God's new "representatives." This story is quite different from what the Catholic leaders are claiming, according to their interpretations and understanding of the Word. The Bible reads, "He [Jesus] saith unto them, But whom say ye that I am? And Simon Peter answered and said, Thou art the Christ, the Son of the living God" (Matthew 16:15-16, KJV). After Peter confesses that He is the Christ, Jesus told him that from then on his name would be Petros, meaning a rock, but the meaning of that rock in itself

216

is faith. Upon that faithful confession, the Church of Christ will be built, and not upon a rock that holds different doctrines and denominations that divide the only faith of the Gospel.

Some good-hearted people of the Catholic faith say that the church came first and then the Word. That is not correct. First came the Word for the ones who had ears to hear, and the ones who heard came to be the beginning of the spiritual church, as intended by the Lord.

Catholicism proposes that such things as confession, infant baptism, and the use of idols are biblical, but they are not. The Bible warns us to be alert for this type of substitution, saying that Satan will use false doctrine to try to deviate souls from the correct path, even those who are saved. In short, the Catholic interpretation of the gospel comes from man, not by revelation of the Spirit of the Lord. Whether the Catholics are wrong or right, God is the only One who can determine who is in the Spirit to understand His Word in the way He wants us to.

What makes us all wrong is our own misunderstanding of what is spiritually right and what is spiritually wrong, while we are living and walking in this world full of rotten, sinful, evil self-righteousness. Instead of having the type of righteousness that makes us come together as one in the body of Christ, with one mind and one spirit, we try to convince each other of who is right and who is wrong.

The Almighty definitely knows who is wrong. The letter of the law kills, but the Spirit gives life, and He is the only One who can see the intentions of man's heart.

The Romans, after too many years of dealing with the Christian problem and having too many questions without answers, agreed among themselves, or with someone else, to assure the Jewish leaders that they would have nothing to worry about if the Romans were to make Christianity their national religion, which would solve any interpersonal or interreligious problems with no harm coming to any side. And with the creation of that first religion, goodness and spirituality came to be conflated.

The new church wished to reflect the Law of Moses, the gospel of Christ, the story of the people of Israel, and so-called spiritual traditions. Catholicism made it so the apostles and the do-gooders of the new religion would be canonized as saints, for which the new church, in its glory, would honor a new spiritual leader, who in the future would be called "the pope," the earthly Holy Father, although Jesus prohibits anyone on earth from being called such a thing.

Whether the tradition existed in the Jewish religion or in the religions of any peoples who knew not of the existence of God before Christ, the practice of praying for the dead was added to Catholic doctrine as a way of remembering those who have departed from this life. Indeed, the Catholic Church thinks that this is spiritually required.

Many believers still pray for the memory of their deceased ancestors as a matter of tradition. Many others raise the memory of their ancestors to the Highest One, whoever that may be according to their faith, and ask for the departed soul's merciful redemption in the afterlife.

What the apostle Paul said in 2 Timothy 1:18 was wrongly interpreted by the Catholic Church as a prayer for the Almighty to have mercy on those souls waiting for judgment. Instead, Paul meant it as a word of hope directed to God for Onesiphorus, who was going through a time of uncertainty in his life, and whom Paul was remembering in a brotherly way, asking God in gratitude to have mercy on Onesiphorus and his family when the day for it came.

A person does not have to be dead to receive God's mercy. Still, perhaps the apostle Paul knew somehow that Onesiphorus had been arrested and that was why he said those words. The Bible doesn't tell us if Onesiphorus was dead, or very sick, or in the midst of adverse circumstances. Given that Christians were persecuted at that time, who can say whether or not Onesiphorus and his family were in danger of ending up in prison and being killed.

Let's say that the apostle wished for mercy not because Onesiphorus was dead, but because Paul knew he was in prison and was about to be executed. That would be a good reason for Paul to wish for God to have mercy on him. The time for a believer to ask God to have mercy upon someone's life is when the person is alive and in need of God's help or, for some other reason, is likely close to the end of his life—not when he is already dead. Paul knew better than to ask God to have mercy on a soul already in paradise or hell, that is, if Onesiphorus was dead.

In 2 Timothy 1:18, the apostle Paul wrote, "The Lord grant unto him that he may find mercy of the Lord in that day," with "that day" being the Day of Judgment, when Onesiphorus will be dead.

It is not known if Onesiphorus was dead. Paul wrote those words to express his hope to his brothers that God would have mercy on Onesiphorus no matter the situation or future outcome.

To take these words of the apostle Paul as something concrete, the way some denominations do, is to forget that no matter how much we would like to intercede for a soul that is no longer with us, we should adhere to the Words of the Almighty when Moses was hoping to see Him. God told Moses: "I will make my goodness pass before thee, and I will proclaim the name of the Lord before thee; and I will be gracious to whom I will be gracious, and will shew mercy on whom I will shew mercy" (Exodus 33:19).

The wishful words of Moses and the apostle Paul, even though the two stories are different from one another, have the same spiritual answer. Whatever man wishes in his heart, even as a prayer, is known to God, and God will pour out His mercy when, why, and upon whom He so chooses.

We might wish for something that is not for us to wish for given our lack of spiritual knowledge and/or revelation. But still we may, no matter our spiritual knowledge, before God, as good-hearted people, hope for something or someone and feel or think that we are correct in doing so. There is no sin in wishing, when before God one's hope is well meant. But the wish for God's mercy is more effective in the life of a person when he is alive than when he is already gone.

If Onesiphorus was already dead, for sure the apostle would have said something about his death, as he made mention of the other companions living him and that sort of thing. But Paul said those words out of the gratitude of his heart, asking God for mercy upon not only Onesiphorus's life (soul) but also the lives of his family members. Paul knew that in Onesiphorus's heart was a list of things he had done for Paul while Paul was in prison in Rome and when he served him before in Ephesus.

In our Christian lives, we must plead to God for mercy in anticipation of any soul in this world who would be saved, for when that day comes. We should do this for anyone we choose to leave within God's merciful protection in and by His Spirit.

To say that Paul was pleading to God for mercy upon the already dead Onesiphorus, or any other dead person, is a wrong interpretation of this passage of scripture. For the Christians who are not of one mind and do not understand things the same way in God's Spirit, they read the Word the way they want. That is why everybody is right and wrong, because there is an absence of one understanding, a lack of spiritual unity, and an absence of revelation.

The Catholic doctrine essentially created a new Christian faith by twisting the gospel and interpreting it according to convenience or misunderstanding, including idolatry so that the people of different pagan beliefs would be attracted to it, as if the real gospel of Christ wasn't enough.

Satan took not a single break from creating his own deceptive gospel, the first iteration of which was Catholicism, which is a very convincing doctrine for the people who Satan knows will never find themselves in need of revelations from God. Nevertheless, no one can accuse the heart of any believer, in their denominational doctrines, of how wrong or right one believes and has faith in the Almighty. The spirit of revelation is always a need, teaching a person to differentiate the deceiving truth of Satan, even when that truth makes use of interpretations of God's Word and God Himself.

One of these deceiving truths is the Catholic idea that there is a person to whom believers may come who will "represent" God on earth and intercede on their behalf.

We could say that nothing is wrong with that. But when people start using the names Holy Father and Your Holiness to describe the church leaders who will help them in their spiritual need, this goes against the teaching of the Lord. Unless the heart of the spiritual leader is free of the intention to take for himself what is prohibited, he will not allow himself to be referred to by such terms. What is in man's heart is unknown to us, but known to its Creator.

The Romans, in proposing their new religion, left the Pharisees free to practice Judaism and to think as they liked, teaching and believing in the law of Moses. According to their rabbinical interpretations, the law as written in the Talmud was to be the guiding light for their faith, with an open road to practice their way of life according to their understanding of the law.

The Romans did not disclose to the Pharisees that in the

future, the Christians would publicly accuse the Jews of killing the Savior of the world, something that up to this day people of the Jewish faith deny. And that is the truth. They did not kill Jesus with their hands; their loud voices were what not only cursed them before God, but also threatened Pilate if he were to fail to deliver their brand of justice to Jesus.

The Jewish leaders accepted the idea of this new religion presented by the Romans because then the world would not be reminded of what they did to the Son of God, the Messiah they rejected. The leaders of this new Christian faith would refrain from reminding the people that the Jews were the ones who had pushed for the Savior to be executed, which was agreed to for the future peaceful coexistence of the two religions, so Christians could preach and testify freely of the gospel of salvation of Jesus. That is why after the agreement about the preaching of the gospel, more than a few truths, not of the whole Jewish nation, but about the spiritual leaders of the House of Israel, were forgotten. Even today, they are not mentioned because of the accepted spirit of conformism and fear.

What exists today is a "gospel of political correctness," from which the real fact of spiritual warfare has all but disappeared, in favor of a half-true interpretation of the Word of God. Perhaps certain facets of Zionism have infiltrated the gospel to make it more palatable for the future preaching of so-called evangelicals.

There are many preachers and teachers who, according to their own gospel, misunderstand, ignore, or are blind to the spiritual truth of the gospel of Jesus, which is the gospel of truth. This truth that is like a sword against all the hypocrites in high places where it is not the Spirit of God in charge of the truth, but a man—a man who is careful of what he is saying when he speaks so that no modern Pharisees, scribes, or Sadducees of any religious or secular institution, establishment, or foundation will be offended by it, as they practice, according to their own "righteous conscience," an unacknowledged double standard policy.

How is it that the Christians of this world, more than anyone else, are unable to understand the real spiritual meaning of the apostle Paul's statement about the struggle, fight, or battle being against the spirits of this world and not against flesh and blood?

Before and during the time when Christians were persecuted in the Roman Empire, the fighting spirit of Christ in the life of His children was different. But after the Roman agreement, we entered a different world, one where that same fighting spirit had gotten weak, where the enemy of our souls became more hideous. Because of this, if we think that the time after the agreement was bad, we should know that today is worse.

Today, God's children do not fully understand what it is to train in the spiritual ring of the gospel and get strong in the Spirit so that God may fight His fight through their faith. Instead, they get involved in the philosophical interpretation of the gospel.

It is imperative to understand that any wrong a man commits under any pretext, any wrong that he knows of, admits to, excuses himself for, rejects, blames someone else for, or accuses someone else for, will negatively affect his future. It is clear that such a person has fallen under satanic control, but still he will deny his guilt. Such a person, in his own "spirituality," believes that he is right and rejects any notion of future judgment or negative consequences.

And finally, the Romans thought that they would be free of any wrongdoing by maintaining their practice of worshipping idols. They were proud to have brought peace with the creation of the first religion, hoping that it would create an understanding among people of different beliefs and a chance to believe in one invisible God.

With the agreement that has lasted up to the present day, a

partnership was forged between the new Roman Catholic Church, with its own understanding of the gospel, and the Jewish faith, with its doctrine based on the interpretation of the law of Moses as written in the Talmud.

It was a partnership where different understandings of historical accounts would no longer give rise to criticism or misunderstanding of each other, as the Romans and the Jews have never had any real heavy consequences for their interrelation. Later on in the history between the Jews and the Romans, there were some bloody encounters where they fought each other for different rights, beliefs, and ideals.

Two different prideful systems were united for the common good of each. And the Christians accepted the Roman–Jewish union and the new so-called religious gospel without having had a say. But they were happy about it because they had been waiting for peace for three hundred years after Jesus died.

This story of the creation of the Roman Catholic Church was derived from a few sources, namely, historical documents filled with imprecise information, and theories proposed by academics, historians, and religious people. But where the documents are short on details or doubtful in terms of being historical truth, researchers have made guesses, which, at the end, won't make any difference for the future of the spiritual well-being of humanity.

There is not only one document or only one source of historical information about the creation of the Roman Catholic Church. For anyone interested in the subject, there is public information at almost any level that is easy to find, that is, if the original historical documents can't be found. Opinions will always be different, even when witnesses stand at the same time and the same place in the midst of developing future history.

Say that the number six is painted on the floor and there is a person standing at each end of it. One of those people will see a six, but the other will see a nine. From their points of view, according to where each is standing, both are right in their understanding of what numeral it is, and because of that, their accounts of the same story may not include the same facts. It is well-known that when a glass of water is half full, a person may see that same glass as half empty. That is the way men see the things of this world, according to their own beliefs, deductions, understandings, or conveniences. And to determine if that six or nine is a six or nine, or the glass of water was already filled and someone drank from it, or it was not filled yet, the witnesses will have to give honest reports. And the truth for the secular world is different, such as in religion or politics. In this secular world, only an honest heart can tell the truth, whether he knows what has happened or not.

But a man may intend, for reasons known only to him, to present his truth in a different format—not a complete lie, but also not the whole truth. This is what people with decision-making power at all levels of life have been doing since ancient times.

For everything that is unknown or secret, the Spirit is the One who can declare by way of revelation the things a man needs to know, because it is the Spirit who knows the truth, and the truth is God Himself. This will happen if the intentions of a man's heart are oriented toward something greater than just pleasing his own ego.

The apostles and many other Christian pioneers in other parts of the world have laid their lives on the line for their beliefs, with the real spiritual goal of their faith being to reach eternal life. At the beginning of any campaign, one takes a calculated risk, knowing there is always a price to pay. Whether in the political world, in wartime, or during some religious situation, or any other, people have laid down their lives to accomplish an ideal.

Not knowing what God was doing at that time when Christians were persecuted and killed by the Romans, we have to assume that the church leaders had to make choices given the difficult time they were undergoing, even when their spiritual connection with God was strong. It was their hope to bring peace and safety to the saints, and they may have thought this Roman action was a sign or an answer from God to their prayers. They didn't stop to think, analyze, or pray for an affirming answer to know for sure if the peace agreement was the answer to their prayers and was really in the will of God.

They never thought or imagined that maybe, just maybe, another unnoticeable spirit was interfering in their emotions, causing them to wish for a peaceful life. Maybe, just maybe, as humans they had wished in their hearts so much for a peaceful life that after three hundred years of persecution and killing, they may have forgotten to react accordingly, that is, spiritually, to get some revelation from God to take the right steps, waiting a little longer for an answer.

The task that they had ahead of them wasn't easy at all. The mix of feelings about their responsibilities and the pressure of doing the right thing created a moment of true uncertainty. Obviously, they were always thinking about God and waiting for His help, wishing for an end to the long-standing terror hanging over their lives. After all, right or wrong, they were people, and their human feelings and emotions may have taken over their spiritual sensibility, instead of hearing the right answer directly from God's Spirit. We may never know exactly what was going on in their hearts and minds.

Again, not knowing what God's plans were, and not having lived in those days as participants or witnesses, we take what we can get from history and apply our own deductions or imaginings to the events of their lives.

For us, imagination and deduction is all we have to try to stand in their shoes. This is because we do not have on hand precise historical information about God's revelation, which otherwise would allow us to understand what these people decided to do under such obligation, pressure, and stress for a better future. There is a chance that God, being God, was testing His people, and the time came when not the sheep but the shepherds failed.

What would have happened if the leaders of the church hadn't accepted the Romans' conditions for a peaceful life? We'll never know the answer to that question. Perhaps, just as people did back then, today we need more patience in God, knowing that He is never late or early in His promises. If the persecuted Christians had practiced patience, then today not only Christianity, but also the whole world, might be different. Maybe nothing of the kind ever happened, and the leaders of the church, after Emperor Constantine and Licinius legalized Christianity, lowered their spiritual guard. Or maybe none of the leaders of the church remembered the promises left by the Lord for their own defense and protection, just like Christians throughout all generations who were slapped and slapped again by evil because of their unguarded spiritual lives, up to the twenty-first century.

Many say that what is currently happening in this world is the will of God. It is not *in* the will of God, but God is allowing what is happening because of people's ignorance and their lack of interest in and rebellious attitude toward Him in terms of their own spiritual future. There are two types of God's will, the first being perfect, the second being permissive. The first type has no need of grace and mercy, but the second type does, as it is what He will use on Judgment Day.

The apostle Paul wrote, "Oh, the depth of the riches both of the wisdom and knowledge of God! How unsearchable are His judgments and His ways past finding out! For who has known the mind of the Lord? Or who has become His counselor? Or who has first given to Him and it shall be repaid to Him?" (Romans 11:33–35).

But what happened has happened, and there is nothing that we can undo. God, guiding His people through His Spirit, knew that they would endure even the loss of their lives. But sometimes, a moment of spiritual disconnection, because of our human feelings, desires, or emotions, can leave us one second short of seeing God's will done in our lives, leaving an open space for the unnoticed, uglier evil spirit to usurp our decision by taking advantage of our emotions and/or doubts.

Sometimes we think that the step we are about to take is the right one, but that type of thinking may cause us to fall short of taking the real right step. If only we allow ourselves to consider and be absolutely sure of our next step, then in our spiritual knowledge we will receive the answer in revelation for our secular and spiritual needs. And the answer to any question or request before God is in our faith, in our surrendering to Him, and trusting and believing in the Lord's promises, then putting them into practice according to the wishes of our hearts.

The evil one is in a fight with our thoughts, feelings, emotions, and desires. In short, he is trying to control our hearts and minds, removing any possible way for us to use our common sense, completely neutralizing our reasoning.

Many times when the moment to make a decision arrives, evil spirits may intervene, especially when we may think we are about to take the correct spiritual step at a crucial moment. That is the moment when we have to be more spiritually aware, knowledgeable of God's warnings, and consciously honest about our faith, declaring that God is the One who is in control, even if our hearts and souls are troubled. Just like Abraham when he raised his hand with the knife to sacrifice his son to God. The precise moment when he was about to lower his hand and plunge the knife into Isaac's body, the angel stopped him.

Abraham knew in his troubled heart that he had a profound faith in his Creator. If God told him to do something, then God was in control of the situation. And because of his faith in Him, he never lost hope in the future outcome, whatever it was to be. And when the angel stayed his hand, Abraham understood that God has the power to do something different for His own glory even amid our worried but faithful hearts.

That second between knowing the will of God and carrying it out is the most important moment in a Christian's life for the will of God to be planted, revealed, or reworked. That second of faith relies on unconditional trust based in faith and an unconditional surrender to God. That trust and belief through our faith requires a complete giving up of our human senses, where we refuse to allow the emotions to battle in our hearts to trigger our thoughts of insecurity, even when our hearts are weary to death.

To rephrase, the key to doing His will in times of trial, when our hearts and souls are trembling, is to fight our senses and emotions, even if such a thing seems impossible.

If we feel fear and have the sense that it is inevitable that something is wrong, that is the moment when we need to be faithful and remember His promises. Then, even if things don't go as expected, we will be at peace with the outcome. Because the Lord says, "And the Lord, he it is that doth go before thee; he will be with thee, he will not fail thee, neither forsake thee: fear not, neither be dismayed" (Deuteronomy 31:8).

This means that during an unfavorable moment in our lives in the flesh, our spiritual lives are secure by way of His promise and the strength of our faith. And the power of His miracle working, according to His will, does not always end with the death of His child.

It's not a wish, intuition, desire, calculated risk, or any other human feeling, but a spiritual knowledge and a higher understanding through faith that God will resolve the case when one trusts God. One must be totally convicted with belief and trust in the Almighty in any situation, including those situations where the believer's life is threatened. We must be edified by the apostle Paul being in prison and writing to the church, telling them that he had almost lost hope in regards to the conservation of his life, trusting to the last in the Lord.

"For we would not, brethren, have you ignored our trouble which came to us in Asia, that we were pressed out of measure, above strength, insomuch that we despaired even of life. But we had the sentence of death in ourselves, that we should not trust in ourselves, but in God which raiseth the death" (2 Corinthians 1:8–9).

That awareness is the knowledge that comes from surrendering in faith, belief, and complete trust, knowing that one will be delivered into the hands of the Almighty according to His will for one's life, no matter the outcome. This is a "secret" that is well advertised but hardly understood or accepted.

In our faith in God, we are ready to physically die. But when we have to wait for a change, when we hope for a miraculous intervention at the needed time, we are often short on patience. We must trust Him and leave matters in His hands, believing in His promise to help us. And that unconditional trust in His promises is the key to receive the knowledge we are given ahead of time by the Spirit.

Faith is our challenge, and it is in that faith—residing not in our heads, but in our hearts—where victory lies. The Lord will never fail us in His promises if we have faith. He said, "According to your faith be it unto you" (Matthew 9:29). Jesus said those words when the two blind men came to Him believing that He could heal them. In another instance, that kind of belief and trust is what amazed the Lord of the centurion's faith when he came to Him asking to heal his servant. The story is in Matthew 8:5–13. There are other stories of miracles produced by a believing faith.

The question is whether the children of God today, according to their belief and faith, are hearing the voice of the Lord through His Spirit, fulfilling their needs, saying to them, as He said to the centurion, "Go thy way; and as thou hast believed, so be it done unto thee" (Matthew 8:13). Does that kind of belief and faith rest in people's hope, instead of their hearts? Or is it like waiting for a miracle in the relaxing horizon?

CHAPTER 23

Historians in their writings have left us a number of invaluable documents recording events that they lived through, witnessed, or heard about from someone else. Whether their stories are correct or not in the way they are presented is another topic. The truth is that any story about history is written from two perspectives, the first being truthful, or at least trying to be, and the second being untruthful, hiding something, hoping to bury some compromising information because of guilt or because there is not enough information about the circumstances for the historian to be impartial. That is why many times the historical truth is not accepted as fully accurate.

What is left for future generations is the task of finding the real truth according to their own understanding, having the so-called historical facts. Such findings, one way or another, will fall short of the truth. Suppositions, opinions, and proof are things that can go either way in terms of theological or philosophical interpretation.

It is the good intention of most historians, those who have nothing to hide, to tell the truth about what happened today, hundreds, or thousands of years past. And people being people, whether today or thousands of years ago, in their hearts, can go any way with their feelings, beliefs, and emotions—even in their own understanding of what truth is.

Still, the human heart remains full of pride, hate, greed, selfishness, incrimination, stubbornness, lies, cunning, and excuses, all presents from the devil. Because of this, intentions often end up being unclear. One may have good intentions to do good, or "good" intentions to cover evil. Or one may consider that it is "necessary" to do evil to bring about something "good." People who have such intentions are twisters of the truth, like Satan when using the serpent in the Garden of Eden to approach Eve.

Yet again, sometimes circumstances in people's lives are taken wrong by others, whether intentionally or because of misinterpretation. Also, as was said before, we mustn't forget that someone could be purposely twisting the so-called truth, for some reason unbeknown to us. In any case, what historians forget to do is to touch upon the spiritual side of the story while it is fresh, at least according to their own spiritual understanding at the moment—if at that moment the spirit of truth is present in the person's heart.

One way of finding and understanding the truth is through the human intellect. Another way is through the revelation of God to our spirits. Without discrediting or having doubts about authenticity or intentions, and depending on who wrote it, we can assume that there is possibly undeclared truth, as with any other historical document, because of reasons of guilt, future judgment, punishment, or curse.

Any written secular or religious history by any author does not have the final say and is not considered the only truth. On the contrary, to the inquisitive intellect, even with its limitations, history is a field providing one with more opportunities to know the past, the present, and maybe the future consequences.

In the spiritual world, there is only one way, and this is not through secular knowledge but through spiritual revelation. Because the spiritual person, being one in Jesus, has one mind and one spirit, in that spirit the person understands everything that is intellectual to a greater degree because the person, as the Word says, has the mind of the Lord for the things he or she needs to know.

The Word of God says, "But he that is spiritual judgeth all things, yet he himself is judged by no man. For who hath known the mind of the Lord, that he may instruct him? But we have the mind of Christ" (1 Corinthians 2:15–16). When historians, theologians, and knowledgeable people of different spiritual fields with master's degrees are trying to find the evasive historical truth and, more than anything, the spiritual side of it without the help of the Spirit, they always disagree.

This doesn't mean that to know the past in a secular or intellectual way is wrong. It is wrong when we mix salt water with fresh, as then it becomes a deduction or guess about spirituality in a very intellectual, secular, philosophical world.

To understand people of past generations is to understand that they were no different in their hearts' intentions from present-day people. And because people do not change in their nature, they are the same today as they were thousands of years ago. To understand Christians of all denominations, we have to look at circumstances since the beginning of Christianity.

From the beginning of time, according to the Word of God, the only people who knew God, besides Abraham and his family, were God's chosen people, the Jews. The rest of the people of the world were pagans, no matter how advanced their civilization or culture. The teaching of the law and the belief in God for the Jewish people was only for them, not for other people, unless someone was interested and asked, because the Jews considered themselves chosen, pure, and unique—a spirit that still exists today in some nations.

After the coming of Christ, there were two kinds of Jews, the ones who followed the law of Moses and the ones who converted to Christianity. The first group, hated or disliked then, remain hated and disliked up to this day.

In reality there are three kinds of Jews. The third type, as the Bible says, call themselves Jews but are not Jews. Who are these people? The ones who believe in the law, or people of another faith who became believers in the Jewish law? Are they not Jews in the flesh or in the spirit, or both?

Before Christ, paganism and Judaism were the only forms of adoration of gods or God. No people of any nation had the special task of proclaiming their religious beliefs as a way of life as Christians would have in the future with the coming of Jesus.

Obviously, people from every one of those religious or pagan cults were waiting for whatever hopes or expectations they placed in their beliefs for this lifetime or the afterlife to come true. But it was a time of change when Jesus came to this world. His presence, His teachings, and His deeds became a sword, separating the prideful way of believing in gods and the humble way of believing in the only God.

It was a time in which the never before heard truth about man's inner being began the process of uncovering his own neutralized spiritual and ignorant conscience, opening his eyes to the truth of this unknown way that would shine light upon the road of salvation, a way that would open people's eyes and allow their hearts to see Satan's hidden intentions, now brought into the open.

Christ's Truth shows the conscience who man really is in the eyes of God and how much evil man harbors in his lifeless soul and hypocritical, self-righteous heart. And with this revelation came a chance for freedom for those who had the wrong spirit, such as the Pharisees, who in their spiritual blindness kept not only themselves but also their people in the spiritual slavery of ignorance with no future of spiritual freedom.

The Pharisees and others didn't believe in or accept the revival and salvation of their own souls. Rejecting the Truth, they rejected the opportunity to walk in the way of knowledge, holding on to the hand of the One who would take them on a free road to heaven. But they chose, for their own convenience, to keep believing in letter of the law, not the spirit, while other Jewish people saw the Light of the gospel, believing in Jesus and accepting salvation from their awaited Messiah.

Jesus in His native land became for the religious leaders of the Jewish nation a revolutionary troublemaker reformist type who did not see eye to eye with the religious oligarchy or condone their rules for a truly open spiritual life of freedom.

To their disappointment, He wasn't the Messiah they thought would free them politically from Roman rule and oppression. They had expected not the spiritual Messiah, but a political messianic leader. They did not see the promises of God come true through their prophets about the spiritual Savior of the people of Israel. And not only that, but because of the gospel of Jesus, people were walking away from the religious way of life in which the Pharisees and other leaders were keeping them.

The purpose of the Pharisees' well-established control over people's lives was to keep the people spiritually ignorant for the Pharisees' own purposes and convenience. That same control leading to spiritual ignorance is still in existence today and is known by God to exist in the lives of some leaders of different Christian denominations, leaders who are keeping their flocks ignorant through the preaching of wealth, through political self-preference, and through the practice of creating a Zionist state. This is no different from any other superficial spiritual teachings of "God's truth," where the people with their amens are ignorant of the Word of God and the intended spiritual meaning of its message.

Some of these leaders retain their "spiritual" way of life and their power in their secular private lives. Jesus said: "By their fruits you will know them." They get upset when they are asked about their wealth because they don't have the peace of mind or the spirit to tell the truth, never mind a working conscience. All the while, they keep their followers in spiritual ignorance, even when they know from memory the Bible from cover to cover, which is knowing the letter, but not the Spirit who reveals His Word.

If God is the one blessing you in your wealth, you don't have to be afraid; He knows how to defend His blessings over your life. You have nothing to hide and no frightening questions to answer. Remember, Satan, through his followers, digs into the lives of Christian spiritual leaders. But don't forget that honest people do the same thing with these so-called "honest" Christians leaders, who are the ones getting mad about the digging into their finances and lifestyles.

The honest ones will say, "Here, everything is on the table to be seen"—even when they have the right to privacy. The other, "honest" ones will say, "My finances or wealth, and my lifestyle, is not your business."

Big difference in their reactions. One is trusting in God, and the other is afraid to be discovered. If any person is honest in his heart before the Almighty, then he has nothing to hide and nothing to be worried about, even if he is questioned by God or Satan.

Because of Jesus, the Pharisees began slowly losing that life of self-indulgence, together with their power, which made them a very angry bunch.

Today, at the beginning of the twenty-first century, something like this is happening in the secular political world, particularly in the United States and Great Britain. Those long-lived democratic systems of government have brainwashed their citizens, who are slowly beginning to understand that they have been lied to and used by the ones who, slowly but surely, have decreased their rights. The established new laws to control the banking and financial systems are creating an impoverished future for their countrymen, because of the greed of those in power.

Democracy is unnoticeably bringing about an end to freedom. This action is very much spiritual, but people do not see it as such because they are unable to switch on the lights of their natural minds to allow themselves to see what is secular and what is spiritual. It's as if they don't understand that at the end both will be judged spiritually.

Democracy is an evil system that, because of the brainwashing, is slowly causing patriotism and incorrect, political interpretations of gospel to overtake the spiritual lives of sincere believers.

Believers are changing their faith by believing more in their democracy and the Star Spangled Banner or, in Great Britain, the queen and the Union Jack. In the name of "democracy" and wanting to live free, believers are rejecting others' truth about the deceptive need for patriotism preached by their own political leaders and many so-called Christian leaders.

A spirit of divisiveness is slowly but surely taking over Christian countries by way of a system not much different from that of the Pharisees, one that keeps the people believing they must show patriotism as a matter of law, so those representatives, in the name of a secure nation, may retain their own personal control and wealth. This is happening not only in individual nations but also worldwide, through people's naiveté or ignorance and their acceptance of putting their lives in harm's way for so-called democracy or any other ideal or freedom, for the interest of a few.

In short, this belief in patriotism that many Christians have is deceptive in that such Christians are not seeing the spiritual side, unaware that it is a lie told by Satan and being repeated by some of his followers.

The religious way of life of the Jews made the Pharisees and others in the higher ranks of the religious leadership a club of very rich and privileged oligarchs—untouchable members of society. Maybe it was at that time when the deep state was born, as we know it today. The elite oligarchs, who are unknown to the common people, declare themselves to be the guardians and "salvation" of their nations, while merely making mention of God.

The fact is that it isn't only the self-righteous "holy representatives" of God, but also politicians, who were and are in the ring of "We are right, you are wrong." In the name of so-called unity, whether political or religious, if a person should offer any criticism, he or she becomes the enemy, something that has been happening through the centuries and up to this day. It has led to the establishment of one strict, yet invisible law against heresy that in the future will increase more insecurity of any individuals who dare to speak negatively of the system or its members. In the time of the Pharisees, any person who even had a thought of such insolence was categorized as a heretic and kicked out of the temple. In people's minds at that time, if they were kicked out of the temple, then God wouldn't be in their lives. They believed they'd be lost souls.

Some people were afraid of the Pharisees, or maybe they were just humble believers who were following everything that the Pharisees and scribes were telling them. It is a similar situation today. People have given up on trying to discern what is true and what is not in what comes from the mouths of their leaders. But the cronies, following not the teaching but the example of the Pharisees in their way of life, were not worried about consequences.

Jesus told the people about the Pharisees' hypocritical life of double standards: "All therefore whatsoever they bid you observe, that observe and do; but do not ye after their works: for they say and do not" (Matthew 23:3). Jesus helped them to understand that the day would come when the Pharisees would have to pay for everything that they had done wrong. Obviously those leaders never believed in those consequences. Nor did their friends.

Just like today, citizens of the United States are overwhelmed by the rules and regulations they have to follow, while those who are to set an example of obedience to the law are breaking laws every minute of every day. In the religion of politics, the people are prevented from knowing the ins and outs of their leaders' internal dealing among themselves. This is because politicians, even when they are corrupt or lying to other people, consider their personal business arrangements to be matters of national security and, therefore, secret. And when they speak their "truth" to the people, they do so with the same deceiving spirit that afflicts most world leaders.

Contrary to this is God's "political" gospel, where the believer, in his faith, is permitted to know in detail, and in advance, God's business so that he may do the best for himself and for God's glory. And according to His promises, while working for the heavenly "country," one will never be lied to or cheated, because God has nothing to hide from His "citizens."

Jesus said, "Woe unto you, scribes and Pharisees, hypocrites! For ye compass sea and land to make one proselyte, and when he is made, ye make him twofold more the child of hell then yourselves" (Matthew 3:15). Ironically, these words can be applied to the makers of foreign policy of the United States, Great Britain, and other democratic European countries. A victory for a corrupt politician, leads to the corruption of "new friends," for who their democracy promises a great future, to the point that those new friends trade their countries and people for the temporary wealth of this world, be it an another politician, influential businessman, human rights activist, dictator, freedom fighter, or any other Judas type. Satan knows how to work.

This statement may sound very political, but it is also the wrong spiritual "gospel" with very different ending consequences.

So if a true believer of Christ looks at this as simply a political statement, without seeing the spiritual side of it, then he or she is not understanding what Jesus said to the Pharisees, scribes, and Sadducees in the temple.

We'll never know what God knows, but we can guess by looking at what is happening in the countries where the United States or Great Britain have a strong foothold for purposes of their own national interest. Their true intentions are hidden behind "democratic" words of empty promises for the "well-being" of whatever nation is being infiltrated.

Today there are Sadducees in spirit who are the same as their ancestors were in the past. That is why it is nearly impossible for people today, according to their constitutional rights, to rid their government of fakers of the truth.

People's rights exist only in words, and anyone who believes that a reformed system of voting is the solution is a dreamer. Replacing one evil with another won't change anything, because politicians' morals and principles are based in the gospel of wealth.

Such is a gospel of lies, where cheating people and killing them for purposes of satisfying greed and grabbing power is done in the name of the nation and its people. The world system is growing its roots in evil, for the conquest of the world through the New World Order or any other name, which is being created to control the nations by instituting the system of the Antichrist. And here is where Christian believers do not understand the secular connections to spiritual realities, especially all the promises left for us by the Lord, so that they could intercede according to those same promises, which are spiritual weapons of defense for the believer to use in faith.

The question is, what is stronger in the believer's life, his faith, his doubts, or something else? The Pharisees, scribes, and Sadducees had their own interpretation of the law, as written in the Talmud, to govern their secular and religious way of life. The same is happening today with the different leaders of Christianity and other religious denominations. They are working on people's consciences and emotions and teaching them nothing, so they grow up ignorant in the knowledge of the Spirit.

The religious leaders in Jesus's day were displeased about people speaking up for their own rights, like Jesus did in the temple. Today, some Christian leaders and their political friends consider themselves to be right and others to be wrong. They are all interpreting the gospel of Christ as a gospel of politics, forgetting that there is only one God, one Word, and one will.

In their confused, prideful state of mind, religious and political leaders alike ignore the spirit of truth, revelation, and unity, believing in their ideal of religion and politics, thinking of themselves as spiritually correct. In that wrong spirit is no space for doing what the Word of God requires us to do: to be of one mind and one spirit. Because even among themselves they have their own disagreements, which lately the world is coming to take notice of. This is not a spiritual union under the One and only Spirit of God for one heavenly understanding. Instead, it is coming from a different spirit, one of deceit and division, where leaders' opinions about each other seem to be pitting one "righteous" person against another, so they can destroy themselves in their own house. The same thing happened to the Israelites after Jesus's words about the future of Jerusalem and Israel itself. But this time it is the whole world that is in extreme danger.

God does not approve of denominations, because they

separate. Denominations are a present from Satan, just as the unacknowledged gospel of politics for so-called spiritual leaders who are too numb to react to the growing evil in the world. And if they can see it, they assume that nothing can be done, thinking that it is impossible for people to agree on such a task.

And they are right: for them it is impossible. But not for God. Because if His children believe and have faith, there is nothing that is impossible for the Almighty to do. The question is, where is that understanding, faith, and belief in the lives of God's children?

If God is not leading your heart, there is nothing that man can do. Even so, God won't do anything if you don't believe that it can be done or question if it is necessary. Doubt will always be present in a faith that is fading away in the lives of Christians who are unable to notice the change in their lives.

Wrongly oriented leaders and many believers are deaf to the voice of their conscience, either because their hearts are proud and arrogant or they have a lack of interest. They do not have in their lives the Spirit of God to guide them, the Spirit having been replaced by man's own understanding. With their own spirits and God's Spirit pushed into a corner and ignored, many believers think they are okay in their self-righteousness.

There was a time when God's prophets, through His Spirit, read and taught the book of the law to the people of Israel in the proper and correct way, so they could understand the will of God in their lives and His promises for their future. But man's self-confidence made him disregard the promises of the Almighty and His caution that something may go wrong if man is not alert.

God, knowing man's heart, is the reason for Jesus having said, "All that the Father giveth me shall come to me; and him that cometh to me I will in no wise cast out" (John 6:37). Is it because of the knowledge of Him that the Father has given all men without exception a gift, namely, a chance for salvation?

But for some, the Word of salvation will be like the story Jesus told the people about the farmer:

> Behold, a sower went forth to sow; and when he sowed, some seed fell by the wayside, and the fowls came and devoured them up. Some fell upon stony places, where they had not much earth: and forthwith they sprung up, because they had no deepness of earth. And when the sun was up, they were scorched, and because they had no root, they withered away. And some fell among thorns, and the thorns sprung up, and choked them. But others fell into good ground, and brought forth fruit, some an hundredth, some sixtyfold, some thirtyfold. Who hath ears to hear, let him hear. (Matthew 13:3–9)

The farmer is the Lord God Jesus. The words of the gospel are the seeds. When in His time He preached the gospel of salvation, His Words were heard by people's ears and received in their hearts, that is, the ground.

With regard to "And when he sowed, some fell by the wayside, and the fowls came and devoured them" (Matthew 13:4), we understand that people's wayside hearts are the ones which are hearing the Word of God, that is the seed of the Gospel, but they are not interested because the things of the world, that is the fowls. People's own beliefs and understandings about life are taking the first place in their heart's devouring, that is, they ignoring or rejecting the chance of salvation.

"Some fell upon stony places, where they had not much earth: and forthwith they sprung up, they were scorched, and because they had no root, they withered away." This means that other people who hear and accept the seed of the gospel receive the message of salvation at that moment, and it grows for a while in their hearts. But because of whatever good or bad circumstances they are having in their lives, distracting their attention to this world, they lose interest in the gospel, to which they were only superficially attracted. The lack of will to read the Word, a lack of interest in the gospel, and an attraction to the things of the world are much stronger in man's heart, becoming like the sun and killing the will and the interest, that is, the roots, in the things from above.

"And some fell among thorns, and the thorns sprung up and choked them." These are the people who have heard of the gospel but for some reason, such as a spirit of weakness, painful experiences, disappointments, rebellion, hate, greed, or immorality, choose not to accept the things it mentions, which in their understanding won't help or are not necessary. And all of these are the thorns that are choking their understanding of the gospel.

These are the people whose hearts are like ground with stony places and thorns—atheists, doubters, the unsanctified, the unsatisfied, the know-it-alls, the insecure, the realists, the proud, the arrogant, the ignorant, the rebellious, the self-righteous, the weak, the disrespectful—people blind to spiritual reality who are unstable in their own emotions for a lack of knowledge and faith. They are slaves to their own unstable feelings coming from an insecure or proud heart who quickly give up hope, lacking a fighting spirit when going through life's trials, with an almost nonexistent belief and faith. These are people who do not believe in God and who wish not to hear or accept a word about Him. Because they refuse to accept God's offer of salvation, one day they will be mightily surprised by the One who they never believed existed and whom they never cared about. About such people, Jesus said, to paraphrase, "If the Father doesn't bring them to Me, I cannot save them or protect them." And that is because the Father knows their rebellious hearts.

"But others fell into good ground and brought forth fruit." The people who give themselves a chance are the people whom God is helping because they have accepted the chance for and the challenge of a better future, which He has given them for their own well-being, not only in this world but also in the one promised in the heavens. These are the people whose hearts are the good soil, with the predisposition not only to accept the seed but also to understand that it needs to multiply and bring forth fruits. And for that, according to each sacrifice resulting in multiplication, God accepts them and blesses their effort. It is through the heart that one understands that without God's Life in them, which is given when one accepts the seed, they also can give life to others through their own received seed.

It is up to man to accept or reject the voice proclaiming salvation. If he accepts, he won't be cast out by Christ. God alone knows the ones who will accept the seed of salvation and the ones who won't. Everyone has an equal chance for salvation.

Jesus told this story to His disciples to describe the people of Israel who accepted Christ in their hearts and those who did not, but it is also for us Gentiles. The spirit that back then was against the heavens and humankind is the same one working today in people's lives.

A spirit of denial in man's heart that deceives and rejects common sense blinds him from understanding the possible coming tragedy. Jesus warned the Pharisees of this type of heart and its consequences on their own future and the future of Jerusalem and Israel.

Among the leaders of the Pharisees, scribes, and Sadducees, they had no intention of freeing people from spiritual bondage. On the contrary, the people were told that to please God, they would have to live lives of sacrifice for their sins. Not only did they brainwash their own people, but also, because of their pride and blindness in rejecting the will of God, God allowed Satan to brainwash the leaders too for hardening their hearts to the truth of God.

That is why Jesus told people that if they wanted to know God in their lives, they had the freedom to do so in Him and not through the law. The prophecies came to a reality when they were fulfilled by His presence as the promised Messiah.

That was a chance in their lives to have the freedom to decide something for themselves, and they did so through self-determination in recognition of their sin, then through repentance and faith, believing in Jesus. This meant they were not obligated to do so according to the rule of law.

I wonder if Jesus saw the same spirit of deceit of those scribes, Pharisees, and Sadducees in the future deep state governments of the United States, Great Britain, and many other countries to their own people.

Why just the Anglo-Saxon world? No other nations in the Western world, since King James of England authorized the translation of the Bible in the year 1611, have been given the privilege to spread the gospel for future generations according to God's plan.

First it happened throughout the West European Isles. Then, perhaps the most important part of God's plan was to bring the gospel to the Americas through the pilgrims, to completely cover the future generations of the world.

Maybe the United States will be the last nation where God will use His people to spread His Word to the ends of the earth. No other nation has spread the gospel as His children in the United States have done in the twentieth century. And who can say that the Azusa Street Revivals in 1906 in the city of Los Angeles were not a spiritual example of unity, where the Spirit of God was working in the lives of those who humbled themselves before the Lord, baptizing people with the Holy Ghost in the speaking of tongues. Even though some have maliciously criticized this movement, it is true that the faith of God's children with His Spirit in their lives got even stronger in terms of power to perform miracles. It was a Pentecostal movement that affected the whole world like never before.

God's Anglo-Saxon children have let another gospel take place of Christ's gospel in their homeland. A similar spiritual situation developed in the first seven churches in Asia. Some of these have fallen under the same evil spell of pride, covering their lives with a secular spirit of arrogance, because they sought financial growth and considered themselves to be intellectually exceptional, instead of seeking God's blessings and His knowledge. Maybe there were other reasons. Satan never stays still; he will always try to divert the children of God from the right path. That is why we need to be spiritually alert. This is the reason the Word of God gives us a warning.

It is hard today to understand where God's blessings begin and end in the secular and spiritual lives of His Anglo-Saxon children, just as it is hard to know when self-sufficiency and a sense of exceptionalism started to replace God's blessings. Or does it make no difference?

These children of God have blinded themselves by believing wrong things and having no humility, but proud hearts, before God. The believers of Anglo-Saxon nations fail to understand that the problems in in their lives are not caused by God but are allowed by Him because of their rebellious hearts and their pride, self-sufficiency, and arrogance, all of which exist in the lives of leaders and congregants alike, which is the consequence of lowering their spiritual guard. They believe more in themselves, the values of their political religious system, their moral self-righteousness, and their material wealth. The same spirit that was with the Pharisees is still around in their descendants.

CHAPTER 24

When the powerful people of any so-called idealistic society that never knew any alterations to its sense of order begin to notice that something is changing in a system so closely and jealously guarded, obviously the alarm will sound very loud. In a so-called democratic society, which can also consist of a dictatorial regime within a democratic system, which also can exist under any other name too, anyone trying to promote anything new is a target of distrust. More than anything, powerful people seek not to lose their control or their wealth.

Any kind of human intention to help and do good for others who are in need is disappearing from all people in positions of power across the world. Unfortunately, man is under the law of sin, so any intention in a man's life to do good could be short-lived. But for people in politics, business, and mainly religion, they see a chance to manipulate others by pretending to perform "benevolent" acts while pursuing their own self-interests. And that is something that people commonly ignore or don't care to know more about. The doctrine of any religion, whether the faithful are in politics or business, presents the religion's established rules and regulations as law for the people to follow in their spiritual or secular lives, not knowing that these "spiritual rules" cannot apply or exist in the real spiritual freedom of a conscious heart before God.

The apostle Paul wrote, "All things are lawful for me, but all things are not expedient: all things are lawful for me, but all things edify not"

(1 Corinthians 10:23). Rules and regulations are established by man to create his own system of freedom under the law, whether in religion, politics, or any other case. But the spiritual freedom made possible in God's Spirit follows no law. The devil has played a fine evil trick to cover people's secular and religious lives with an aura of hypocritical self-righteousness that many of them don't realize they have because of their ignorance of spiritual revelation and the Word of God.

On the other hand, only God knows who has a humble and sincere heart before Him, whether the person is religious or spiritual, ignorant or knowledgeable. People who do not know the real life made possible by Christ through faith and the power of the Spirit working in people's lives are wrong when they choose to trust man or themselves.

In this secular world, man can believe in man but not trust him, because sooner or later, he will betray that trust or lose it for reasons beyond his control. When such a thing happens, very unpleasant, if not tragic, consequences may materialize in the life of the one whom we chose to trust. A person may never know the questionable intentions in the heart and mind of the one who is trusted. It is for this reason—a change in intentions and perhaps uncontrollable circumstances in a man's life—that God does not want us to put our lives in the hands of people about whom we are uncertain.

"That saith the Lord, 'Cursed be the man that trusteth in man, and maketh flesh his arm, and whose heart departeth from the Lord'" (Jeremiah 17:5). This means that God is more worried about your soul than about your flesh. In your confidence and trust in man, you may lose not only your life in the flesh but also your soul, even if you sincerely believe and trust in someone in the spirit of his religion.

Spirituality is completely another reality, and therefore it is not reined in by rules, rituals, and perhaps obligations. It is reached by having a spiritual understanding of the Word, which brings freedom and is where trust is in God through faith, and where through that faith, belief is always rewarded by God Himself for the one who submits to His will and His wisdom.

The apostle James says, "Pure and undefiled religion before God and the Father is this: to visit the fatherless and widows in their affliction, and to keep himself unspotted from the world" (James 1:27). This means you should free your heart of any wrong intentions and act humanely at all times, having no moral blemish or blemished conscience. Most, if not all people consider themselves as having a clear conscience, but in reality, they don't even think of their conscience when they are helping someone.

James said nothing about spirituality. Why? Because even an atheist, who thinks himself to be correct and righteous, has the same ability to help another being in need as the everyday religious believer or spiritual person. You don't have to be spiritual to help another person; it comes naturally. As for the keeping of one's conscience unspotted, many of those who have a troubled conscience may decide to ignore it, thinking that everything is fine.

Unfortunately, too few religious leaders and politicians allow their consciences to work, and among those of them who do, it is a rare event. People with power have an ever greater motive to silence the conscience. But spirituality presents you with a different perspective, not what you think of yourself, but what God is saying you are. That best version of yourself is something you have to fight for.

Religiousness is not spirituality, but a set of rules for people who have accepted the wrong teaching to follow, rules upheld by those who have twisted the gospel to make it sound spiritual, as if to bring people to God. It may sound simple, but if one is honest, has a clear conscience, has good intentions, and has a curious heart, then he or she will be able to tell the difference between religiousness and spirituality with God's help, if he or she seeks Him.

Neither the Pharisees nor their close friends had a clear conscience or a good-intentioned heart. Because the same evil spirit that had used them to kill Jesus, that is, Satan, was still in control of their lives. And most of them never had any decency or honesty to begin with. The Pharisees hated Jesus for opening people's eyes to the way of salvation. In a way, Jesus was taking away their profits by challenging the Jewish practice of making sacrifices. And that was not what the Pharisees had expected of Him.

To make their sacrifices, people would come from many miles around. There was a great deal of money coming into Jerusalem from those sacrificed animals, as the owners donated money to the high priest to perform the sacrificial ritual and say the blessing in the temple.

Those who brought no animal to offer had to buy animals from the Pharisees. In addition to the tithes and the regular offerings of gold and silver to the temple, the amount of money from these sales was astronomical. So when Jesus explained to the common people that salvation of sin was through Him, not through rituals or sacrifices, they accepted His words and began to follow His way. Because of this, fewer and fewer people were coming to make sacrifices and offerings to God in the temple.

The Jewish leadership at the beginning were jealous, and then became really mad, upon seeing that hundreds and, later, thousands of people were following Jesus. Simultaneously, they noticed over time that there were fewer and fewer offerings made at the temple. This was because the new Christians took it as their task to spread the gospel and to help their brothers in need. They put into practice the Jewish system of tithing, but for them it was understood as an offering in gratitude to God for His blessings in their new lives in Christ and not as an obligatory sum they had to pay for their sins.

The Pharisees had no love for Jesus at the beginning, but when He began telling them what they were, knowing their hearts and thoughts, in front of their own people, saying that they had kept the people as sheep all their lives, the Pharisees really hated His guts. Obviously they were talking not about money but were accusing Jesus of breaking the laws about the Sabbath, on top of any other accusation they could think of.

Jesus, making short quips on a number of different occasions, told the people to be careful of the scribes and Pharisees and their teachings. But there came a day when He was teaching in the temple and all the Pharisees, scribes, and Sadducees were there. That day the temple was packed. After reading from the book of the law, Jesus looked at all the people present and, pointing, said to them, "For I say unto you, that except your righteousness shall exceed the righteousness of the scribes and Pharisees, ye shal in no case enter into the kingdom of heaven" (Matthew 5:20).

People were shocked and amazed by the way He spoke. Looking at each other, they whispered about the things He had said, marveling that he had challenged the scribes, Pharisees, and elders in their own temple where they taught. In the way He spoke about them, Jesus showed no sign of respect in regards to their positions or of being intimidated by any one of them; He was acting with authority and knowledge of the law, unlike the Pharisees, the scribes, or their peers.

The Pharisees knew that Jesus had come from a family of commoners with no higher education, so Him being in a lower social position and yet having the gall to lecture them was infuriating. They couldn't take the humiliation, but they couldn't say anything about it either, because deep down they knew He was telling the truth. They were not expecting anything like that and they were in shock. He had not only corrected them according to the letter of the law but also told them that they were snakes in the eyes of God and the eyes of their own people.

The Pharisees, in their great pride, neither took this well nor appreciated it. In their hearts, they declared war against the Son of God. Because of the hardness of their hearts, they wanted to see neither the truth about themselves nor the light of salvation.

From the beginning, the Pharisees covered up their double standards and their hypocrisy with religiousness, just as some religious leaders do today. Jesus was no respecter of such persons, because He knew who the Pharisees were. Not all of them were prideful and set against Jesus. They knew their leaders were doing wrong, but because they were afraid of them, they remained silent—which made them accomplices to their deeds.

The Pharisees were dictators, wolves dressed in sheep's clothing, rulers of people's conscience. Because of how they abused their high position, they were intimidating to people, so the people were intimidated by God. The Pharisees were untouchable to the common people, just like many religious leaders and politicians of today. But Jesus cared for none of them and, using the same law that they held their people accountable to, told them the truth to their faces.

Today if someone were to do what Jesus did in a government building, that person would be democratically escorted out of the building, arrested, booked, jailed, fined, marked for life, and then sent home, maybe with some bruises to remember his constitutional rights, that is, if he is lucky. Jesus wasn't.

CHAPTER 25

The expected day came. Surrounded by all the Pharisees, the scribes, the other high-ranking Jews, the common people, and His disciples, Jesus said the following:

> The scribes and the Pharisees sit in Moses's seat. All therefore whatsoever they bid you observe, that observe and do; but do not ye after their works: for they say, and do not. For they bind heavy burdens and grievous to be borne, and lay them on men's shoulders; but they themselves will not move them with one of their fingers. But all their works they do for to be seen of men: they make broad their phylacteries, and enlarge the borders of their garments, and love the uppermost rooms at feasts, and the chief seats in the synagogues, and greetings in the markets, and to be called of men, Rabbi, Rabbi. But be not ye called Rabbi: for one is your Master, even Christ; and all ye are brethren. And call no man your father upon the earth: for one is your Father, which is in heaven. Neither be ye called masters: for one is your Master, even Christ. But he that is greatest among you shall be your servant.

And whosoever shall exalt himself shall be abased; and he that shall humble himself shall be exalted. But woe unto you, scribes and Pharisees, hypocrites! for ye shut up the kingdom of heaven against men: for ye neither go in yourselves, neither suffer ye them that are entering to go in. Woe unto you, scribes and Pharisees, hypocrites! for ye devour widows' houses, and for a pretence make long prayer: therefore ye shall receive the greater damnation. Woe unto you, scribes and Pharisees, hypocrites! for ye compass sea and land to make one proselyte, and when he is made, ye make him twofold more the child of hell than yourselves. Woe unto you, ye blind guides, which say, Whosoever shall swear by the temple, it is nothing; but whosoever shall swear by the gold of the temple, he is a debtor! Ye fools and blind: for whether is greater, the gold, or the temple that sanctifieth the gold? And, Whosoever shall swear by the altar, it is nothing; but whosoever sweareth by the gift that is upon it, he is guilty. Ye fools and blind: for whether is greater, the gift, or the altar that sanctifieth the gift? Whoso therefore shall swear by the altar, sweareth by it, and by all things thereon. And whoso shall swear by the temple, sweareth by it, and by him that dwelleth therein. And he that shall swear by heaven, sweareth by the throne of God, and by him that sitteth thereon. Woe unto you, scribes and Pharisees, hypocrites! for ye pay tithe of mint and anise and cummin, and have omitted the weightier matters of the law, judgment, mercy, and faith: these ought ye to have done, and not to leave the other undone. Ye blind guides, which strain at a gnat, and swallow a camel. Woe unto you, scribes and Pharisees, hypocrites! for ye make clean the outside of the cup and of the platter, but within they are full of extortion and excess. Thou blind Pharisee, cleanse first that which is within the cup and platter, that the outside of them may be clean also. Woe unto you, scribes and Pharisees, hypocrites! for ye are like unto whited sepulchres, which indeed appear beautiful outward, but are within full of dead men's bones, and of all uncleanness. Even so ye also outwardly appear righteous unto men, but within ye are full of hypocrisy and iniquity. Woe unto you, scribes and Pharisees, hypocrites! because ye build the tombs of the prophets, and garnish the sepulchres of the righteous, and say, If we had been in the days of our fathers, we would not have been partakers with them in the blood of the prophets. Wherefore ye be witnesses unto yourselves, that ye are the children of them which killed the prophets. Fill ye up then the measure of your fathers. Ye serpents, ye generation of vipers, how can ye escape the damnation of hell? Wherefore, behold, I send unto you prophets, and wise men, and scribes: and some of them ye shall kill and crucify; and some of them shall ye scourge in your synagogues, and persecute them from city to city: That upon you may come all the righteous blood shed upon the earth, from the blood of righteous Abel unto the blood of Zacharias son of Barachias, whom ye slew between the temple and the altar. (Matthew 23:2–35)

It was not for nothing that day that the House of Israel rejected Jesus, as they still reject Him today. Their hearts were hardened, not only because they were spiritually blind, but also because they carried anger, pride, and arrogance, failing to recognize their Messiah before the Almighty. And because of that, their own people, those who were innocent, did pay, are paying, and will pay the price in their lives for the decision of their leaders.

I wonder if in Christian nations such as the United States and Great Britain, the words of the Ten Commandments are allowed to be hung in a big frame in Congress, the White House, and the British Parliament, where some of the representatives of the people pray every morning before starting their workday. Next to it, in a smaller frame, could be hung these words of Jesus:

> Judge not, that ye be not judged. For with what judgment ye judge, ye shall be judged; and with what measure ye mete, it shall be measured to you again. And why beholdest thou the mote that is in thy brother's eye, but considerest not the beam that is in thine own eyes? Or how wilt thou say to thy brother, Let me pull out the mote out of thine eye; and, behold, a beam is in thine own eye? Thou hypocrite, first cast out the beam out of thine own eye; and then shalt thou see clearly to cast out the mote of thy brother's eye. (And for the common people about their representatives this advice) Give not that which is holy unto the dogs, neither cast ye your pearls before swine. Lest they trample them under their feet, and turn again, and rend you. (Matthew 7:1–6)

The warning is that believers must be wise in choosing in

whom to place their confidence. Trusting someone in the secular or religious world can be a mistake with terrible consequences if such a person is not guided by the Spirit. And about judging, *if the judgment does not come by way of revelation of the Spirit, then we have no right to judge.*

The people in whatever high positions whom we approach with trust should treasure that trust we place in their hands. Unfortunately, we have to be careful, as many times that trust is "mistakenly" or intentionally mishandled for a preferred outcome of a behind-the-scenes plot, or for the desired result of manipulation, including political.

The people of Israel trusted their so-called spiritual leaders to be right in their decisions when they were shouting before Pilate to put Jesus to death. And in terms of that trust, we know what happened later on to the city of Jerusalem and the nation of Israel because of the prophetic words spoken by Jesus.

To paraphrase the scripture, we might say, "Don't trust your life to man, nor leave your valuables under his protection, because he may change his mind about his goodwill promises and may kill you in order to keep your valuables." Another person whose promises we trust may be harboring unseen jealousy, greed, lies, treason, or some unfavorable trait. Jesus's words work not only as a warning in the intended spiritual way He meant them to, but we can also apply them in our secular lives when we trust somebody with our life, wealth, or some secret.

Picture how interesting it would be when some representatives finish their speeches accusing other nations of being enemies against their good democratic intentions, and to hear from a citizen who disagrees with how his representatives, whether political or religious, are spreading their "morality" and other "good intentions" for humankind around the globe. That citizen has the favor of exercising their Constitutional freedom of expression, rebuking in disagreement the "righteous well-wishers and defenders" of freedom, comparing their spoken words to their vile deeds around the world. But now picture this on live TV, a common citizen having the gall to lecture them in their own "temples," such as the Senate floor, the House of Lords, or the House of Commons. The free and the brave of the country can see who the enemy is and who the creator of enemies is in a God-given country whose Anglo-Saxon people are about to lose their own freedom. Again, in repetition of what was said previously, if someone today were to do what Jesus did in a government building, that person would be democratically escorted out of the building, arrested, booked, jailed, fined, marked for life, and then sent home, maybe with some bruises to remember his constitutional rights, that is, if he is lucky. Jesus wasn't.

When Jesus finished talking, not even the wind would blow. There was a complete silence. The people were in shock that a man could come to the place where they were taught the Law of Moses and tell the almighty Pharisees and scribes to their faces what kind of hypocrites, cheaters, liars, lawless snakes, and dirty, rotten murderers they were, in front of the people in what was supposed to be their "kingdom". The people were speechless because at that moment, they knew He had brought to them the knowledge of the evil secrets within the hearts of their religious leaders out into the open.

After a few moments of unprecedented quietness, people in a soft whispering broke the silence. The Pharisees, the scribes, and their followers were sitting as if hypnotized by what had just happened. The weight of the heavy truth was out in the open, pressing on their pride and arrogance, all while keeping them silent and glued to their seats for the people to see.

People were looking at them, expecting some reaction, but before anything happened, Jesus stood up and left, and the people followed Him. After the temple was empty, the Pharisees and their friends came to the reality of what had just happened and, in silence, stood up. Their faces had changed.

The image of Satan's hate could be seen in their persons. Coming to terms with the reality, they devised an evil agreement, not only about Jesus, but also about everyone who would be His disciples.

Truly there was nothing that the Pharisees and their cronies could appreciate, respect, love, or reason within their selfishness, evil, and pride.

Satan put things into gear by amplifying the feelings and emotions in their hateful hearts. Jesus had slapped their pride so hard that, from that day on, He was a dead man to them. And the consequences of the decisions they made would, unbeknownst to them at that time, result in a great misinterpretation of the gospel in the future, through the newly created Catholic religion of the Roman Empire, which challenged people's faith and belief in God.

Once Satan got a grip on the Jewish leaders, his evil plan for man's life came together like a puzzle. The Jews were used and later abused, because of their own selfish pride, and brought upon themselves an accursed future.

The Pharisees and scribes made but one mistake, that is, not giving themselves a chance to come down from their high horses. If only they had given themselves a moment to discuss, listen, compare, and reason with Jesus, then perhaps the story of the Jewish people and the Christians would be different today. But their rebellion against Christ and the cursing of themselves before Pilate in their role of Jesus's death condemned them before the heavens. In the eyes of the world, they became the scapegoats for everything that happens on this earth. Satan is still playing in the lives of people on both sides, for and against themselves.

CHAPTER 26

The evil spirit that used the Pharisees and scribes to kill Jesus is the same one that, in the future, would persecute Jews and try to exterminate them. Their attitude against Jesus, the Son of God, made them the rebellious children of the Creator. Their anger and hate against the Messiah whom they rejected has darkened their destiny.

The day for Jesus to be judged by Pilate arrived, and the Pharisees had instructed their people not to allow Pilate to free Jesus under any circumstances.

> Pilate saith unto them, What shall I do then with Jesus which is called Christ? They all say unto him, Let him be crucified. And the governor said, Why, what evil hath he done? But they cried out the more, saying, Let him be crucified. When Pilate saw that he could prevail nothing, but that rather a tumult was made, he took water, and washed his hands before the multitude, saying, I am innocent of the blood of this just person: see ye to it. Then answered all the people, and said, His blood be on us, and on our children. (Matthew 27:22–25)

If only the Jews had realized what they had just said, they would fall on their knees and ask for forgiveness. But they cursed themselves and their descendants, to the last generation in this world. If they don't repent of those words, accept their mistakes, and recognize the Messiah as their Savior, then they are doomed for the rest of eternity.

Those words were the scissors that excised God's presence from the lives of these rebels against heaven. They rejected His protection and blessing when they chose to reject their own salvation, offered by the sacrificial death of the unaccepted Messiah.

Today, all the Jews who will not recognize Christ as their Savior are not the Israelites of the Almighty, nor are they under God's blessing or care, because God stopped caring for them once they rejected Him. And by rejecting Him, they rejected everything that is from Him.

God, according to His own promise to Himself, will protect Israel at the end of time, not allowing their complete extermination at the hands of the Antichrist, whose system they themselves will create unwittingly in the future, because of their spiritual blindness, in a faraway land on the other side of the world.

Besides the writers of the Bible, no other writer or historian has written about the curse that the Jews brought upon themselves that day when they demanded in their satanic fury that Jesus be put to death.

It is true that many Bible scholars, historians, Christians, and Jews have tried to explain what "His blood be on us and on our children" means according to their own understanding and point of view. Those words speak to the destiny of the people of Israel in this world, as they are the chosen people of God.

In the spiritual world, words have power, so one needs to know how to use them. God has created this world through the power of His Word, and whether we like it or not, words can be a blessing or a curse. They can protect us or lead to the destruction of our lives, whether anyone believes this to be so or not.

The Jews threatened Pilate for trying to free Jesus because he saw no fault or guilt in Him. They said that they would tell Rome that he was trying to put himself higher than Caesar by not complying with Roman law and the Jews' demands to execute someone who was threatening not only the peace of Israel, but also the Roman Empire.

Pilate, being a man who had heard but did not believe in the living God, according to historians, and also being an experienced man, knew what kind of people the Jews were, and he saw that it was their hate, pride, and jealousy leading them to accuse the innocent Jesus. No one can confirm or deny whether Pilate had a change of heart upon seeing the Jewish determination to convict Jesus and sentence him to death. After going through such an ordeal, who can say whether or not Pilate became a believer.

After speaking with Jesus, Pilate did not see him as a criminal or any other kind of outlaw breaking any law of the Roman Empire. What he saw was a man at peace with Himself who was about to be condemned for calling Himself king. For this, His own people wanted to get rid of Him, and also because He proclaimed Himself to be the Son of God, with a new message of faith that, according to the Pharisees, was against Jewish law.

For Pilate, this particular incident was something new. Knowing Roman law, he saw nothing that applied to Jesus's case. Pilate knew that the Jews were outraged by Jesus for reasons pertaining to their religion. But according to the law, because the majority of the people were against Jesus, Pilate had to act. He saw no wrong in Jesus after he talked to Him, so he said to the people, "I find no crime in him." He had hopes to let Him go free, but because of the roar of the people, he asked them, "What should I do with him?" Everyone, including the priests, shouted, "Away with him! Crucify him." So he said to them, "I'm innocent of the blood of this just person. See ye to it" (Matthew 27:24).

Pilate, according to historians, was not a saint. When his wife told him about the dream she had about Jesus, and when he thought about the questions he had asked Jesus and Jesus's answers to him, he was afraid. And maybe because of his conscience, he washed his hands of any guilt.

Jesus's willingness to die for His belief in something much greater than His own life made no sense to Pilate. Pilate did not know that Jesus's death was a chance for the spiritual redemption of His own people, but because the people had rejected Him, Jesus granted that opportunity to the whole world. At that moment, Pilate had no idea that he was in the midst of a brutal satanic war. He was amazed by the people's hysteria and noise upon seeing Jesus, who said not one word and stood as someone who had surrendered, peacefully accepting the end of His own life. That is why Pilate believed that Jesus was an innocent man. Given the conviction of faith that Pilate saw in Jesus, even unto accepting death, he may have had a change of heart to believe in God.

The historians have written many things about Pilate, such as that he was a tyrant, a criminal, and a coward, which may or may not be true. Whatever history records is always someone's opinion, whether it is the truth or a lie. What would make the difference would be concrete proof of what a person has in his heart, which is impossible for us to know, but not for God.

We always judge what we think we know, whether in favor or against. With the case of Pilate being, to some, the evil that destroyed the good and, for others, the necessary evil, we have to ask ourselves one question. According to historians, Pilate mixed some of the blood of the people whom he sentenced to execution with his sacrifices to the Roman idols. If he was such a bad person, then why was he putting so much effort into freeing Jesus?

If the spirit of evil was in Pilate and his job was to carry out Satan's wish to kill Jesus, and given that Pilate understood the Jewish people's hatred of their rejected Messiah, he wouldn't have had any reason at the beginning to ask the people if they would agree to let Him go free.

Maybe Pilate was a coward, afraid of what the Jews would do against him, such as contacting Caesar, if he were to decide against executing the Savior. But there is something we must constantly remember: whether you are a secular believer, a religious person, a spiritual Christian, or an atheist with a heart to do well, evil spirits or Satan himself will interfere in your life to make you take the wrong steps. Whether you take a step in full knowledge, naiveté, or ignorance is your choice.

Pilate knew it wasn't a question of politics between the Jews and Jesus. He understood the matter was a religious one, with Jesus offering some approach that was different from their Jewish beliefs about God, the law, faith, and the person of Jesus. But there was no limit to the roaring hatred of Satan in the hearts of the Pharisees and their accomplices manipulating the people to act against Jesus. And that is what Pilate saw.

What if Pilate, going against whatever the Jews were saying about him not being a loyal friend of Caesar, had decided to free Jesus?

Was Pilate guilty for handing Jesus over to the Jews to be crucified?

Wasn't it God's intention to save the human soul through Jesus's sacrifice? If Pilate was to let Jesus go, how would God's plan have been accomplished? Maybe God knew that Pilate, unbeknownst to himself, would be part of His plan?

The truth is that only God knows of how Pilate ended up in life. No one has any proof about his life after Jesus's death, or him going back to Rome. Also, no one has any knowledge of Pilate's life before he was a Roman governor. What we do have is a lot of guesses.

Whether we blame Pilate or excuse him, the fact of the matter is that the life of Jesus was in the hands of the Jewish leaders at that time. Paraphrasing, Pilate said to the Jews: "I see no guilt in this innocent man. I am innocent of the blood of this person. You said, 'Let His blood be on us and on our children.' Well, you want His blood, then have Him according to your will and your wishes. I'm washing my hands of any guilt."

Was Pilate guilty of something that was out of his hands? If he had let Jesus go, how would Jesus have accomplished His heavenly task? Someone else would have killed Him, but who? If God's plan was for Jesus to accomplish His mission, what was the time frame for Him to do so if Pilate had decided to let Jesus go free against the will of the Jews? As always, the questions are many but the answers are too few.

Jesus came to save the Jewish nation first, not the Gentiles. The Gentiles, because His people rejected Him, were given the chance of salvation, and the ones who are called to salvation will at the end be together with the Israelites in the arms of the Almighty.

The Pharisees, having been looking for a reason to kill Jesus, found one through false accusations and statements, according to the Bible, by paying false witnesses. The Pharisees allowed themselves to be under evil influence. This is the time to remember what Jesus told them: "Ye are of *your* father the devil, and the lusts of your father ye will do. He was a murderer from the beginning, and abode not in the truth, because there is no truth in him. When he speaketh a lie, he speaketh of his own: he is a liar, and the father of it" (John 8:44; emphasis added).

Today, our lives in the very secular world of government, where leaders are lying and dirtying their own nations and their own people with others' blood, are no different from the lives of people in the time of the Pharisees, who lied in order to have other people killed for their own convenience. And the leaders of today's governments, whether politicians, religious people, or businesspeople, are brainwashing their constituents with "righteous" beliefs against others who are in opposition to them, calling them enemies for not agreeing with them or for being uncontrollable.

The people of the world are suffering because the diabolical deeds of these leaders are caused by just a few evil followers. A political, religious, or business statement, whether or not made by someone with authority, has spiritual roots, even when the person making the statement is telling a lie or speaking the truth. The purpose of telling lies to those who do not possess inquisitive minds is to kill off any future reasoning about the truth. Those leaders who lie forget that the truth can never be killed—nor be reached by an evil heart.

Satan believed that if Jesus would only die, he would be victorious. He did not know that the day Jesus died would be, for him, the beginning of the end of his sorry existence. Satan did not know that the death of Jesus in the flesh would fail to kill the person of His holy soul.

The hatred against Jesus and His disciples that Satan spread through his followers throughout all the nations crossed even the borders of the Roman Empire.

Christians were accused of being troublemakers, not only for the Jewish nation, but also for the world. The Romans in reality didn't believe everything that they were hearing about the Christians from the Pharisees. The Romans despised the Jews, knowing that they were a tricky and hateful people. The Romans in their investigations never found anything against the Christians that the latter could leverage as a political reason to be rebellious against the Roman Empire. They had no proof whatsoever.

Romans knew that the small Christian sect, as they called them, had never presented any threat to them. They knew that the Christians were obedient to their laws and never tried to force anyone to believe in their faith or cult, never mind try to act politically against the empire.

The Romans, in their faith to their gods, being in the majority and being a well-established culture, were not afraid of the Christians. Even when many Roman citizens declared their belief in the living God, there were no problems with this new faith to the Roman system.

What made the Christians seem dangerous was the hateful propaganda the Jewish leaders spewed against them. That is why some of the Romans, but not all, were eager to look good in the eyes of the Jews. Money was the main reason the Roman governors allowed the Christians to be persecuted. The voluntary payment, disguised as "compensation" or "contribution," of large sums of money, in addition to the Jewish tax, made by the Pharisees to different regional prefects and to the main government in Rome, was the grease that moved the gears of some Roman leaders to do their job against the Christians.

It is true that Christians were killed in different places and even in the Roman Colosseum for entertainment. But we lack precise information about the real number of believers who were killed. Some estimate that in a span of three hundred years, the number killed was between a few thousand and three million, until Christianity was legalized. Obviously, this does not account for the Christians who were killed in the future at the hands of different people controlled by the same evil.

The purpose of those payments made to Rome by the Pharisees was for "understanding" and cooperation against the "deceptive and seditious" Christians, who allegedly were against the Jewish nation, the Jewish people, and the Roman Empire.

When people see a white blanket with a small dark spot on it, the first thing they notice is the spot. Compare this to God, who has a quiet nature, and evil, which has a loud nature, even when the evil itself is small.

One of the Pharisees, a man of stature, went by the name of Saul. He was a respectable man, an educated and well-known professor of Jewish law. He said of himself after converting to the Christian faith that he had assisted in the killing of believers with the blessings of the high priest.

"I verily thought with myself that I ought to do many things contrary to the name of Jesus of Nazareth. Which thing I also did in Jerusalem: and many of the saints I shut up in prison, having received authority from the chief priests; and when they were put to death I gave my voice against them. And I punished them often in every synagogue and compelled them to blaspheme; and being exceedingly mad against them, I persecuted them unto strange cities" (Acts 26:9–11).

Even with all his hate against the Christians, Saul of Tarsus, before his conversion to Christianity, later known as the apostle Paul, ended up being persecuted by the long, unjust arm of Jewish law and killed by the Romans. It is believed that because of Saul's conversion to Christianity, the Jewish leaders lowered his status or, better yet, ignored him and denied their former close relationship because he had revealed to the world that the chief Jewish priests had authorized him to eliminate Christians everywhere the Jews had their synagogues. In other words, Paul pointed his finger directly at the head of the House of Israel.

The motive of the Pharisees was to hide their guilt by ignoring the history of who the apostle Paul really was before his conversion. They did this because they were enraged that one of the members of their inner circle had revealed to the world their plan to do away with the Christians.

For this reason, there is little written by Jewish people about the life of the apostle after his conversion. And whatever is said about him is a commentary on his irrelevance as a member of the Pharisees. The oligarchical Jews of the Great Sanhedrin and the Lower Sanhedrin have placed the blame for the tragedies that have historically befallen them, not even on Paul, but on the whole world, in a full-blown effort throughout the generations. The Pharisees avoided remembering the curse they brought upon themselves at all costs, by denying Paul's testimony against them for what they had said and done to condemn Jesus to death.

Christ, the gospel, and Christianity were not, are not, and never will be a religion like Judaism, if Judaism can be called a religion. Christianity was never sheltered by Judaism, but Jews were sheltered by Christ's sacrifice for their salvation, a salvation that most of them disregarded with hate. The killing of Christians was a tactic established by the devil, manipulated with extreme prejudice against all believers of Christ, through the Jewish authorities and the Romans.

Satan will always try to destroy the lives of believers, never admitting in his hate that God Himself was, is, and will be the main reason for his fighting. Understanding that he can't even come close to being a threat to his own Creator, he takes out his hatred on the lives of every person who, through Jesus, has or may have eternal life.

When people die, their lives are history, but their spiritual lives have no history because such a life is always present now, whether the person's soul is in hell or heaven. And God is the One who has the record of saved souls with Him because He—never "was" and never "will be"— but forever is.

The people of the world have been given the Word of God, which is the Bible, the only spiritual Word of Truth that has been given to man inspired through His Spirit. The Bible was written for the people of all generations, past, present, and future, to offer them a chance of salvation. There is no found contradiction of the truth in the lives and circumstances of all the people, believers or not, in the Old and New Testament. And the Bible is for the Jews and Gentiles alike, being not only a book of historical facts but also a proven spiritual document with a profound statement on the spiritual condition of the human being. As it was in the past, it is the same today.

Whether accepted or rejected, the Bible is a book approved and rubber-stamped by the power of the Spirit of God, that is, by God Himself. His Word is given by His Spirit to the spirit of man, in the inspiring power of His love, grace, and mercy, for man to develop understanding in his heart for the salvation of his soul.

The Bible was written by more than one person under the inspired guidance of the Spirit of God, in which case it is not only a historical document but also, more importantly, a defined spiritual declaration. It is to be understood only when it is revealed, as Jesus said, by the Father to the ones who accept, not reject, His Word, which is Him, in revelation for their own salvation.

All other historical documents written by man as testimonies for the future require historical proof of whatever circumstances man has lived through. Unfortunately, many times such documents are short on many details, so we have to do research, and not always be successful, to find the truth.

Many distorted minds have said that historical documents, even when they are not 100 percent correct, are better resources than the Bible. Obviously the people saying this have sick minds and hearts under the control of evil. In their atheism, they say that the Bible presents an imaginary story without any proof of its truth.

What is most important is the spiritual directive to believe in God, which occurs not through the deductions of a guessing instinct. The only way to reach God is through faith, a gift given by Him to man, with faith being a spiritual tool leading one to believe in God's spiritual world through an understanding heart in need, not through a mind with its own intellectual principles and arrogance.

There is a big difference between being inspired by the Spirit of God to write and tell His truth and gathering together one's best intellectual, theological, and historical knowledge to write of that same truth. The latter is the situation for anyone who writes of the truth according to his own understanding without the guidance of the Spirit, whether the person is a witness to or a participant in an historical event. The Spirit is the Original Truth, who inspires or reveals to the spirit of man the wisdom of God at the needed moment, with God's wisdom being higher than man's natural wisdom. God's spiritual wisdom in man's heart, not his mind, is all that is needed for man to come to a spiritual understanding of life, which will be of benefit to his intellect.

The intellectual interpretations of the gospel have been dreamed up by people whose minds are confused about spirituality. This is the reason why the Lord said that things will go wrong in this world, will go against us, or will go from bad to worse, because we have neither the understanding nor a fighting spirit to do battle, according to the promises left for us, with the dark spirits of this world.

And because those same spirits interfere with our accepted denominations and human doctrines, our wrongly directed faith and lack of spiritual knowledge of the Word is like an invisible wall that will keep us divided in our own "spiritual" knowledge—an invisible wall that will allow us to recognize each other as Christians but prevent us from hearing and coming to an agreement to take that wall down. God wants us to be of one mind and in the same spirit, unified as members of the same spiritually healthy, functioning body.

If anyone believes or thinks these words do not come close to the truth, then what explanation can be made as to why we cannot be in the same spirit of understanding if God and His Word are one? And if we are in the same spirit, how come we cannot understand each other according to God's Word and will? We may say that we understand each other despite our doctrinal differences and interpretations of God's Word and will, but we are certainly not united with the same understanding in the same Spirit. Believing we are one in Christ is what makes us say, in our different beliefs and approaches, that we are one. But what if that is not true? Then what is our excuse?

A lack of knowledge, not theological or historical, but spiritual through faith and revelation for one understanding, is why there is no unity among those in the spiritual body of Christ. It is not denominations or different doctrines and interpretations of the Word that make us one in Christ, but the working Spirit of the Lord in the humility of our hearts with believing faith in the teaching and guidance of the Spirit, making us as one in the life of our Savior.

In Luke 9:49–50, Jesus's disciples came and told Him, "'Master, we saw one casting devils in thy name; and we forbade him, because he followeth not with us.' And Jesus said unto them, 'Forbid him not: for he that is not against us is for us.'"

This is a very interesting story about the truth of the gospel. It sounds very simple—a man casting out evil spirits in Jesus's name. This man was in the Spirit of the Lord, and in His name he was doing the right and correct spiritual work. But the disciples did not understand why the Spirit was imbuing the man with power. They believed that if the man was not physically following Jesus, he was not doing the right thing.

Today if a person refuses to follow along with what others of his denomination believe, then he is regarded as wrong. The ones who are "right" are those who follow the denomination's interpretation of the Word. And according to such people, the rest misunderstand the teaching of the gospel, when they themselves fail to notice that it isn't a spirit working for God's glory in their lives, but a spirit of competition. A working spirit in the life of a believer makes changes to the believer's heart and to the world. This is what Jesus did, entering a pagan world and changing people's lives, causing evil to become afraid.

Because people are what they are, they became easily convinced by Satan that there is something more, good, better, lighter, and easier out there, being told that they are able to keep living with one foot in the church and the other in the world. Those are not the people whom God has chosen to serve Him.

Returning to Jesus's story, the thing is that this man perhaps previously followed Jesus, heard Him, and believed in His words, and having a believing faith, was doing what was allowed by God's will. Otherwise the man wouldn't have been able to cast out evil spirits in His name.

The spiritual content is simple to understand for those who have ears to hear. God knows the ones who are failing to preach the real spiritual gospel. He also knows their hearts and their reasons, and His children in the Spirit know the difference.

Some of God's children, as the apostle Paul said, are living on milk and thinking it is solid food. But the ones living and being guided by the Spirit through revelation are those who are eating solid food. Some people who have no knowledge of the Spirit guess that the man in the story is just someone good who is taking it upon himself to help God out. This is reminiscent of when Jesus's disciples came to Him and told Him about the man casting out evil spirits. They were still in the learning stage, so Jesus taught them the difference. But some will never learn the true spiritual meaning of the gospel.

The apostle Paul was a man in the Spirit, like many others, and in the Spirit he rebuked a spirit speaking through a young girl when he was going to the temple with some other brothers. The story is in Acts 16:17–18. To know the Word of God and His will is to know God in the Spirit through Jesus, who works in the life of every real spiritual Christian. Everything that is related to His Word, to His person, and to His world is in the Spirit. And it is *only* in the Spirit, living in our human spirits and our obedient, humble hearts, that God has His place in our lives. God does not live among our theological and historical knowledge, or our so-called spiritual interpretations of everything that is of God. Some think that knowing the Bible from cover to cover will make them acceptable to God just because they have more knowledge, but they are wrong.

If there is no understanding in the same Spirit, then no knowledge will, by any means, bring about a change to any heart full of knowledge alone. And if anyone thinks that a weakened or wrongly directed faith is sufficient to give knowledge of the things from above, then such a person should think again about the results of such thinking and its failure to produce spiritual fruits in this messy world we live in.

It is faith, belief, and a wish from a spiritual heart, one in which God lives, that will move God's hand. Wishes and hopes in the heart where the Spirit of God has no place, do not work. And for the lack of spiritual wisdom in a Christian life, things are going from bad to worse, and instead of us conquering the world, the world is conquering us.

Nevertheless, a very few people who fit this description may eventually find the spiritual help they need from God. God will never, in His grace, let go of a heart in need, if that someone has given his or her testimony of help or salvation, with a clean and clear desire to serve the Lord. Jesus said of the man casting out demons in His name, "Forbid him not, for there is no man which shall do a miracle in my name, that can lightly speak evil of me. For he that is not against us, is on our part" (Mark 9:39–40). Those words were said about the man casting out evil spirits, but they easily apply to anyone whose heart is filled with a pure intention to give his testimony of the gospel for God's glory.

We seek the love, mercy, and wisdom of God because many times in our spiritual ignorance, we walk through trials without living by the wisdom of His Spirit within us, the way God intended for our lives. And that is the difference between the one who has faith in Christ and the one who merely seeks to do good in His name. One is spiritually inspired; the other is inspired by the good-intentioned human heart wishing to do well. A similar principle is found in the Bible, given by the apostles as personal advice, according to their faith, experience, knowledge, understanding, and belief, to help warn people about other people and the actions of the Deceiver.

CHAPTER 27

What will be different within us if we know the historical truth according to our wishes? Will we seek to understand the historical truth so we can be better as secular or spiritual people? Will it help us to change our future, giving us the ability to forgive and be better, or will we hate more and do nothing about it, but merely be informed of what happened in the past, thereby pleasing our intellect and ego alone?

People's intentions in the past and people's intentions today are no different at all. Good and evil are still fighting for souls, and they are working in people's hearts. No matter how we slice it, if we do not have the correct spiritual understanding, or at least a reasonable idea of what it means to have one mind and one spirit, then we will always be defeated.

If we Christians fail to align in our spiritual understanding and become unified in the knowledge of God's Word, then we'll continue being divided. The Father won't be able to bring to salvation those who will not allow themselves to see farther than their own noses, because of pride, arrogance, stubbornness, or too much knowledge. Jesus said, "No man can come to me, except the Father which hath sent me draw him, and I will raise him up at the last day" (John 6:44).

Any person who does not believe in the existence of God or

the salvation of the human soul through the acceptance of Jesus's sacrifice on the cross is a person who, according to the gospel, will see none of the heavenly promises spoken of in the Bible.

Researching historical documents to find the truth, and putting the truth under a magnifying glass either to excuse someone or find someone guilty, won't make any difference. Although we like to exercise power to have the last word, this is something of a dream because truth and judgment belongs to God, not to man. The truth of one man over the truth of another man is something that is always open to discussion. But under God's eye, man is guilty, unless He says otherwise. Our accusations or excuses are invalidated by the righteousness of the ever-watchful Almighty and His justice.

No man, at any time, could please everyone when it comes to determining justice of another man by law for things done in the past, such as what the Pharisees and their accomplices did to Jesus and the Christians. But every person has their own reason for approving or rejecting whatever actions have marked this world by other people. The world itself is not justified because today, as in the past and in the future, we are told by Jesus, "Render therefore unto Caesar the things which are Caesar's, and unto God the things that are God's" (Matthew 22:2). We know what He meant when He said those words, speaking about this secular world, but we also have to understand His spiritual meaning. Whatever we choose to do, according to our own understanding of that advice, will depend on the intentions of our hearts.

Instigations and persecution of Christians did not exist in some places where people of different pagan beliefs lived and had no knowledge of the new faith. And when they were told about Christianity, they listened with interest about this new God and had no problems with those who followed Him. The problems would start when a Jew would show up and begin to stir people up, leveraging their ignorance of the matter.

The Bible tells us of different situations when the apostles and other Christians were doing their job of testifying about the kingdom of God with no problems, until a Jew showed up, and then the problems began. That means that the influence of the devil over any people, mainly the Jews, was powerful not only in their land, but also around the world. This is the same influence Satan has today at every level of people's lives.

When someone is under the devil's influence, that person has the devil's power. When Jesus was tempted by the devil, the devil said to Him, showing Him the kingdoms of the world and their glory, "'All these things will I give thee, if thou wilt fall down and worship me.' Then saith Jesus unto him, 'Get thee hence, Satan: for it is written, Thou shalt worship the Lord thy God, and Him only thou shalt serve'" (Matthew 4:9–10).

Satan failed with Jesus, but he had a good grip on the Jewish leaders who had accepted his spirit of a blind arrogance, pride, greed, and glory, which has followed their descendants up to this day. The same is true of the Gentiles. So Satan began the hunt not only for Jesus, but also, later on, for His disciples. That is why Jesus said, "If they have persecuted me, they will also persecute you too" (John 15:20). About this topic and many others, Jesus says the following:

> But take heed to yourselves: for they shall deliver you up to councils; and in the synagogues ye shall be beaten: and ye shall be brought before rulers and kings for my sake, for a testimony against them. And the gospel must first be published among all nations. But when they shall lead you, and deliver you up, take no thought beforehand what ye shall

speak, neither do ye premeditate: but whatsoever shall be given you in that hour, that speak ye: for it is not ye that speak, but the Holy Ghost. Now the brother shall betray the brother to death, and the father the son; and children shall rise up against their parents, and shall cause them to be put to death. And ye shall be hated of all men for my name's sake: but he that shall endure unto the end, the same shall be saved. (Mark 13:9–13)

Even though those words were spoken about the brothers and sisters of that time, they are still applicable today. This is because we have not yet learned to prevent the enemy from attacking us, as the apostle Paul warned us: "For we wrestle not against flesh and blood, but against principalities, against powers, against the rules of the darkness of this world, against spiritual wickedness in high places" (Ephesians 6:12).

This verse mentions Satan's spirits working in men's lives to make them miserable. According to the promises left for us by the Lord, we need to discover the secret spiritual weapon for our own defense and learn how to use it.

This is an inquisitive challenge to our own faith in our knowledge of the Word, living in the Spirit believing that through God everything is possible. And this was the reason that Almighty God said, "My people perish for lack of knowledge" (Hosea 4:6). Having all the Lord's promises and believing in Jesus's name, we have been given the authority and power to battle the spirits of the air. We must understand that we have the ability to change what seems to be impossible if we believe and have faith. The amount of faith and belief we have in the Word of God determines how much we will be able to do against the evil spirits, as the apostle Paul mentions.

That is something the Lord has left for us to understand in the spirit, not with our brains—the understanding of the mind comes later, with a translated spiritual revelation. Fighting human beings won't help us conquer the evil spirits that are persecuting us, but if we fight and conquer the evil spirits controlling man, then man won't persecute us.

Many Christians say that it is not their job to fight evil spirits. If this is true, then how do we understand the words of the apostle Paul when he talks about the struggle being not against flesh and blood, but against the spirits of the air? And what does the Bible say about our rights and the wishes of our hearts in the promises of the Lord? How do we understand what Jesus said about the things He has done and Him telling us that we'll do even more than He has? These are questions that many, who unfortunately are not in the Spirit, understand poorly.

If we do not understand or admit that, in God, the impossible is possible, then we have a problem of our own. Someday we will have to answer for the lack of investment in God's promises, along with any doubt in our faith, belief, and wrong personal interpretations of the Word without spiritual revelation. Our faith is not only our spiritual weapon to defend ourselves, to neutralize, or to attack our enemy, but it is also our wealth. If we don't have that wealth, just like the poor of the secular world, we will be poor in the spiritual world.

We Christians need to come out of the religious box that we have been living in for so many generations. Some of the things that the Lord has said are not definitive. They become definitive when we ignore them or do not take the chance to challenge our faith and ask Him if whatever we seek is acceptable according to His promises. He hasn't mentioned anything that we should not ask about, and if we ask for something that is not in His will, we will find out soon enough.

Jesus said, "Verily, verily, I say unto you, He that believeth on me, the works that I do shall he do also; and greater works than these shall he do; because I am going to the Father. And whatsoever ye shall ask in my name, that will I do, that the Father may be glorified in the Son. If ye shall ask anything in my name, I will do it" (John 14:12–14).

Here is another strong promise made by Jesus: "Verily I say unto you, if ye have faith and doubt not, ye shall not only do this which is done to the fig tree, but also if ye shall say unto this mountain, Be thou removed and be thou cast into the sea, it shall be done. And all things, whatsoever ye shall ask in prayer, believing, ye shall receive" (Matthew 21:21–22).

The apostle John wrote, "And this is the confidence that we have in him, that, if we ask anything according to his will, he heareth us. And if we know that he hears us, whatsoever we ask, we know that we have the petitions that we desired of him" (1 John 5:14–15).

Both of the two foregoing declarations are correct, but in order to receive the promise, the believer must not challenge the promise. Jesus was more direct in His promises when he said, "If ye have faith and doubt not, whatsoever things ye shall ask in prayer, believing, ye shall receive." The apostle Paul said, "This is the confidence that we have in him, that if we ask anything according to his will, whatsoever we ask we'll have the petitions we desire of him."

It is all the same, but the difference is in us, in our faith, knowledge, and confidence. We must be confident in our own selves, that is, have a strong faith and believing trust in our Lord and His promises.

Jesus never promised anything that He could not deliver; He was always direct. When Jesus said "if," that was a direct challenge to one's faith in the impossible, like the "will"—that is, the knowledge of decision—that the apostle Paul mentioned when talking about the confident trust in our hearts before the Trinity of heaven.

We need to ask ourselves how submerged we are in the Spirit, and in our faith, belief, confidence, and trust, regarding all the direct promises of the Lord. We'll see how effective the "if" of Jesus and the "will" of the apostle Paul are, according to the faith we have, when we try it.

We read in Proverbs 3:5, "Trust in the Lord with all thine heart and lean not unto thine own understanding," that is, your own deductions, interpretations, calculations, feelings, emotions, and so on. The difference in the life of a believer and non-believer, according to Jesus's promises, is that the believer has faith, belief, trust, and confidence with no doubts. Everything that is good in the will of God, against the evil hordes, will become a reality for the glory of the Father in the name of His Son. We'll do what Jesus has done and, as He said, even more things for God's glory. Everything that we seek to do for the glory of God, not our own glory, will be granted without doubt.

Even when we are in the flesh, experiencing all the inconveniences of the secular world, we must fight against the secular on a spiritual level. Always remember that whatever happens in anyone's life, good or bad, is the consequence of direct spiritual intervention of either God or evil spirits in a man's life, spirits that either make us strong, or weaken us and destroy us. Nothing happens in any life just because.

We Christians in the name of Jesus need to become combatants in the Spirit of the Almighty, seeking to conquer all spiritual principalities, powers of this world, rulers of darkness, and the spiritual forces of evil in the heavenly realms. We must stop Satan by eradicating evil spirits from those who are possessed, using God's Spirit to accomplish this, as we have direct assurance in

God's spoken Word: "Be strong and of a good courage. Fear not, nor be afraid of them; for the Lord thy God, he it is that doth go with thee; he will not fail thee, nor forsake thee" (Deuteronomy 31:6). This is a promise to protect us against not only physically strong people, or their laws and systems, but also, and mainly, the hordes of evil spirits in man that fight against us through those same physically strong people, their laws, and their systems. Again: "Trust in the Lord with all thine heart and lean not unto thine own understanding" (Proverbs 3:5). We need to be in the Spirit to be the strong people Jesus spoke about, and have the weapons of His promises for our defense as the apostle Paul mentioned in Ephesians 6:11-17.

"The righteous cry, and the Lord heareth, and delivereth them; out of all their troubles" (Psalms 34:17). This tells us, as do many other promises in the Old and New Testaments, that we have the assurance that if we are in Him and He is in us, He won't let anyone hurt us.

We believers can be certain that no one will be able to touch the Almighty if He is in our lives, certainly protecting us as He promised He would do. He gave us His Word. All it takes is faith. The rest is up to the will of God.

There is no better insurance for us in this world than His promise. To see it fulfilled, we need to be united in one mind and one spirit, fasting and praying. If we do this, then we will accomplish all that is possible to accomplish, if we have the will.

If we don't take a chance, then every Word spoken by the Almighty about the future tragedies for the human race will come true. We need to challenge ourselves to have faith in His promises. What is happening today in this world is a sign that we are not even close to being in the spiritual positions that we need to be standing in if we are to stand in the spiritual body of our Lord and God. We cannot win any battle against man if first we don't conquer the evil spirits controlling them.

We need to trust God for whatever adverse circumstances we are going through in our lives, believing to the end that whatever the outcome is according His will, we are, one way or another, by His mercy, conquerors of faith in His promises, whether in this present world or the one to come. But in this world, while we are still here, we need to put up a spiritual fight, or at least try.

What makes a person or a nation powerful? Is it the power of wealth? Many may think that in this world there are two kinds of people with power since the beginning of time, namely, politicians and military leaders. But now there are powerful people of other types, such as religious people and businesspeople who, ironically, went from the bottom of the list to the "top of the food chain". These people may not even know that the power they have has its origins in darkness. This, in what looks like a plain secular example, is absolutely a spiritual task of a deceiving spirit in the life of the ones who may have God only on their lips.

Today, politicians who have at their disposal, the strong arm of the law, are there to serve the ones on top, those who work behind the scenes. This is the modern-day Sadducees and Sanhedrin of the deep state. Those who became first, along with their political servants, are the ones who have sold their integrity, honesty, decency, and honor to mammon, together with their word, which they gave when they promised their people that they would uphold the truth and defend the Constitution, Magna Carta, or whatever other document outlines their country's system of law. Not all of them, but most of them.

Humanity has left a legacy of decadence from the time of Abel and Cain to the present day, with no national, cultural, religious, or belief system expected. As the Word says, "For the love of money is the root of all evil" (1 Timothy 6:10).

If not for money, then how does one understand the misery created in this world by rich, powerful, and greedy people under the control of evil? The regular working citizens of any nationality or faith are not the ones waging war against their own people. The ones taking their people to war are the politicians, pushed by the businesspeople to uphold their "country" in the name of their "god," money. These powerful, "good-intentioned" businessmen who claim to have national interests in mind when they make their business deals are trampling on the rights of defenseless nations.

For the last four or five hundred years, we have seen how empires, including those of England and France, and perhaps the last one the world will ever see, the United States, have co-opted parts of the world in their own national interests. Some of those countries' presidents, prime ministers, or dictators are like Judas, who have been converted to the Anglo-Saxon style of democracy, having spent their people's and their country's wealth on the Babylonian "church" of Wall Street, in search of soulless pleasure. What Jesus said to the scribes and Pharisees could be said about certain US senators, congress people, British Lords, and so on: "Woe unto you, scribes and Pharisees, hypocrites! for ye compass sea and land to make on proselyte, and when he is made, ye make him twofold more the child of hell than yourselves" (Matthew 23:15).

Those same leaders are the ones who, in the name of their nations, under some Western democratic political, patriotic, or other type of ideal, and being well paid for their service, are using people's ignorance or naiveté to brainwash them, including many Christians, for their own interests. And when such leaders no longer need the support of their constituencies, they dispose of them one way or another. This is Satan's political gospel, practiced in the lives of those who are blind to the future consequences once they stand before the heavenly court to be judged. People, thinking that their leaders are telling the truth, are ready to do the "right thing," when in reality they are deceived and kept blind to the real intentions. Behind the scenes, their leaders' only intentions are to use them for their own personal interests.

Such people are not unlike the Pharisees and their dealings with the Jewish people. Using the name of God, along with claims of justice, truth, and the unity of their people, under God's promise of blessings and protection for Israel, they covered up their lies and deeds. Taking advantage of the things their people brought to the temple as a sacrifice, they were in pursuit of wealth and glory, which they gained through a well-coordinated system where tithes and offerings were coming into their coffers in exchange for the preaching of obedience to God's law.

There is no difference in what is happening today in some denominations where so-called church leaders are taking what belongs to God for their own personal use, thereby robbing God. Whether it is one person in his own ambition acting this way or a whole system under the law, there is no difference. Whatever those leaders may have said five thousand years ago, two hundred years ago, or today, as recorded in history, and whether their intentions and actions were right or wrong, nothing has or will change in the lives of people who haven't changed their hearts.

The Jewish head priest, the rabbis, the Pharisees, and the scribes sought to make people believe that Jesus was destroying their perfectly created system of developing belief in God through following the Law of Moses. The Pharisees claimed that Jesus had said the Law of Moses was no longer important, when in reality Jesus said that the coming of the Messiah had been fulfilled according to God's prophets and that the Mosaic Law had been replaced. It had been replaced by a new law, if it can be called as such, which is love, mercy, compassion, forgiveness, and a whole new covenant, based no longer in a future hope, but in a belief and acceptance of the already present Messiah. His presence was the proof that the prediction had come true. No longer did one have to make animal sacrifices to reach God; what is required now is a believing faith in Jesus as the prophesied Messiah.

In a way, the Pharisees were given a chance to foresee what would become of their "perfectly" schemed system if people were to decide to believe in Jesus. Trying to protect their underhanded resource stream, they said that Jesus was a charlatan, a deceiver, and a blasphemer of the truth by calling Himself the Messiah.

The Pharisees used the legalistic rituals that the people were to perform under law (just as bankers use loans), to indebt those who are in need, naïve, or ignorant. The common people are unlikely to distrust the ones whom they ask for help, whether spiritual or secular. The Pharisees had created a very sophisticated and profitable system of scheming in God's name.

Now the question is, did these Jewish leaders unintentionally help create the Roman Catholic Church by soliciting the participation of the Roman Empire in the trial of Jesus? We'll never know. What we do know today is that something happened, and to find anyone in particular to pin the blame on is simply impossible. No historical documents on the matter exist. If they do exist, they are among the most dangerous documents in existence in this world. If they exist, they are very well guarded. Surely someone is waiting for a chance in the future to find these documents and show them to the world. Perhaps such documents were kept to show what happened and the reason why it was done—evidence that the Roman Catholic Church was keeping to prove to the world that they did the right thing. That is, if for some other compromising reasons the documents were not destroyed. And if they were, someone is covering up the guilt of the Roman Catholic Church before the world.

Man can cover, bury, or destroy any proof of guilt, but God

knows the truth, and we, the outsiders, are the ones always guessing. How many historical documents will we need to have in our possession before we are certain of the truth? We'll never know. But there is one thing for sure: the intentions of man's heart are known to God.

There is one certain and undeniable truth: the most important historical and spiritual document, with more value than all the rest put together, one that contains the irrefutable truth about man, is the Bible. And because it is a living document, many people may not accept it as proof of what will happen to man in the future.

Any of the why, when, how, or who, of reasons, intentions, truth, lies, guilt, excuses, motives, curses, and times, is water under the bridge. What we know for certain is that Satan is, through worldly minded people, creating his plan for a future spiritual takeover "legally," by using false doctrine to make it look spiritual. He places this plan in the heart of man, for many to believe that it arises from religious or secular law.

The spiritual ignorance in people's lives exists because of the lack of personal interest to seek a higher knowledge based in the Word of God. In their spiritual blindness, they are filled with rebellious emotions of righteousness, a state of ignorance. In people's carelessness, Satan successfully introduces his imitation of faith and belief, deceiving them through religion and politics, and a twisted confidence, where faith in God becomes trust in man by way of the rules and regulations of their own secular "spiritual" gospel.

Nothing is new under the heavens, and whatever side of secular history man is choosing to side with, it may or may not make a difference to this world and humankind. But a person may experience a difference in his own personal life, if he gives himself the chance to know God's Spirit in his own heart.

The world won't change, because people won't change. The

day people change their hearts in Christ will be the day the world will be different. People have become too philosophical about life and human actions, having an understanding of spirituality as a religious way to know God. God's real spirituality in people's lives is not hollow, and is visible to the natural eye of man, with positive results, both spiritual and secular.

CHAPTER 28

The words Christ used to accuse the Pharisees and others of hypocrisy, saying they were rotten in their religious hearts, can be applied to the same kind of people of all generations in high positions.

Many historians are preoccupied with the past, wondering if it is possible to know it in detail and to discover why things happen the way they happen. Some say the purpose of this is to learn from history and not to repeat the same mistakes. Unfortunately, humans are full of pride and stubbornness, and many are too intellectual and spiritually blind to perform the impossible without God, like living in peace without wars. And whatever man does reach, he will again come to a point of catastrophic failure. We are seeing the same tragedies occur over and over again.

Reaching blindly in their greedy ambition, people dismiss the future consequences, instead of reaching for knowledge and understanding to see if the goal they are working toward is the right thing to do or not. That is a very ignorant way to try to be successful.

The apostle Paul said in 1 Corinthians 6:12, "All things are lawful unto me, but all things are not expedient: all things are lawful for me. But I will not be brought under the power of any." Every person needs to know if the intentions of his or her heart are correct before God. Sooner or later, people will pay the consequences for their actions for using God's name with the intention to create or promote a deceptive idea. The Pharisees never believed in this principle, or if they believed in it, they just ignored it.

Thinking of the creation of the Roman Catholic Church, we may think that it was born from an agreement between the Romans, the Jewish leaders, and the Christians. We might guess it was a religiopolitical agreement. But what people are maybe unaware of are the spiritual consequences of that agreement, which were not even known by the participants, because the agreement by itself was a spiritual one which was struck by Satan's deceptive "goodwill."

Likely at that time, the spiritual Christian leaders were hoping, in terms of their own personal interests, for peace and good intentions among all three parties in the future. But they failed to notice Satan's intervention in their decision.

The gospel would come to be transformed by Catholicism, the church unnoticeably introducing, over time, in a very sophisticated way, Gnosticism, Zionism, Calvinism, and other teachings that deviate from the intended spiritual teachings of Christ. They sought something more theological and maybe philosophical, directed toward the intellect to be understood, instead of directing the believer to spiritually challenge himself in his faith.

When man is humble before the Lord and holds the best of intentions in his heart, he seeks the true spiritual way to reach God's wisdom and Spirit of revelation, and it is not through man's deductions, guesses, and so on.

In the future, those who seek in the Spirit the wisdom of the Almighty will receive the challenge to become part of a praying fellowship where the Spirit of God reveals His Word. Not man but God is the only one who knows in what spirit people teach His Word.

We read the following in 1 John 4:1–6:

> Beloved, believe not every spirit, but try the spirits whether they are of God: because many false prophets are gone out into the world. Hereby know ye the Spirit of God: Every spirit that confesseth that Jesus Christ is come in the flesh is of God: And every spirit that confesseth not that Jesus Christ is come in the flesh is not of God: and this is that spirit of antichrist, whereof ye have heard that it should come; and even now already is it in the world. Ye are of God, little children, and have overcome them: because greater is he that is in you, than he that is in the world. They are of the world: therefore speak they of the world, and the world heareth them. We are of God: he that knoweth God heareth us; he that is not of God heareth not us. Hereby know we the spirit of truth, and the spirit of error.

It is important to note that the tragic division of the true Christian faith based on the Gospel occurred after the birth of the Roman Catholic Church and after the agreement was made. With the Catholic Church preaching a new doctrine, the spiritual Christian leadership refused to change their apostolic ways. A small group of leaders who understood the present danger decided to unite under the correct way of believing in the gospel of Christ as an apostolic orthodox faith, without any changes to the doctrine. The laws of the time did not prohibit apostolic faith because the Christians were an unnoticeable, quiet minority, unlike the new, supposedly benevolent Roman Church.

Unfortunately, like in many other denominations and with the passing time, the apostolic church, now called orthodox, unnoticed in the purity of its people's faith and belief, began adding things that did not exist before the creation of the new approach to the faith, namely, rituals and images of so-called saints to honor those who served the Lord. For many, this is accepted practice, and for others it is deemed incorrect, as it is not found in the Bible. And for those who do say it is in the Bible, they are taking the warnings of the Almighty out of context. As always, it is not man, but God, who knows man's heart and his reasons.

The core of orthodox Christianity is faith in God, whether the person who seeks that faith is on the right path or has deviated from the spiritual doctrine of the real gospel of Christ.

A change of name doesn't mean a change of faith, but a change in doctrine may cause the faithful of any denomination to deviate from the right path, which makes a believer ineffective in his faith. And the depth of any person's spirituality is known only by God.

Faith is good because it comes from God, but when that faith is twisted by man's own understanding of the gospel, leading to a different doctrinal interpretation without spiritual revelation and guidance, faith is ineffective. And if the faith in any believer does work, it's because God knows the heart of the person in need. Sometimes a sincere humble heart before God is more effective than the heart of someone who knows the Bible by memory from cover to cover.

The war the Jewish leaders and the Romans waged against the Christians in reality was a spiritual war against the real Israelites, the children of God. Only some people thought the war was over differences in ideas, creeds, and so on. Living in the secular world, many times we forget that life in itself is a spiritual reality, a reality that is something very difficult to see and understand because we are secular people guided by our own intellectual understandings, feelings, desires, emotions, and self-righteousness. More than anything when we are dealing with history in terms of philosophy and secularism, we forget that there is a spiritual side with consequences.

The devil never misses a chance to intervene in human affairs. In this particular case, he took advantage of the situation that he himself had created by appealing to the greed and mutual interests between the Jews and Roman leaders.

When Christians were being killed, everything was okay with Satan because he was manipulating the situation. When the Romans saw that the killing of Christians was without any benefit to them, they came up with a plan to align doctrinal belief with the Christians, keep the Jews in their peace of mind, and remove themselves from violent acts against believers. We must understand that evil is always around when man intends to make any situation better.

With the agreement to live peaceably, Satan had a chance to create a quiet war of spiritual ideals, called denominations and doctrines; in one word he created "religion." Not the kind mentioned in the Bible, but the type that future teachers of the gospel would use to confuse people into thinking that man's natural instinct to do good is in fact spiritual.

All these things put together may have one goal, but are not in solid unity. The ideal, God's ideal, is to be of one mind; to be of one mind is to be of one understanding; and to be of one understanding is to be of one spirit. One spirit, one mind, and one understanding means no disagreement, and no disagreement means peace. And that is one thing Satan doesn't want—peace.

Through human emotions, Satan creates a sensible masquerade of spirituality through religiousness in people's mind, which replaces God's spiritual knowledge of his Word to a knowledge based off of intellectual interpretation. Such interpretation is mistaken as spiritual revelations of his Word. When people are spiritually ignorant or naive due to their lack of interest in receiving spiritual knowledge of the Word, "God's representatives" can bring out their guilty conscience. They do so by teaching them to believe and trust in God with their minds, not their hearts, and to listen to and lean on man for their spiritual needs, because those "representatives" are interceding between their flock and heaven. This is not the way to spirituality, but a way to philosophical religiousness.

Instead of lecturing people on religious doctrine, religious leaders should be teaching people to discern the presence of God in their human spirits and helping them to understand the Word. A person needs the Spirit of God to reveal the Word to his heart, but instead of imparting spiritual understanding, religious leaders keep the people entertained with philosophy and theology. They should be guiding the curious believer to direct spiritual knowledge, not intellectual knowledge. The Spirit of God is like a sword separating the true from the false, no matter how spiritual we think we are.

If anything we read in the Bible offends us or makes us feel uncomfortable, injuring our pride as if someone has just said that we are wrong, it means that we do not have the spiritual knowledge of the Word we thought we had. There is only one true gospel, and whenever believers of any Christian denomination fail to agree among themselves and be of one mind and one spirit, as God wants us to be, they are lying to themselves.

The truth causes no discomfort, anger, or pain to a clean and clear heart because such a heart is at peace with itself in its Creator's truth, where His Spirit gives man new life. This is the promised world and the promised truth that those believers in Christ have not yet reached or understood. The reason for this is that our world, as His Word says, is going from bad to worse.

For a heart to be spiritually educated, it must learn to be

humble and wise. It must be persistent in its dedication to fight spiritually against its own weaknesses, whatever they may be, and make personal sacrifices in order to conquer them. This sort of education involves a spiritual battle within the will and life of a person with a weak heart and mind. And this internal fight is the only and right way to reach God for enlightenment, wisdom, and revelation. The first thing Christians must conquer is themselves to begin receiving God's promises. But people don't know this, of which they are warned in God's Word, because they have been given an alternate, sophisticated "spiritual truth" by their so-called spiritual leaders.

Man can show man the way to know God, but God's Spirit will teach man's spirit according to His will and man's faithfulness to do His will. Jesus said, "Neither be ye called masters, for one is your Master, even Christ" (Matthew 23:10). And that teacher is the One whom we may only reach by getting down on our knees.

Being a good person who does good deeds and enjoys a quiet conscience with a passive heart and an inactive spirit means that one is acceptable before God, according to man's new teaching of the gospel, but certainly not according to God. This deceptive teaching was given by the prince of this world so that man, because of his inactive spirit and passive heart, would misunderstand how he could come to know God.

Most religions profess that having faith, doing good deeds, obeying man's laws, and making sacrifices in life is what one must do to earn happiness in eternity somewhere up in the sky. There are religions in the world that take a different approach to God's love. The Bible calls this "prostitution of the nations," which means that man has misunderstood which pathway leads to the love of God. God's will for our lives is that we love Him and love our neighbor as ourselves. This was Jesus's greatest commandment. But a newly-created belief through denominational doctrines, where images, rituals, and ideals are dividing the interpretations of the Gospel, was not what Jesus left for us.

Perhaps Catholicism was created by people who were very confused, having good intentions but lacking in spiritual knowledge of the Word and God's revelations. That is if the Catholic Church wasn't the product of an evil mind, hoping to deceive people as to the way of salvation by twisting the truth of the gospel. In Catholicism, personal sacrifice and obedience to the rules are of first importance, instead of Jesus Christ, the living Son of God, through whom, and through whom only, we have the chance to approach the Father.

Religious people have forgotten what God Himself, through His Spirit in King David, has said: "But our God is in the heavens: he hath done whatsoever he hath pleased. Their idols are silver and gold, the work of men's hands. They have mouths, but they speak not: eyes have they, but they see not: They have ears, but they hear not: noses have they, but they smell not: They have hands, but they handle not: feet have they, but they walk not: neither speak through their throat. They that make them are like unto them; so is every one that trusted in them" (Psalms 115:3–8). Idols include modern-day pictures, drawings, or images on walls or on trees, and any other "supernatural" appearances of saints.

Catholic representatives of God claim that the saints intercede before God on our behalf, but this is false. The saints are dead. The Bible says that the only One between man and God who may intercede for us is Jesus Himself, and when we pray for someone in need, we are to do so in Jesus's name, not the name of any person, dead or alive.

The Bible advises us to test any spirits so that we don't get deceived by evil, whether coming from out of the blue or existing within man. This is a very fine line, where it is almost impossible to distinguish between the real and that which merely looks real to the person who is incapable of spiritual discernment and understanding.

The ones who know the Word of God not by spiritual discernment and revelation, but theologically, will never see or know the difference between the material world and the spiritual world. Clearly, Satan has created this spiritual confusion among so-called Christians, making them incapable of understanding His Word or doing His will. The Bible describes such people as being ignorant of the Word and therefore incapable of spiritual discernment. Believers who were once on the right path but who switched to some other religion or denomination, seeking the truth elsewhere in their failure to have found spiritual fulfillment in revelation, have cheated themselves out of knowing God.

Some people live their whole lives believing that because they know the Bible from cover to cover, in addition to theology and biblical history, they are experts on God's spiritual world. Those believers who, having been deceived, departed from the Truth, and the ones who remain in the Truth without moving forward, failing to grow up spiritually, are walking on thin ice. The ones who fast, pray, and meditate on the things of the Almighty will never be deceived or caught "sleeping," as the apostle Paul has said of some in the Christian church. What was supposed to be the will of God has been covered with deceiving explanations and man's interpretations of love, goodness, and so on. The spiritual things spoken of, which are not disclosed in God's Word, are made to look convincingly spiritual so that the person who has a passive heart and is ignorant of the Word accepts it.

When your common sense is inactive and your reasoning is skewed, it means that your mind is being controlled and you are unable to analyze or discern for yourself. Your mind in such a state is neutralized or asleep. But it is not the Spirit that prohibits the mind from working independently; it is the man with a title to whom people go to make their confessions, rather than going directly to God. Instead, they will kiss a man's ring for the forgiveness of their sins, calling him "Father," "Your Holiness," and many other names of glory and greatness that he has picked for himself. He ensures, in people's ignorance, the belief that he is the one between them and God—when Jesus clearly says that there is no one, through whom man can come to the Father, except through Him, Christ, the Messiah. "No man can come to me, except the Father which hath sent me draw him: and I will raise him up on the last day" (John 6:44).

Jesus says not to call anyone father: "And call no man your father: for one is our Father, who is in heaven" (Matthew 23:9). But many leaders ignore the spiritual teaching of Jesus and practice their own rules, participating in their own condemnation by allowing people to call them father. Some leaders, whose hearts are known only to the Lord, may be doing it for their own glory, deceiving people knowingly and unknowingly, and preventing them from being guided towards a real spiritual fellowship in the Spirit with the real Father.

How do those who ask or allow people to call them father, fail to heed the warning of Jesus? Some will say, "Well, if you call your spiritual leader 'pastor,' then why can't we call the spiritual leader of our religion 'father'? It's common sense, right?" No, it is not common sense. Some believers, who do not know the Word of God, may accept the spiritual connotation of a male called father in a spiritual sense as an equal with the One in the heavens, when in reality it was merely given by God to man for recognition of natural fatherhood by his descendants. Jesus warned the naive, but respectful, people not to call their religious leaders father, who, like the Pharisees, were exalting themselves above the people. Even when we don't know if the Pharisees were ever called fathers, for some reason, Jesus said what He said.

In some countries with cultures thousands of years old, younger people call older people whom they don't know "father" or "mother" because it is part of their culture to show respect to the elderly and address them as they would their own father and mother. Sometimes elderly people might call a young man or young woman to whom they are not related "son" or "daughter," which is normal in some cultures.

Jesus told us not to call anyone Father on this earth, in the spiritual sense, for people to understand that in our spiritual life we all have one Heavenly Father. It was a spiritual mandate for the people to know that there is a spiritual difference between the Heavenly Father and the human "father" with a religious title, both of which cannot be related, by blood, to each other. In the Spirit, we are all brothers and sisters as believers.

The responsibility of religious leaders, if they understand the difference themselves, is to tell their people to distinguish between the heavenly Father and a religious leader. Then it is up to the believers to decide what to call their spiritual guides, showing love and respect but also knowing who they are in their spiritual role. Perhaps believers could choose to call their leaders "brothers" or "shepherds." Jesus was a shepherd, the Good Shepherd.

There are other gospel controversies amid different denominations. These disagreements exist because these denominations lack spiritual revelation and an understanding of God's will. This is required if we are to have in our hearts the wish to be of one mind and one Spirit. That unity will allow us to have the same understanding of the gospel, as the Lord wants us to have. If we don't have that, then no matter how we cut it or slice it, we are doing something wrong.

Some religious leaders of the gospel are no better in their "spiritual" way of life than those who are practicing religion by leading their people into believing in idols or performing rituals.

Even if such leaders do not asked to be called Father, Pastor, or some other title, some are putting themselves almost at the same level as the throne of God in the lives of their naive believers. About such leaders, the Lord Almighty said, "Not everyone that saith unto me, Lord, Lord shall enter the kingdom of heaven; but he that doeth the will of my Father which is in heaven" (Matthew 7:21)

An idol has come to dwell in the lives of believers, who have accepted it blindly, without any discernment, and without asking the leaders of the church what that idol truly represents in the life of a Christian. That unrecognized idol is like the demon that Jesus expelled from a herd of pigs. When Jesus asks the demon its name, it responded, "Legion." The story is in Mark 5:1–12. That legion today has a new name, and it works knowing God, but separating believers who are otherwise unified in the gospel, diverting the believer away from the truth of God and an understanding of His will.

The name of this unrecognized spirit that has been keeping believers in the gospel in a state of togetherness without union is called Denominations. A spirit of religiousness and passiveness has come to dwell within people, causing them to accept what they are taught without any skepticism, without discernment of any kind, just because someone in a position of authority is supposed to speak the truth.

A Christian world without a guiding Spirit has come about because of a lack of interest. The human spirit is ignored by the lazy, dormant heart, which rejects its own awakening in favor of believing that it is on the right path. Anything that detracts from or numbs the heart to the reality of its spiritual future is one of the spiritual legions within the heart of man. These spirits darken the light of a person's understanding so that he does not comprehend how another spirit is claiming that there are different ways to believe in God, confusing the person's heart and also confusing doctrine.

It is amazing to see the spiritual blindness of those who fail to see what denominations are doing to the church. The birth of the first denomination of the Christian church, which later was called the universal church, has brought to the world a different understanding of the gospel, confusing people's faith. Such faith and beliefs as the Catholic Church espouses would in some nations cause people to be regarded as fanatics in their religious way of life. Among religious people, only God knows which leaders are honest and real. Many believers who are ignorant of the Word as revealed by the Spirit, in their honest and sincere faith, remain under God's grace, mercy, and protection.

The devil has created such an incredibly misleading system of spiritual doctrines that man cannot distinguish between the true and the false, to the point that some deny God's commandments, will, and truth. For such people, the will of God is to be interpreted through man's intelligence, not revealed by the Spirit. A "revelation" that one considers to be from God, will create spiritual disunion, if it divides people instead of uniting them in one understanding of the gospel as revealed by the Spirit.

From paganism to Judaism, from Christianity to religiousness, from religiousness to occultism, and from occultism to atheism— one "truth" mixed with so much deceitfulness that not even a "spiritually" religious person can find the right path. The revelation of God's Spirit alone will open men's eyes and hearts to the truth of God, enabling them to see the difference. But that is if the man in need of God gives himself a chance through Jesus, without any preconditions or reservations, to see God's real spiritual truth.

The accepted belief that we are with God, not that God has His Spirit in us, is what is keeping spiritual revelation and declaration of God's truth out of our grasp. Religious people follow their own agenda according to their understanding of the will of God and His Word. Spiritual Christians seek and follow God's will through prayer and fasting, searching for wisdom, revelation, knowledge, understanding, and vision—big difference. Jesus said, "But seek ye first the kingdom of God: and His righteousness; and all those things shall be added unto you" (Matthew 6:33).

Read this verse as if listening to the words of a friend who is giving you advice and telling you to seek God's will and His righteous justice, and He will provide for all your secular needs. That is the first door you must enter if you are to get from God everything that is needed to do His will, with the fringe benefit of keeping your own will at your disposal, without any intermediary between you and God.

There is only one task we have in this world, and that is to train ourselves to see the difference between the truth and that which merely looks like the truth. The real intention of God is to unite people in one mind and one spirit in peace, with no loss of life. Religion involves a code of man-made rules that were created to "unite" people who had a different understanding of God or gods. Given that these rules were created by men, those same people also planned to present an imitation of the gospel to the people so it would be wrongly understood. We shouldn't forget that Satan was involved in man's plan for the new religion, where rules were to be followed and rituals were to be performed, in the end resulting in bloodshed because of the internal disagreements.

In the era when the Jews were persecuting Christians, they allied themselves with the Romans because it was convenient to do so. They bribed them with money in exchange for political favors, chief among things being the execution of Christians. A similar thing happened a few centuries later when the Roman Catholic Church instituted the Inquisition for the "salvation" of lost souls.

Every denomination in this world has its own truth, each

single person in the world has his or her own truth, and that truth depends on faith, understanding, intention, and conviction. From the most sincere and pure intentions to the most diabolical beliefs that a person's heart may hold, it is easy to implant religious doctrine in an ignorant or naive heart that has only a superficial knowledge of, or has never even heard of, the Word of God.

Religion today does not deliver the force necessary to fight spiritual warfare. The people who have devoted, solemn, and reverent faithfulness to the rules of their doctrine, treat religion as status quo, which is maintained by their church leaders. At the end, God is the only one who knows the hearts of His believers, whether they are right or wrong in their faith.

There are three kinds of teachers of the Bible. First are the spiritual ones, who understand that if a Christian is to grow in faith and do God's will, he will need wisdom and revelation from the Spirit. Second are the intellectuals, who describe God and discuss Him according to their own interpretation of the Word and their knowledge of historical arguments, but without spiritual revelation. And the third are those who teach according to denomination, where one comes to a knowledge of God through learning the Word by having theological discussions, with historical arguments and psychology added to make it more philosophical.

Such teachers who believe that they are spiritual, that have the necessary wisdom, and that have good intentions, become undisputed religious leaders spouting their own theology. In studying theology or the Word of God, one must understand why different doctrines and denominations exist, and what is important to accept or reject, and why. It is also important to be aware that all Christians, no matter their denomination, believe they have been spiritually illuminated by God and His Word. Rare is the Christian who wants to admit that he has chosen the wrong denomination. But still, who's to say who is right and who is wrong?

The difference between intellectual knowledge and spiritual knowledge is that the latter comes via revelation. That is why in the learning of God, His Word, Jesus, or Spirit as the personal connection between humankind and God, those things are not especially emphasized in how to access God's wisdom and to achieve the spiritual goal. The Almighty Trinity is spiritual, the learning is for the purpose of intellectual understanding, but the teaching should be understood as spiritual.

Lastly, as with many other things and no matter how we slice it, if the well-intentioned way to help a person understand God, Christ, the gospel, salvation, and service is something that has been created by man, then it may mislead the person and blind him to God's desire that we Christians be of one mind and one spirit in the spiritual unity that is required from us.

Man's unnoticed introduction of philosophy into the gospel was to make it more widely understood and more easily explainable, and this philosophy many times is accepted as spiritual because it is taught as having come straight from the Word of God, whether we hear this from someone behind a pulpit in church, from someone in Bible college, or any other way. The interpretation is still an intellectual one, and many times it fails to direct the believer to a more practical way of finding his own personal road to spiritual revelation and forging a personal relationship with his Savior.

Even when the study of God and the broad teaching of the gospel in the so-called theological way is correct in terms of intention, it may fail to teach beginners and seniors alike how to personally challenge themselves to reach their spiritual goals. The real knowledge of God in the spirit of revelation is found in direct fellowship with the Lord, something that is known as a "mano a mano," or hand-to-hand, encounter. And to get to that point, man needs to understand the kind of heart he is approaching that learning with if he is to learn directly from the Spirit. God declares Himself, His truth, and His will to us according to the intentions and understanding of our heart. If we fail to be in one mind and one spirit as He wants us to be, then our spiritual practice may be without results. This may sound difficult to follow, but remember: God will direct the process of learning about the Trinity.

The Word and the Spirit are one, but if a man does not understand that those two things are the same in God, then intellectually it will be impossible for him to know God. Without spiritual revelation, it is impossible to know the things of the Spirit, which are required if one is to understand God and His Word. The Bible says: "But the natural man receiveth not the things of the Spirit of God: for they are foolishness unto him: neither can he know them, because they are spiritually discerned" (1 Corinthians 2:14).

The apostle Paul in 1 Corinthians 1:10–31 talks about spiritual unity in Christ, as opposed to divisive beliefs about Him, saying that in the future, Christians would profess their brotherhood within their own denominations. Different doctrines separate Christians, leading them to be in direct conflict with God's wish that they be of one understanding as members of one body working together for the same purpose. And due to the of lack of spiritual unity among believers, the body of Christ has been growing increasingly weaker, proving that the world will be going from bad to worse, as the Word mentions.

In chapter 2 of 1 Corinthians, Paul explains the difference between real wisdom from God and human wisdom. God's wisdom is revealed by the Spirit to man, while human wisdom is man's IQ. In chapter 3, Paul repeats the reason why we remain as children in the gospel. He adds that we will fail in whatever we do without the required knowledge and understanding to form our foundation in God, and then we will have to answer for our lack of spiritual inquisitiveness, our laziness, our concern for our own comfort, and our arrogance.

Nothing we do to learn about God will bring us closer to Him if the Spirit does not dwell in us, guiding us. Failing to understand this, Christians are not united under one same thought in the will of God, although they do agree on the theological meaning of everything that is of, and maybe from, God, according to different doctrines.

If theology is about the divine person of God or His personality, and if philosophy is our deepest form of knowledge, then in our attempts to understand Him, our human intelligence can never become a higher knowledge if we are not living in the world where discernment is revealed by the Spirit. By relying on our own intellectual interpretations and teachings of the Gospel, our spiritual knowledge is far from the teaching of the Spirit.

In order to know the celestial life, the believer has only one option: to walk the road of his spiritual faith—nothing else. Intellectual wisdom and academic knowledge, even when needed for other purposes, will never achieve unity of mind and spirit if it is not through the Spirit itself. The reason for this is that human knowledge provides a religious understanding but not a spiritual connection, even when a person believes he has such a connection. In that case, only the Almighty can say whose heart is in His Spirit, both in the teaching and in the learning.

Many good-hearted Christians find it hard to understand how spiritual sickness enters and causes division in a healthy body. The teachers of the gospel, who are supposed to be the "doctors," are failing to see denominational doctrine as a disease. For failing to make a diagnosis, the spiritual body becomes infected, causing neutralization to our spiritual "immune system" which then alters the heart the ability to speak to reason.

So-called spiritual leaders, whether unintentionally or on purpose, have accepted wrong doctrine and spread it, asking people to believe that their doctrine offers a spiritual cure, saying that if one would adopt their beliefs, they would come to enjoy a healthy and prosperous life in God. Instead of healing the members of the sick body, the leaders, unknowingly or on purpose, just give them the same spiritual "medicine." Instead of getting rid of the evil of illness, the "pill, injection, or syrup" of their different "demon-inations" simply mask the symptoms for a while. So when a believer returns for a spiritual cure again and seeks a leader's help, the believer does not realize that the expected "spiritual medicine" will never be able to heal a soul from an ill or weak heart just by listening to a "doctor" who may prescribe medication that does not work. Due to the lack of spiritual knowledge and revelation, the above is the wrong understanding of God's promises of help. And because of that misleading spiritual teaching of offering a "medicine" as a solution to all problems to the believer, one must show obedience to God through offerings and personal sacrifice while serving the so-called religious leaders. Believers are warned about losing something if they should turn away from the said path. It is implied that since God is first, whatever little you have, give it to the church anyway to have God's blessings in your life. Religious leaders who demand such things do not encourage spiritual awakening, because spiritual awakening is another "corporation" that the "demon-inational doctor" does not want you to know about, because it could create competition for them in their "spiritual pharmaceutical" business.

Here is where the "patients" need to realize that they can look for God themselves. They can do so by getting on their knees, not by going to some doctor, specialist, clinic, preacher, teacher, or church, but by taking the time and, from the bottoms of their hearts in all humility, doing what Jesus told them to do in the beginning: "But seek ye first the kingdom of God: and His righteousness; and all those things shall be added unto you" (Matthew 6:33).

Try Jesus's medicine of fasting, meditation, and prayer. Ask in your heart to know His Spirit and His will; ask for the knowledge of His "medicine" of wisdom, revelation, and vision. Meanwhile, as with a red-hot iron, keep branding His Words of promise onto your faithful believing heart.

The division among good-intentioned Christians exists because of their different doctrines in the knowledge of the gospel, which is believed to be a revelation from God. The reason for this is because the believers approach the Word with their minds, or intellectually, rather than their hearts. A refusal to read the Word with the heart instead of the mind is the reason why spiritual revelation cannot be achieved. And to achieve revelation, one must have a humble heart patiently waiting to hear God's voice and feel the presence of His Spirit. His Spirit will first heal any spiritual misunderstanding, and then will rid the believer of any secular inconveniences, such as in their physical body, in the material world, or in their financial life. This spiritual power is impossible for man to comprehend if he is not in the Spirit.

Whether the believer is new to the gospel or not, he needs to allow God's Spirit to give his human spirit understanding to translate to the human intellect the dictates of the Spirit. God works in and through the heart, not through the gelatinous thing in our skulls called the brain, and it is our intellect which needs to understand that our human mind is unable to comprehend what is spiritual.

It is important to understand that before Adam and Eve sinned, we were spiritual. Only afterward did we become secular, superficial. That is why the Son of God came to us in the flesh, to show us the way back to the spiritual world, the way we were before, deep in the life and right knowledge of the Spirit.

As long as we fail to achieve the same understanding, we'll never be spiritually united. And it doesn't matter how solid our theology is, we'll never be one in Him.

Philosophy and theology are academic studies where knowledge of the Word of God is consigned to the field of religious doctrine. Logical discussions about the gospel and God might be good for religion, but they are not good for the purpose of achieving spiritual understanding through spiritual revelation.

Intellectual interpretations of the gospel are not always correct, and therefore make it difficult for us to reach spiritual unity. Spirituality is a higher knowledge revealed by God to man, according to the sincerity of his heart, but not according to his mere intellectual curiosity.

God will reward man's heart if he seeks His will for the right reasons, for God's glory, not man's own. If intellectuality is impossible to explain, then spirituality is even harder.

Spirituality, according to man's understanding, is short in knowledge, even when a believer goes through spiritual experiences. There are things that can't be explained because the human mind cannot comprehend that things are happening in the spiritual realm.

Go back to the example of a person seeing the number six on the floor, not realizing that someone standing on the opposite side sees it as the number nine, or another person seeing a glass of water as half full, while the other sees it as half empty. To understand why someone declares something as the truth, one must be able to see through that person's perspective at that moment. The same goes for knowing God's Word and will, with the difference being that the latter requires a spiritual approach. Even though each offers its own understanding, one depends on human intellect and the other is based on the spirit, the heart, and revelation.

There is nothing wrong with studying the things of God with our human intellect. It becomes wrong when we confuse our intellectual knowledge in the understanding of the Word with spiritual revelation.

When the Spirit of God is allowed to be in charge in our hearts, He gives our hearts the ability to understand His will through spiritual knowledge. And that spiritual knowledge comes as a revelation only when we are in a close relationship with God, seeking first His will and then the wishes of our own hearts. This only comes about if man's heart understands that only in Him we are spiritual. Just because we may know the Bible from cover to cover or have a PhD hanging on the wall with people calling us doctors or professors, does not make us experts.

There are only a handful of spiritual Christians who are guided by God's Spirit, when at the same time, most religious believers think that they are also spiritual. The truth is that the majority who call themselves Christians are entirely ignorant of God's will, the real will. And the proof of that is the condition of Christianity in the world today.

In this world, people seriously misunderstand everything from faith to love, from morals to justice, from peace to war, and from hell to heaven. It is because they are confused and self-righteous, living outside God's will, love, and grace. People of all socioeconomic levels, whether religious believers or not, are allowing evil to move from bad to worse. The proof of this is the condition of the world in which we live, and this world is in terrible condition because people think they know better than the Almighty. But people in their religious knowledge, even when they see where this world is heading, refuse to do something about it, thinking that everything is in the will of God.

To understand God's will is to be of one mind and one Spirit, not only to be united as one for the salvation of the human race, but also to keep us strong against the hordes of hell. If believers of Christ won't accept the challenge to determine if what they wish for are things that God wills, then certainly they will be destroyed in due time, and He will have to intervene to save the world at the prophesied end of times.

What is worst of all is the dying and slowly disappearing gift God has given us called faith. When one approaches faith with one's brain but not a working mind, then the heart is putting the soul in danger. A close fellowship with our Lord is made possible through fasting and praying, just like our Savior did when He was on earth, with His Father in heaven.

According to the Word of God, our salvation is not to be found in the way we criticize people of other faiths and denominations, saying that we are right and they are wrong. According to our hearts, our knowledge and understanding of Him, and the things we do in this world, we will one day stand before our Creator to be accepted, not rejected. Every single day someone writes the story of someone or something that will be the recorded history for future generations to read, then take on the same task of finding out the truth.

People, political institutions, and religious outfits deny the evil within themselves, though there is a secret well-guarded in the deepest of their internal system, or heart, and it doesn't matter how powerful or weak the person, institution, or nation is, the secret of greed, ambition, envy, jealousy, self-interest, distrust, fear, treason, or corruption remains hidden even when the person or institution allegedly are believers in God. Evil came to exist in human nature since the time Adam and Eve were expelled from the Garden of Eden.

In every country, in every generation, the blood of innocent people is spilled under the direction of some self-righteous evildoer, who to some is a hero, and to others is a mass murderer, even if he claims to be a believer in God. Some kill in the name of their "religious" political ideals of democracy, communism, socialism, or libertarianism; and some in the name of religion.

Those crimes, from the psychological corruption of morality to the taking of someone's life, are committed by people who have in mind greed and control, who feel no remorse upon spilling blood in the name of some "benevolent" person, organization, or government. Satan knows how to manipulate those who are religiously and spiritually blind in high, low, or no positions at any level of society. But the end goal of whatever atrocity is committed, is power. Money is wealth, wealth is power, and power is control. And those things combined create an aura of untouchability around the murderous individual or group of wealthy people, religious people, or government representatives, making it easier for them to achieve whatever goals they may have. All the while, the poor man will try to convince himself he is living in a secure and peaceful world, not knowing that unpleasant circumstances may arise in his life when he puts his trust, not in God, but in the one whom he has voted for.

That world is the dark kingdom in which Satan is keeping his "truth" through men's religious, political, and other beliefs. He gives off a superficial intellectual light of knowledge in the darkened places of the lost or confused heart where religion and self-righteousness dwell. He provides a false peace, a state of mind where a person may convince himself he is not living in darkness, which is spiritual death. God is waiting for the moment when the will of that soul, using its intuition and common sense, will realize that it has within it the gift of self-determination. This knowledge allows the neutralized spirit to help revive the soul as the heart reaches for the Light of Life that it knew so long ago.

CHAPTER 29

S piritual religiousness today is like the paganism of the past, in that those who profess it believe in something imaginary, hoping that it will materialize through an act of goodness by a person. That is Satan's philosophy, a philosophy of "the righteous goodness of togetherness," a way of life suggested to people to get them to rally around politics and religion but not be united. And if they are united, they are united in groups called denominations, and not in one consolidated mass under God's will alone, believing in the same things for the purpose of being unified, that is, being of one mind and one spirit.

Christians who are truly united practice a spirituality free of personal opinion. Those who subscribe to an intellectual interpretation of the Word think and believe it has been spiritually revealed to them, when it has not, because they lack unity of Spirit with no disagreements, because God is not the one guiding them through revelation. If something causes serious disagreement, it is usually of an intellectual nature, and that is when one must be aware of the present spirit.

Some brethren, for failing to achieve the spiritual growth required to understand spiritual revelation or a dictate from the Holy Ghost, are confused by their "spiritual knowledge." If any disagreement should exist, then all the brethren should pray to

God and ask that He clarify the situation in their hearts. But first they must humble themselves before God.

Being spiritually blind in your own interpretations, deductions, or opinions is a sign of pride in your self-sufficiency and a lack of humbleness. The letter kills, but the Spirit gives life and wisdom.

You will learn of a higher knowledge with which to understand His will if you humble yourself before God and seek His guidance through His Spirit. Intellectual interventions in God's spiritual Word and world are a waste of time. In God, the future is now, not tomorrow, because life in Him is now and is in the Spirit.

Moreover, moving away from the intellectual and spiritual aspects of human nature and to the secular life of man, Jesus says, "For what shall it profit a man if he shall gain the whole world and lose his own soul?" (Mark 8:36). How many people understand these words? How many powerful people understand the consequences of imposing their greed, to get what they will own for only a few years, over the lives of people who have been calculated to be miserable?

The greedy people who live this way do not know of the eternity of painful punishment that awaits them when they leave behind their power the day they die. God cannot be cheated. God from eternity is the same. Lucifer, since he lost his citizenship in heaven and became the ruler of his own burning kingdom, also is the same, as are we the people—still the same.

God and Satan won't change because they are who they are, and they are that for eternity. We are like them in spirit, but with the difference being that we have a short fuse, and enough time to choose to which side we'll make a run for our lives, for our own better or worse ending in eternity.

God has given us a chance of eternal life through His Son, which is from whom all humanity is given an understanding of hell and heaven. Thus, if man does not harden his heart, like many have done throughout human history, then he will have a chance to be with the righteous in the right place. Religion and intentions, whether good or bad, will always keep people short of reaching God. It is not with the mind, deeds, or the sacrifice of idealistic goals that man will reach God's grace and mercy, but with the recognition of wrong in his heart, leading him to repent in humility with a believing faith.

The Pharisees, Sadducees, scribes, and others had an agenda to keep power for themselves. Religion, like politics, is a powerful weapon to control people's ignorance, naiveté, hope, or conscience, more of it, if some individuals have a specific deceitful plan besides playing servant to both God and other people. The painful reality is that common believers don't take the time—no matter their denomination—to look deeper, to investigate, or to pray.

God's revelation of His truth and will, to whatever religious organization people belong, will come to the ones who are looking for the truth in their hearts, if their hearts approach God without extremes or preconditions. The majority of believers are such conformists in their faith that they "grow up" spiritually blind to the reality of God's power. Even when they are supposed to know that power, they always think a cent short of a dollar.

Conformism is the biggest enemy of Christians of all time, the mentality of *I'm safe and active in church* is robbing Christians of the chance to investigate God's will by themselves, and not just in church. Christians should desire to look into any question that may arise in their hearts, comparing what the Bible says to the circumstances of their daily lives. They should not only ask questions of the leaders of the church, but also go directly to God because there are questions that no man will be able to answer. But God will.

Consider Jesus, who looked not toward man to determine what His next step should be, nor was he thinking about or planning things to do on His next workday by soliciting someone else's opinion. No, He called out to His Father, our God, for revelation of His wishes to serve Him. The truth is an offensive weapon; an excuse, an ineffective one. Some leaders of the church today are modern Pharisees; they have too much pride and not enough spiritual knowledge, never mind humbleness or spirituality. And some believers are ignorant, lazy, or offended by the truth, just like their leaders. And all this because the leaders are holding a long spear in front of them and protecting themselves by thinking, *I know what the Bible says,* thereby preventing anyone from coming too close to their self-sufficiency.

The events lived by people at any time in the past, whatever the results may have been, are no different from the events lived out by today's people. In the end, the result is always the same: someone is offending and someone else is offended, whether the circumstances of the moment are true or false. People lack the spirituality, common sense, and goodwill to understand other people. And that is because an unnoticed spirit of division exists within people who are ignorant, self-righteous, or arrogant, ignoring the Spirit and thereby negating any chance of help.

Moments in the life of someone with a secular spirituality and an irrational mind may be recorded for future analysis. That is something for a person to agree with or disagree with, to either forgive or accuse, or to simply add something extra to what is already history, making it more interesting or more confusing, but never definitive.

Yesterday is already history, and what happened yesterday cannot be changed. Yesterday already has its guilty and its innocent to be analyzed by future experts. In the end, as always, none of the experts will come up with a solution for man's past actions.

Because the fight for the human soul is ongoing, true spiritual believers are the only ones who can make a change with their prayers, without getting anyone upset or spilling anyone's blood, leaving in God's hands what is impossible for man but possible for Him. This is a very different spiritual solution from man's political gospel for the betterment of man's future.

People of this nation once and for all have to understand that if anyone in the name of God or under any other banner is calling to defend some national interest, whether political, religious, or business-affiliated, in any other nation by shedding blood through somebody else's hand, that call is not from a sane person. It doesn't matter who that person may be, of God or from God, whether on the inner or the outer limits of Christ's teaching, the provocation from such a person may result in an outside attack where their own citizens will be forced to defend their homes and country. The only exception to justified bloodshed is if a person is defending their country and home from whoever is attacking. An example of a person rightfully defending his home can be found in Luke 11:21-22: "When a strong man armed keepeth his palace, his goods are in peace: But when a stronger than he shall come upon him, and overcome him, he taketh from him all his armour wherein he trusted, and divideth his spoils."

Christians should have a real understanding of peace with a wishing heart before the Lord, remembering what the Word of God is teaching us when it says, "For kings, and for all that are in authority; that we may lead a quiet and peaceable life in all godliness and honesty. For this is good and acceptable in the sight of God our Savior" (1 Timothy 2:2–3). The Anglo-Saxon believers in Christ should have the responsibility to pray for their leaders and their nation.

The only legitimate time to take up arms is when someone is trying to forcibly enter your home. This is according to the example of the strong man. An honest, decent, and respectful strong man will never go to someone else's house with the hidden pretext to help, do justice, or secure his own peace at home, while using personal reasons as an excuse for some ideological, geopolitical, or national business interest.

The accusation that an enemy a few thousand miles away is putting our country in danger is a premeditated satanic lie, more of it when the accused nation does not have a competitive armed forces.

We are not living by the law of the Old Testament given by God to His people. We are living in the time of a different understanding of God's will for us, which is under the law of love, grace, mercy, and understanding. He said, "I will have mercy on whom I will have mercy, and I will have compassion on whom I will have compassion" (Romans 9:15).

It looks as if the Anglo-Saxon "gospel of democracy" is taking God's Word as its own, forgetting that God is much more merciful than their democracy, with justice and respect for a human life. No one in this world is better than anyone else. That is what the Christians are not seeing, and for not seeing, they forget what it says in 1 Timothy 2:2–3. Anglo-Saxon believers are praying to God to protect their soldiers in faraway lands. Though well-intentioned, that is the wrong prayer.

You pray to get rid of your enemies, yet God's mercy and compassion will go to the ones whom you would never expect in your "righteousness", placing them under His protection. Undoubtedly, this principle goes both ways. If you don't want to have intruders, then don't leave your doors or windows open on purpose. If you don't want enemies, then don't make them, or don't look for an excuse to have them.

Religious people have appropriated the words *mercy*, *compassion*, and *righteousness* for themselves, according to their own convenience, in their wrong beliefs about the gospel, whether the undertone is political or religious.

God's Spirit in people doesn't kill people; evil spirits in people kill people in the name of their own interests, using the name of God by sending them "with God's blessing" to take another's life. Why? Because people, even when they have heard of Christ, don't know Him, never mind know how to be in Him. There are those who reject Christ or have Him only on their lips. This happened in the times of the Pharisees and the Romans, as it happened before them and after them, all the way up to the current time.

War is based on Satan's greed and the hatred in man's life. Religiousness, with its false spirituality, is the driving force of the weakened nature of man who does not have the Spirit of God, but thinks he does, as he performs his evil in the world, whatever his goals are. The wish of a man, who knowingly or unknowingly, has allowed his heart to weaken in his pursuit to conquer the world and accumulate wealth for the power that comes with it, and to control other people's lives and needs, is to be rewarded by Satan.

The new man has the power of Jesus, but unfortunately he doesn't know how to use it for his own defense. The Word says, "Resist the devil and he will flee from you" (James 4:7). But the man who lets evil get into his heart as he represents that which is "good" in his own interests or the interests of his people or country, having in mind the idea of a great empire with power and control, is a man controlled by Satan. That man does not resist evil because he may not even notice its presence in his life or understand the destruction he is creating around him. That person is in a world where he is failing to notice that he is killing himself. By way of his own belief and greed, he has created an illusion of a heavenly future.

Today in our churches, we pray to God to protect our soldiers, while they are off in some distant land killing the citizens who are defending their own country. Soldiers are destroying lives, land, and infrastructure, and being killed themselves, for "political justice" and many other reasons, but the real reason is their leaders' greed for wealth. Our soldiers are not even fighting for justice or the security of their own country, even when that is exactly what is being preached to their fellow citizens.

We are not living under the Old Testament's law of an eye for an eye, nor are we the strong man defending our home against someone who lives on the other side of the world. After two world wars and with close to one hundred million dead people, if not more, we are living in what is supposed to be a new world.

By now the leaders of the world, at least some of them, understand what peace is now that their own countries have had that monster of destruction called war tear through their lands. They are trying to bring some sense of understanding for peace and a spirit of cooperation to avoid another cruel human tragedy. And those who want peace are the ones who are accused of every imaginable evil. In some countries, the leaders wrongly believe that God has given them the moral right to destroy those who do not want to accept their Christian civilization or their preaching lies about the well-being of humanity.

The Western world believes in and preaches peace, but it does not practice it. Human understanding, respect, and care for others are religious ideals for us to put into practice, as the apostle James said: "If any man among you seem to be religious [thinks of himself as a good person] and bridles not his tongue [does not care for the lies he speaks] but deceiveth his own heart [lies to himself], this man's religion is in vain [that man's goodness is fake and worthless]" (James 1:26).

That "democratic religion of American goodness" story that is sold to us is about our democracy helping faraway nations in need. Even when helping those nations, the help is not for the people, but is for our national interest through their Judases in power. When these Judases for some reason cannot be controlled thousands of miles away from us, they and their people become our enemies, and now we have to agree not to help them but to punish them, because they are our enemies, putting our nation and our way of life "in danger."

No, their people are not our enemies. The enemy of the people of any country is probably their no-good leaders. And those leaders who choose to listen to their people become enemies of our own no-good leaders, as opinionated by some citizens. Leaders who have become instruments of evil act according to the will of Satan, setting their people against others for their own purposes, while people on both sides are thinking that they are the ones right in their killing.

The ones who are right in the killing are the ones defending their homes, their families, and their own land from the invaders. The others are labeled as "the thief [who] cometh not, but for to steal, and to kill, and destroy" (John 10:10). Invaders often have some "legitimate" reason to execute their evil intention, viewed by themselves as a "right" for their own evil purpose in the eyes of the world, but not in the eyes of God.

Some people praying to God are asking for peace and justice and to put their misery to an end, while blood of the innocent is spilled. Others are praying to God to protect their soldiers, when they are killing those praying to that same God to protect them from those same soldiers. Ironic combination.

When will we Christians learn to pray, not to protect our soldiers, but to ask God for peace, putting all those war-loving evil creatures that look like man in God's hands according to the wishes of our hearts? Or perhaps we don't wish for peace, understanding, and the love of Christ for the people of this world, knowing who the real enemy of our lives is?

How naive are we when we believe and trust in man's ideals for justice and security, leveraging our love for our country? How is it possible that the Christians of the Western world don't see what is happening in the spirit? Enemies are not created by God, but by Satan in man's ambition for greed and power in his own distorted understanding of political or moral justice and religious righteousness. We the people are not the ones politically dealing in our nation's destiny.

If we don't want any enemies, we should respect other people's ways of life. God will judge them for the way they practice their faith in Him, whether right or wrong. We need to respect their ways of doing business, their borders, and their political ideals just as we require that others respect ours.

Respect for other people's rights in their own homes results in peace. If we think we are better than other people, as evil makes us think we are, accusing others in our tendency to believe that we are right, correct, and justified in our actions against them, that same evil that we have created will sooner or later turn against us in our own homes, our own families, and our own land.

If in our faith and belief as real spiritual Christians, and not as so-called religious believers, we fail to do something to fight the spirits of the air, as the apostle Paul mentioned, then we'll harvest in our own lives what we have planted or helped to plant through other hands. And that will be the payback for our arrogant, self-sufficient, proud self-righteousness, all because the whole nation lacks humbleness in its unrecognized spiritual ignorance and blindness.

This is a well-known secret that many don't understand or accept as a truth. A boomerang always returns to the one who throws it. This is what Jesus has said: "Give not that which is holy to the dogs, neither cast ye your pearls before swine, lest they trample them under their feet and turn again and rend" (Matthew 7:6). Those words can be perfectly applied to some people in the governments of different nations and the citizens who believe in them.

With these words, Jesus was saying to the people to be cautious and prudent. He said, "Behold, I send you forth as sheep in the midst of wolves. Be ye therefore wise as serpents and harmless as doves" (Matthew 10:16). These two examples of Jesus's warnings are to be understood not only spiritually, but also intellectually for our secular lives, when we put our lives, in trust or hope, in the hands of people with power.

We the people are supposed to be co-participants in the future of our nation, but we are not co-participating, nor are we the ones who are acting in our own interests for the future. For that we have our representatives of different "denominations".

Here we are speaking of the "high priest"; the people's representatives in the House and the Senate; and their bosses behind the scenes—people with power who are running the country according to their own interests in our name, affecting our destiny and the destiny of our country.

Such people one day, if it's not happening already, will find that the Christians and the gospel are their enemy. Because it is the gospel of truth, as in the time of Jesus, those Pharisees are labeled as pigs, as their ancestors were in the Lord's analogy, for the evil they have done in people's lives that trusted them, as even today, in the name of humanity and justice around the world.

The only thing the citizens can do to participate is to vote; the rest is out of their hands. If someone says differently, well, not everyone is naive or ignorant enough to believe in such a "truth." The proof of this truth is in the lives of people around the world whom we read about in the daily news. People are protesting because their needs are not being met by their own governments, including in the richest countries of the world, after they have voted and waited for their elected leaders to make good on their promises.

A better way of voting is needed, we are told. Although there is a legitimate reason for voting reform, our leaders leverage this in pursuit of the real reason: to hold onto power so they can continue to satisfy their greed. They give to the people a bag of phony promises that they have made to look like the truth, and the people believe them because their politicians are supposed to know better. Incredibly, people still hope, believe, and trust that what their representatives are saying is the truth.

Maybe if we had real spiritual understanding, according to the teaching of the Lord, and knew what to expect in this life, we'd spend more time in prayer and less time living a life of false hope in human beings. There is no difference between people's lives today and people's lives thousands of years ago. Speaking of this kind of trust in man, God said in Jeremiah 17:5, "Cursed be the man who trusteth in man, and maketh flesh his arm, and whose heart departed from the Lord."

Not many believers are able to spiritually discern man's intentions, and of those who do, they are not making any difference. No one cares enough for wisdom and higher results to bring about a different situation in this world. This is something that "spiritual" Christians, who say they know God's power, should be concerned about. To know God's power is one thing, but to understand how to use it in the spiritual world for our defense, our own benefit, and His glory is a different thing altogether.

Instead of praying to God and asking that He help us to avoid war and bloodshed, we keep trusting politicians and hoping for a happy ending that never comes. Maybe the highest spiritual state our minds can reach is patriotism, which blinds us in our faithfulness to the Stars and Stripes, and to the man who is lying to us. Our patriotic and civil duty is, as the apostle James said about religion, not to kill, but to help another human. This is what we should be practicing on the other side of the world, instead of destroying the people.

What kind of a Christian nation were we before, and what kind are we today? Our form of so-called punishment is based only on greed, called by a false name to defend someone else's interests in the name of humanity no matter the order of the day. All of this is because someone in our government felt that on the other side of the world, somebody whom we are not able to bully should become the enemy. And the explanation of why they are the enemy is according to the politician's convenience, not according to the real truth. Jesus said, "Ye are of your father the devil and the lust of your father ye will do. He was murdered from the beginning, and abode not in the truth because there is no truth in him. When he speaketh a lie, he speaketh of his own: for he is a liar, and the father of it" (John 8:44). Satan's children are doing exactly that. Who gave those people the moral right, in the name of the United States, Great Britain, and the people of those nations, to kill other souls for their corrupt "democracies"?

Jesus says about these people, "Woe unto you, scribes and Pharisees, hypocrites! For ye pay tithe of anise and cumin and have omitted the weightier matters of the law, judgment, mercy, and faith: those ought ye to have done and not to leave the other undone" (Matthew 23:23).

Can we place all the promises of our Lord about our Christian nation and lives on a high shelf, instead of man's word? Perhaps we'll do so when we feel the pain, suffering, and death that we are causing others by way of the same sword. By then it will be too late to be sorry because the pain that we'll feel someday will be caused not by the people of the faraway nations that we have punished, but by the same people who are now telling us to punish others.

The enemy of the people of any country is not outside the

country's borders; they are sitting in the country's own government and institutions. And the blood of their own people and others around the world is on their heads and the head of every individual who knowingly creates suffering, misery, and death, together with the ones who support their actions, that is, those who, under a fake ideology, are not only destroying the infrastructures of foreign countries but also killing those nations' people with the help of corrupt traitors. Remember one thing: everything political has spiritual ramifications whether you accept this or not.

Are the people of our nation so naive that they fail to see what their representatives, like the Sanhedrin, are doing? Don't we sometimes look like the Pharisees, ignoring or rejecting the truth, being spiritually blind and lacking of knowledge and vision because we are bereft of the spiritual wisdom of God? Do we need God's wisdom when we are able to see what is going on in this world? How much do we believe in prayer, or are we so spiritually wise in our own minds that we have questions about whether or not God will hear us pray to fulfill His promises? Being believers, are we not manipulated in our spiritual ignorance through the intellect?

Are we not like the people of Israel, manipulated by the "high priest" and the "Pharisees" in the capitol of some country, who in their hidden agenda and in the name of justice and God are telling us, "Kill, kill"? Is our spiritual understanding of Christ's teaching stronger than our intellectual belief about our spiritual understanding? Or are we so confused about our secular spiritualism, in our own interpretation of the Word, that we think it is God's will to be small-minded? Or we are just content with our spiritual knowledge, believing more in the law of man than we believe in the law of God?

"Beloved, believe not every spirit, but try the spirits, whether they are of God: because many false prophets are gone out into the world" (1 John 4:1). This is a secret we need to know, and not only know, but also understand: not all Pharisees, scribes, and Sadducees are evil in their deeds.

Satan doesn't require a person of a specific nationality or belief to ruin a life or spill blood. Anyone who believes in his heart, in its self-sufficiency, that he is doing "his duty" for the "good" of the people and the "good" of the nation, according to the law of his land, and with a greedy heart known only by the Almighty, is a good candidate to be the devil's advocate, even when he invokes God. Not everything that glitters is gold. We have to crush the human knowledge and pride within us if we want to be like Jesus.

CHAPTER 30

O ur enemy is not a man. It is the evil in that man that makes him our enemy. The apostle Paul wrote, "For we wrestle not against flesh and blood, but against principalities, against powers, against the rulers of the darkness of this world, against spiritual wickedness in high places" (Ephesians 6:12).

We Christians need to learn how to separate one thing from another, and then we will understand and make a difference. Some men can be convinced that evil exists, but others may never be. It is our fight as Christians to restrain, control, and arrest—that is, neutralize—the enemy of humankind. The difference between a real Christian and a person of the world is that one will give himself a chance in the understanding of right and wrong, whereas the other will reject the chance for different reasons.

Meanwhile, when we know much but understand little to nothing and become offensive, defensive, and self-righteous, we make it impossible to come out of the hole of our religious mentality, thinking that we are right and even spiritual. For some reason, evil still has the upper hand in most people's lives.

What is happening to Christians? Are we dead again and need revival? The apostle Paul said, "Many in church are sleeping"—not the sleep of death, but the sleep of laziness, comfort, self-sufficiency, hollow pride, and passiveness, which we need to get rid of in our Christian lives if we really are spiritual people.

In 1 Corinthians 11:30, we read, "For this cause many are weak and sickly among you, and many sleep." The apostle Paul meant to say that Christians in church are not spiritually healthy or strong. Many are living worldly lives. Many are lazy. Some have simply lost interest in everything, especially those who are inactive (the sleepy ones). But all of them, for whatever reason, keep coming to church, thinking that because they are in church, they are okay.

That is a very dangerous state of mind where common sense is dysfunctional because the mind is being controlled by a wrong spirit. We need to be awakened spiritually and become strong and healthy if we are to be able to open the "box" that we are supposed to have in our grateful hearts full of love for our Lord. With that commitment in our lives, we must, in gratitude for our salvation and the awakening of our spiritual awareness, do the will of God all the way to victory in eternity.

We the people are so good at creating history that we are now writing the same story twice, both here in this world and in the heavens, in the book of life. In one of these histories, we may excuse or accuse each other, but in the other, no excuses will be accepted for what we know and don't do, or do when we don't have to.

In this book of life, we'll read of the real acts we have performed and of the intentions of our hearts—something different from that which is written in the earthly record of our actions. In our knowledge or ignorance, any excuse we offer for our weakness won't fly according to the righteous freedom of God's justice.

Knowing what happened in history won't help us if we don't change. And given the results we are seeing, we are doing a poor job. Who is to blame if not ourselves? If God is with us, who can be against us? Well, if God is with us, it seems that we are the ones not close enough to Him, never mind being in Him. Otherwise how does one explain our failure to gain victory over this world? The apostle Paul said, "So likewise ye, when ye shall have done all those things which are commanded you, say, we are unprofitable servants: We have done that which was our duty to do" (Luke 17:10). Here is where we can try to go the extra mile, putting the wishes of our hearts into action. But it could be said that not even in this we are dependable.

We are so "knowledgeable" in the Word that we "understand" everything that the Bible is telling us about what to do or not do. That attitude is found not only in our laziness, but also in our lack of faith in God and in the failure of our hearts to seek and find the will of God in our lives. Simply put, in reality, we do not understand what it means to go the extra mile, not for ourselves, but in gratitude for our salvation and for the glory of the One who died and gave us the gift of eternal life. The only thing that is saving us from total destruction is the protection of His Spirit of love, mercy, and grace against evil. As it was in the old times, it is the same today.

We have gained much from the world, including science, progress, information, knowledge, philosophy, interpretation, and a whole bunch more of intellectual, educational news, but we have neither the understanding nor the spiritual audacity to challenge our own faith, so we can be guided by God's revelations to make the most of our spiritual gifts or the wishes of our hearts.

One of the biggest detractors in people's lives is their lack of knowledge and spiritual understanding, and the reason for this is that they have, unbeknownst to them, accepted a wrong spirit of passivity, with their uninquisitive minds and lazy hearts more interested in the things of this world than in the things of God. And because of this, they lack faith, and desire quick spiritual results, having secular goals in their lives while being members of the Christian church. Their worldliness will always cause them to fall short of acquiring God's wisdom, spiritual knowledge, and revelation, and may even prevent them from entering heaven. If we don't have the extra "oil" that we need for that time which could come at "any moment," we'll miss the chance to be present on the day of victory (Matthew 25:1-4).

Christianity is always the same, one God, one Christ, one Holy Spirit, one Trinity, one gospel, one faith, and one salvation, but Christians are different. Under one doctrine, not two or more, of Christ's teachings, we Christians are supposed to have one right understanding of the gospel and be of one mind and one Spirit. But we have managed to let denominations and doctrines separate us from the power of victory in our daily lives, perhaps causing our daily struggles to be in vain.

Usually we blame adverse circumstances or other people for our troubles, but we never stop to think about the reality of the evil influence that exists unnoticed in our daily lives. Why is that? Because we are not allowing ourselves to be guided by the Spirit of God like Jesus was. In God's spiritual world, man's common sense and deductions don't work, unless in your common sense you understand that the One that needs to be first is the Spirit, not your knowledge, your intellect, and so on.

The tragic consequences many people experience in their lives are the result of a lack of spiritual knowledge and an understanding of that knowledge. To receive such things, one must be open to the revelation of the Spirit in one's daily life, including all secular and spiritual occasions. That is the way to be in Christ. And it corresponds with what Jesus said: "But seek ye first the kingdom of God and his righteousness and all those things will be added unto you" (Matthew 6:33).

In every generation since the time the first crime was

ever committed, evil in man's life has led him to commit an unimaginable number of atrocities. People forget that it is not the creative nature of God, but the evil nature in man that incites man to ruin, break, and destroy anything that is good, sane, moral, or pure. A man will have evil spirits in his life until, once and for all, he decides to fight back with God's Spirit. When those evil spirits begin to disappear from men's lives, then we will attest to victory in Jesus's name, being free from evil interference and strong in the Spirit, just like Jesus.

From the time even before the Pharisees, the time after them, and throughout the centuries, all the way up to the modern day, every generation has seen the evil in man lead to a great number of massacres. It is hard to accept that a human being is able to commit such atrocities against other human beings. We almost never see, remember, or realize that these are acts performed by way of the dark power in man. What we see is the man himself in his act, forgetting or not noticing the inhuman power within him behind those actions. The natural intellect is unable to discern different spirits.

People must understand that when God chose His people to be descendent from Abraham, Satan got involved, taking the side of whomever he thought he had a chance to corrupt. That was the beginning of what we know about Satan's intensified meddling in people's lives.

Before God chose His people, Satan had no "competition," but afterward, Satan had to triple his effort in terms of evil intervention in people's lives, which God knew. Even though we have been kicked out of Eden, we still have a choice about what we do. We have self-determination and free will; God hasn't taken it away. And the evil one, knowing that, attacks with more intensity everything that belongs to God in our lives.

Satan never puts so much effort into messing up the lives of those who do not look for, or try to live as an obedient child for God. People who don't know God, or don't care to know Him, are an easy target for Satan. But the ones who know right from wrong and who avoid doing wrong always uphold a more difficult task to keep themselves clear of that which exploits their own weaknesses, which are under constant attack by the devil.

The dark forces are not concerned with people who are easy prey. No, they are much more diligent about tormenting the ones who invoke God's name, people who truly seek God's will.

Satan first blinds and confuses people, as he did with the Pharisees when they insisted before Pilate, the Roman prefect, to execute Jesus and, later on, persecute His disciples. After the creation of the Roman Catholic Church, Satan used the same scheme with the Gentiles, applying it to the Inquisition, an effort to convert so-called heretics who were breaking the law or had different beliefs. It was a system of terror in which many people lost their lives. With that kind of evangelizing, Satan made the church believe that they were serving God by punishing people in an effort to lead them to God, and sometimes to their death, in order to "save" people's souls. What is a greater triumph for evil than to gain victory of someone who is using God's name to perform atrocities?

There are two types of Jewish people. One type is stubbornly arrogant and prideful, feeling themselves to be unique, unparalleled, in their right way of life. The other type are those who just want to be one among the anonymous crowd. The first type either don't notice or don't want to admit that Satan has very sophisticatedly and delicately infiltrated their lives, turning them against God. In their arrogant, erroneous belief, they disbelieve that Jesus is the long-awaited Messiah.

The modern Pharisees of the Jewish nation, the rabbis, keep their people in the belief system of centuries ago, thereby denying them the chance to soften their hearts and to ask God, their own God, the One to whom they pray for deliverance every time, to talk to their hearts. The rabbis believe themselves to be so right that they would not permit a person, or God Himself, to talk to them.

Given the way the House of Israel behaves against God, are they really God's chosen people, or are the chosen ones a different group? The Jews are very proud, not wishing to humble themselves neither before people nor before their own mighty Creator. They are deaf to God, ignorant of the truth of His mercy, and blind to their spiritual and secular historical tragedy. They believe themselves to be victims of the world, because of what they are, both chosen and Jewish, not wanting to remember or admit—and even actively trying to forget—that they have brought the curse upon their own heads. In their rebellion, they refuse to accept what God, through their own prophets, has told them about their Messiah in the person of Jesus, in their Torah.

For lack of vision, spiritual vision, the Jewish people fail to see God's love for them. They believe in the law of Moses, a man used by God, instead of believing in the love and mercy of the One heavenly man sent by God as their Messiah. Jesus Christ the Messiah, the Son of God, was sent not for the Gentiles but for the Jews, sent by their own Jehovah for their salvation, a salvation they pushed to have killed with extreme hate and prejudice.

The apostle Paul said the following about the Pharisees and the rest of the Jews in 2 Corinthians 3:13–17:

> And not like Moses, which put a veil over his face, that the children of Israel could not steadfastly look to the end of that which is abolished. But their minds were blinded. For this day remaineth the same vail untaken away in the reading of the

Old Testament: which vail is done away in Christ. But even unto this day, when Moses is read, a veil is upon their heart. Nevertheless when shall turn to the Lord, the veil shall be taken away. Now the Lord is that Spirit: and when the Spirit of the Lord is, there is liberty.

Satan has made the Jewish people deaf to the voice of God, having robbed them of their common sense, their spiritual understanding, and their spiritual vision, turning them numb and blind. Instead, he has positioned them on a wide and solid rock of pride and arrogance where they cannot see the security of their own existence. The empty hope they are standing on is the reason that's been killing them throughout the centuries. Jesus knew that they allowed themselves to fall under Satan's power, whether they knew in their hearts or not that that is what they have done. Jesus said to them, "Why do ye not understand My speech? Even because ye cannot hear my word. Ye are of your father the devil, and the lust of your father ye will do. He was a murderer from the beginning, and abode not in the truth, because there is no truth in him. When he speaketh a lie, he speaketh of his own, for he is a liar and the father of it" (John 8:43–44).

The apostle Paul said, "For we do not wrestle against flesh and blood, but against principalities, against powers, against the rulers of the darkness of this world, against spiritual wickedness in high places" (Ephesians 6:12). He said that not only for the Jews, but also for any Christians, believers and leaders alike, who fall short of understanding God's Word and His spiritual world. The things Paul makes note of are the dark forces living in a man's life who blind man to his understanding and common sense. Believers at all levels and in all trades fail to even notice how close these spirits are, interfering in their spiritual lives.

Most Jews, considering what the apostle Paul said about the veil, are the blind being led by the blind. This is not because they have no chance to seek for themselves and read without prejudgment the gospel left for them by Jesus, but because they are afraid to challenge themselves, according to the gospel, about their failure to recognize the Messiah. When they truly think about what their prophets said, describing the Jesus who has already come more than two thousand years ago to save the souls of Israel, without any pretensions of their own justice and righteousness, their veils will fall away and they will see the truth. But because of their pride, they will not admit that they were and are wrong.

The teachers of the Law of Moses will be held accountable before God for misleading people from the belief of the salvation of their souls in Christ. The Lord said to them, right to their faces, "But woe unto you scribes and Pharisees, hypocrites! For ye shut up the kingdom of heaven against man; for ye neither go in yourselves, neither suffer ye them that are entering to go in" (Matthew 23:13). However, a Jewish person who has a chance to consider the gospel with an open heart and knowingly rejects that chance will undoubtedly fall under God's judgment.

Even though they saw that God has offered salvation to the Gentiles, they could not be moved to jealousy or reaction because of their arrogance and careless rejection of Christ. They have hardened their hearts, preferring to perish than admit their mistake. Evil has erased common sense from the minds of rabbis and Jewish scribes, leading to a failure to understand the way to salvation, and thereby robbing their own people and nation of the chance to be saved.

The enemy of the Jewish nation are not the people of the world who dislike the Jews. The Jews are their own enemies, having had a real spiritual enemy among them since before they left Egypt, causing their belief in Zionism. Their stubborn self-righteousness and pride as the chosen people of the Almighty, along with their spiritual blindness, separates Zionists from other Jews, who are against Zionism.

The responsibility for teaching a wrong belief about the way to salvation is on the shoulders of the Jewish leaders, from the time after Moses, to the time of Jesus of Nazareth, and up to this day. The fury of God has hung over their heads throughout all generations for giving over His only begotten Son, whom they killed in a satanic rage through someone else's hand.

We the Christians of the world should all, as an everyday commitment, pray not only for the protection of Israel, but also that Israel would accept their Lord and Savior Christ Jesus into their hearts. With equal intensity, we should pray that God open the eyes of the spiritual leaders of the physical nation of Israel and illuminate their common sense, saying, "Father, in the name of Jesus, give the leaders of Israel and their people, your chosen people, the common sense to discern. Remove the blinding veil covering their hearts, making them see and understand. Have them repent, acknowledging their wrongs, and accept the sacrifice Your Son Jesus made in love for the salvation of their souls."

Our job as children of the Almighty is, according to our heart's desire, to plant before God, in the name of Jesus, a seed of hope and faith for the House of Israel, and God will act accordingly. This way God will help the Israelites to remove the blindfold that evil has placed over their spiritual eyes, leading them to admit their part in, and repent for, the curse that they have brought upon themselves. Then God will soften their hearts and open their minds to reason and understanding, when they give themselves a chance in Christ, if only they turn from their ways and return to Him.

Salvation is only through admitting one's sin, repenting of one's rebellious heart, and recognizing Jesus, Son of God, and accepting Him as Messiah, the God of all the prophets who spoke of the coming of their Lord. Israel will be saved and covered with the shining light of His glory, together with His chosen people, for the whole world to see.

It is never too late in this world, whether for a single Jew or Gentile, or for a whole nation, to repent and be saved in Christ Jesus. As long as one's heart is pumping blood, one may accept His offer. But the Antichrist, who lives in the heart of anyone who does not recognize Jesus, who is under the command of the evil one, and who went against the heavens and then humanity, will try to prevent this from happening. Those who have God only on their lips and not in their hearts have bowed down before Satan for the glory of this world, a world in which Satan, through those people, is creating the system of the Antichrist.

Printed in the United States
by Baker & Taylor Publisher Services